ELIE

1845-1916

BY
OLGA METCHNIKOFF

TRANSLATED BY
Sir RAY LANKESTER

PREFACE

It has been a great satisfaction to me to carry out the wish of my dear friend Elie Metchnikoff, and arrange for the production of an English translation of his biography. The account of his life and work written by Olga Metchnikoff is a remarkable and beautiful record of the development and activities of a great discoverer. It is remarkable because it is seldom that one who undertakes such a task has had so constant a share in, and so complete a knowledge and understanding of, the life portrayed as in the present case: seldom that the intimate thought and mental "adventure" of a discoverer presents so clear and consistent a history. It is beautiful because it is put before us with perfect candour and simplicity guided by rare intelligence and inspired by deep affection. Madame Metchnikoff has drawn the picture of the development of a single-minded character absolutely and tenaciously devoted to a high purpose—the improvement of human life. It is a story of "struggles and adventures," but they are wholly in the field of the investigation of Nature. We read here little or nothing of the quest for personal advancement, for fortune or official position. These things had no attraction for Metchnikoff. He left[vi] Russia and took an unpaid post in Paris in order to have a place to work in. He had many devoted friends in whose company he sought refreshment and relaxation, but all his immense energy and industry were concentrated on the development and establishment of his great biological theory of "Phagocytosis" and its outcome, the philosophy of life called by him "Orthobiosis." This volume tells truly of a simple life—a life in which the social incidents which fill so large a space in most lives were either non-existent or unnoticed because, by the side of the great purpose which dominated Metchnikoff's every thought and action—namely, the advancement of Science—he was not touched by them. He was affectionate, kind-hearted, and truly considerate of others, but was, in a way which is traceable to his racial origin, a practical idealist concentrating his whole strength and reason on the realisation of what he held to be the highest good.

I had as an eager reader of memoirs on biological subjects become acquainted with Metchnikoff's earliest publications in 1865, when he was twenty years of age and I two years younger. I wrote short accounts of them, as they appeared, for a chronicle of progress in the Quarterly Journal of Microscopical Science, then edited by my father. Those on a European Land Planarian, on the development of Myzostomum (the parasite of the Feather-Star), on Apsilus, a strange new kind of wheel-animalcule, and his protest against Rudolf Leuckart's treatment of him in the matter of his important discoveries concerning[vii] the Frog's lung-worm—Ascaris nigrovenosa—remain in my memory, and later, in 1872, I was especially struck by his important demonstration of the true mode of development of the gastrula of the calcareous sponges in correction of Professor Ernst Haeckel. Many other papers of his became known to me, until in 1881 he published his first observations on Intracellular Digestion in Lower Animals, which was the starting-point of his life's work on "Phagocytosis," to which all his subsequent researches—during thirty-five years—were exclusively dedicated.

In 1888 I was introduced by my friend Lauder Brunton to the great Pasteur, and called on him at his laboratory in the rue d'Ulm. There I met Metchnikoff, only lately arrived from Russia, and welcomed as one of his staff by Pasteur. The next year, 1889, Pasteur was installed in the new "Institut Pasteur" in the rue Dutot, and I met Metchnikoff there in his new quarters. Pasteur's assistants were carrying on daily his system of inoculation against rabies, and many British subjects were amongst those treated. I persuaded the Lord Mayor of that year, Sir James Whitehead, to visit the Pasteur Institute with a view to taking steps to make some recognition of the services rendered by

Pasteur to our fellow-countrymen in treating over two hundred of them threatened with hydrophobia. Sir James called a meeting on July 1, 1889, at the Mansion House, and placed the management of it in my hands. As a result we obtained subscriptions to a fund which[viii] enabled us to assist many poor British subjects to visit Paris for the purpose of undergoing M. Pasteur's treatment, to make a donation of 30,000 francs to the Pasteur Institute, and to initiate with a sum of £300 the formation of a fund for the purpose of establishing an Institute in London similar in purpose and character to the Institut Pasteur. That initial fund has step by step received generous additions and given us the "Lister Institute" on Chelsea Embankment possessed of buildings, site, and capital valued at more than £300,000.

After 1889 it was rare for a year to pass without my visiting Paris both in spring and summer, and seeing a great deal of Metchnikoff and his friends Roux, Duclaux, Laveran, and the great master of the Pastorians, who died in 1895. Metchnikoff took me to his home and cemented his friendship with me by bringing to me that of his gifted and devoted wife.

Madame Metchnikoff had when a schoolgirl studied zoology under her future husband at Odessa, and now was able to give serious help in some of his researches. She published some experimental investigation on the sterilisation of the alimentary canal of tadpoles and some other researches, and having a thorough knowledge of English, which Elie did not possess, she helped him in reading and translating from that language. But her chief talents were in the arts of painting and sculpture, and when they purchased their country house at Sèvres, she built a studio in the garden in which to pursue her vocation.

Metchnikoff on several occasions came to England[ix] to take part in "congresses" or to give special addresses, and often stayed a day or two with me in London.[1] I was with him at the Darwin Celebration at Cambridge in 1909, and the last occasion when he came was to give the Priestley Lecture of the National Health Society in November 1912. At my request he selected "The Warfare against Tuberculosis" as his subject, and gave a most valuable account of the history and actual condition of that enterprise, relating the important results of his expedition to the Kalmuk Tartars for the purpose of studying the immunity from and the liability to infection by tuberculosis among that nomad population. The lecture was delivered in French, and I made a translation of it which appeared with numerous illustrations in the journal called Bedrock, published by Constable & Co. I mention that publication here as it is the only one excepting the three lectures on "The New Hygiene" (Heinemann, London, 1906) originally published in an English form by Metchnikoff, and deserves more attention from the English medical public than it has received.

I found Metchnikoff a delightful companion. He always had something new or of special interest to show to me at the laboratory—some microscopical preparation, the digestive process in Protozoa, the microbian parasite of a water-flea, a new method of[x] dark ground illumination with high powers (Commandant's method for film production), the newly discovered Treponema of syphilis, or the experimental inoculation of a disease under study. Sometimes I would lunch at his house, when, although he neither smoked nor took alcoholic drinks himself, he made a point of giving me first-rate claret and a good cigar. It was about the year 1900 that he arranged for the preparation of a pure "sour milk" made by the use of a special lactic ferment (selected and cultivated by himself), and this he took regularly. I found it a most agreeable food, and for several years made it an article of my own diet. He was very careful about the possible contamination of uncooked food by bacteria and the eggs of parasitic worms, and in consequence had "rolls" sent to him from the bakers each in its separate paper bag, whilst he would never eat uncooked salads or fruit which could not be rendered safe by "peeling." This was not an excess of caution, but resulted from his characteristic determination to carry out in practice the directions given by definite scientific knowledge, and to make the attempt to lead so far as possible a life free from disease. Often when I arrived in Paris he would invite me to lunch at one of the leading cafés, and though he ate very simple food himself took keen pleasure in ordering the best for me and thoroughly enjoyed the change of scene and the amenities of a first-rate restaurant. During one of his visits to London, I remember that he was invited, and I with him, on two or three occasions, by leading London[xi] physicians to dinner-parties. He was greatly shocked at the amount of strong wine which his hosts and fellow-guests consumed, and assured me that in Paris it would be injurious to the reputation of a physician were he not to set an example of either abstinence or great moderation.

Metchnikoff was not only exceedingly gentle and courteous in his treatment of servants and employés, but he and his wife contrived on a very small income to help in a most substantial way poor neighbours and those who had met with misfortune whether they were of French or Russian nationality. They had many friends in the world of science and art, real workers and thinkers, including those who had not and those who had "arrived." With them I met and spent a long and interesting day with Rodin the sculptor and the son of Léon Tolstoï, who was working in a Paris studio. Among the pleasures which I have derived from the Life are the accounts of places such as Naples and Messina, where I stayed in order to study the embryology of marine animals as Metchnikoff did; and also the appearance in these pages from time to time of old friends such as Nikolas Kleinenberg, whom Metchnikoff met at Messina in 1883. I had formed an intimate acquaintance with Kleinenberg at Jena in 1871, when he was working at his classical monograph on Hydra, and continued it at Naples in 1875. From Messina, where he became Professor in 1875, Kleinenberg sent me for publication in the Quarterly Journal of Microscopical Science his valuable memoir[xii] on the embryology of a species of Earthworm, and also rare and interesting specimens of Cephalopoda.

Another great and noteworthy figure about whom all zoologists are glad to learn as much as possible is Kovalevsky. Metchnikoff made his acquaintance at Naples in 1864, and they formed a close friendship for one another. Later, in 1867, they shared the Baer Prize of the Petersburg Academy for their discoveries in embryology (p. 58). In 1868 Metchnikoff had a dispute with Kovalevsky as to the origin of the nervous system of Ascidia (p. 62), concerning which he subsequently admitted that he was wrong and Kovalevsky right. There is no doubt that Kovalevsky, by his numerous important investigations of invertebrate embryology, and especially of that of Ascidia and Amphioxus, laid the foundation of cellular Embryology, and the modern study of the embryology of Invertebrates. Metchnikoff's contributions were also of great value and importance (pp. 51, 52, 53, and pp. 72 and 73), though he has not so great a triumph in animal morphology to his credit as Kovalevsky's discovery of the close identities of the development of organs in Ascidia and Amphioxus. I had long cherished profound esteem for Kovalevsky when in 1896 I met him and his daughter at Wimereux with Professor Giard. He came in the autumn of that year to London, but left unexpectedly owing to some nervous fear of annoyance by the police. The great position of Kovalevsky was deliberately ignored in a German history of Zoology,[2] published just before[xiii] the Great War. Metchnikoff describes Kovalevsky as a young man, small and timid, with shy but cordial manners and the clear sweet eyes of a child: he had (like Metchnikoff) for Science an absolute cult—"no sacrifice was too great, no difficulty too repellent for his ardour."

It is, I think, desirable to assure the reader of this book that the actual state of knowledge in regard to various subjects discussed in the Life at the time when they were made the subjects of study by Metchnikoff is fairly and correctly sketched, and the growth and development of his views and original discoveries are correctly given. But it must be remembered that this Life is not a critical discussion of the steps by which our knowledge of cell-layers, of intracellular digestion, and other factors contributory to Metchnikoff's doctrine of Phagocytosis and its outcomes were reached. Others played an important if a subsidiary part in building up that knowledge. What we have here is an account of the growth of Metchnikoff's own observations and theoretical inferences, which were so independent, and founded on such decisive original observations, as to make him a solitary figure contending, and successfully contending, during the best years of his lifetime for the recognition of a great generalisation for long opposed by most of the medical and physiological authorities of the time, and finally established by his lifelong researches and those of his faithful pupils and coadjutors. The recognition of the validity of[xiv] the doctrine of phagocytosis in relation to wounds, disease, immunity, and normal healthy life is the triumphant result of the scientific insight and boundless energy of Elie Metchnikoff.

E. RAY LANKESTER.

INTRODUCTION

On a calm summer evening we were seated together on our terrace.

On the preceding day, one who hardly knew my husband had come to ask him for information concerning his life, with the object of writing his biography. We were saying to each other how inevitably superficial and incomplete such a biography was bound to be; how difficult such a task is for a biographer, even when fully informed; how necessary it is to be thoroughly acquainted with a man and with every phase of his existence in order to give a truthful picture of his character and of his life. The intimate side is bound to remain more or less closed to a stranger; in order to decipher it, it is indispensable for the writer of a biography to have lived in complete communion of spirit with its subject. Our long past, spent together, fulfilled all these conditions.

My husband's whole life was well known to me. My mother-in-law had often told me vivid stories of his childhood; he himself willingly talked to me about his past. As to the second part of his existence, we had lived it together.

In order clearly to understand his character, at[xxii] once both complex and one-sided, it was necessary to possess the key to his psychology. In his life, as in his work, everything was so closely knitted that it was impossible to understand the whole without knowledge of every link of his evolution.

In the soothing calm of that summer evening, I submitted my reflections to him; he warmly encouraged me, and I then and there resolved to write his biography. He advised me to relate his whole life without any reticence, considering that thus alone does a biography justify its existence. That advice was to guide me, within limits, for to dissect an individual life without touching other lives as well is not always possible.

Numerous were the difficulties before me; yet, I considered the task as a mission, hoping, in spite of all, that this biography would present a true picture of the life and evolution of Elie Metchnikoff.

We talked over this project for a long time. The moon now appeared above the trees, the soft light tracing silver designs through the ivy leaves. The lawn, the walnut tree in front of the house, and everything around us was bathed in peaceful radiance. Under its mysterious charm, we ceased to speak, we listened to the inward voices of nature and of our own hearts.

In youth, vague reveries fill our minds; after a long life, distant memories.... He whose life I describe is no more.... Without his help my task could not have been accomplished.

Often, when he was not too tired, he would sit[xxiii] comfortably in his armchair and recount to me with his usual spirit and animation some period or episode of his past. I read to him a sketch of the first part of this biography and a few chapters only of the second, which was hardly begun. Thus we spent many evenings, never to be forgotten.

He wanted this biography written, for he held that the evolution of a mind, of a character, of a human life is always an interesting psychological document. During his long and painful illness, he urged me to relate the "last chapter" of his life; he hoped that his attitude in the face of death might diminish the fear of it in others. Also he considered that men are rare who are conscious until the end; even rarer, those who reach the development of the "death-instinct." Therefore, according to him, an example would be interesting.

I have tried to accomplish his desire within the measure of my strength.

The only object of this simple and truthful story is to show Elie Metchnikoff as he was, a help, a support, and a lesson to others.

I dedicate this book to his dear memory.

OLGA METCHNIKOFF.

Sèvres, 15th Dec. 1918.
[1]
CHAPTER I

Panassovka — Metchnikoff's parents — Country life in Little Russia.

In Little Russia, in the steppe region of the province of Kharkoff, is situated the land of Panassovka, which belonged to the Metchnikoff family. It is now sold, it has passed into strange hands, but it was once the patrimony of Ilia Ivanovitch, father of Elie Metchnikoff.

The country around Panassovka is neither beautiful nor rich: steppes, hillocks covered with low grasses and wild wormwood; a poor village, meagre vegetation, no river; the whole impression is a melancholy one. But what boundless space! What soft, silver grey colouring! And, in the mornings and evenings, what fresh, cool air, and what a delicious aroma of wormwood leaves!

The house of Panassovka, a little way from the village, is situated on a hill which slopes gently towards a pond. It is like that of any other middle-class landowner in Little Russia. It has only one storey and two flights of steps on the principal façade, opening into a deserted courtyard with no view but the high road. On the other side a semicircular terrace, with columns and steps, leads to the garden, composed of a few meagre flower-beds and fruit trees, reaching to the pond. On the bank, a distillery and a very well-kept kitchen garden.

[2]

The house is arranged inside in a commonplace manner, with no claim to beauty or comfort. The furniture, devoid of style or elegance, neither comfortable nor fashionable, is distributed quite inartistically. On the other hand, great care is evident in everything that pertains to the table: the cellars and larders are full of provisions, and obviously constitute the principal preoccupation of the masters of the house. And indeed the hospitable table of Panassovka is renowned throughout the neighbourhood.

According to a very fine portrait, painted in 1835, Ilia Ivanovitch was at that time a handsome young man with regular features, tender blue eyes, and curly fair hair. He was very intelligent, but his mind had that sceptical turn which prevents men from taking life seriously and which paralyses activity. Moreover, he had an Epicurean temperament and was in the army.

He had married, when very young, Emilia Lvovna Nevahovna, sister of one of his brother officers in the Imperial Guard, a very attractive and unusually intelligent girl. Her beauty was of the Jewish type, with splendid dark eyes, and she had a bright and lively disposition as well as a kind and tender heart. Her friends called her "Milotchka," which, in Russian, means "charming"; in her old age she loved to relate that the great Russian poet, Pushkin, once said to her at a ball, "How well your name suits you, Mademoiselle!"

After his marriage, Ilia Ivanovitch remained in Petersburg, leading a merry life with his brothers-in-law, and giving no thought to the future; it took him but a few years at that rate to spend the whole of his wife's inheritance. And three children were growing up whose future had to be thought of. It was[3] then that Ilia Ivanovitch's distant estate was remembered, away in a remote part of Little Russia. What energy, what perseverance had to be displayed by his wife before she could persuade him to take refuge there! and how hard it must have seemed to the gay officer to leave the capital for the lonely and monotonous life of the country! However, departure was decided upon. The two boys, Ivan and Leo, were placed in a school at Petersburg, to be prepared for the Lycée and the Law School. Ilia Ivanovitch obtained a post as Remount Officer for two Guards regiments, and started with his wife, his daughter, an aunt, and a younger brother, to settle down in the country.

The family settled at first in the old Ivanovka house, where a son, Nicholas, was born. Though they wished to have no more children, one more child was born two years later, on the 16th May 1845—Elie Metchnikoff.

The Ivanovka house was old and inconvenient; Ilia Ivanovitch decided to build a new one at the other end of his estate, in a place called Panassovka, which thus became the family home.

Emilia Lvovna threw herself into her domestic occupations with her usual energy and ardour. She was anxious to improve the situation, which had become precarious, and wished at the same time to create for her husband an environment suited to his Epicurean tastes. Ilia Ivanovitch loved cards and the table, both tastes easy to satisfy in the country, and which became the pivot of life at Panassovka. The great daily problem was the question of meals, and long conversations had to take place with the cook and with the housekeeper concerning catering.

[4]

Thanks to serfdom, servants were very numerous and everything could be manufactured at home. The "diévitshia" (maid-servants' room) was crowded with maids, seamstresses, needle-women, washer-women, etc., under the direction of a fat, middle-aged woman named Duniasha. She wore a silk kerchief on her head, and was invariably clothed in a white dressing jacket and a brown skirt with white spots. A regular autocrat, she ruled her little world with a rod of iron; as soon as her heavy, felt-slippered steps were heard, the maids whispered to each other, "Avdotia Maximovna!" conversations ceased, and every one became absorbed in her work.

Among the male retainers, the first place was held by Petrushka, the valet. Careless and often drunk, he was nevertheless a good fellow; he was usually to be found asleep behind the screen in the hall. The upper servants, the cook, coachman, and others left their work to be done by their underlings, the scullery boy, postilion, page-boy, etc. In fact, everything followed the routine usual in every Russian household in the time of serfdom.

Emilia Lvovna directed the children's education; her personal teaching consisted chiefly in tender indulgence, but it was she who chose the nurses and teachers. As long as the boys were small, their great-aunt Elena Samoïlovna looked after them; afterwards they were handed over to tutors and professors. Ilia Ivanovitch's activities consisted in buying horses at fairs and in studs and in convoying them to Petersburg. These journeys took a long time, by stages and relays of horses. Ilia Ivanovitch took advantage of them to gamble heavily and to enjoy pleasures which the country did not offer.

[5]

Agriculture was very restricted at Panassovka, for the property consisted mostly of pasture land for horses and sheep. The younger brother, Dmitri Ivanovitch, had undertaken the management of the estate. He was entirely devoted to the family of his elder brother, whom he had followed into the country. Though only a few years younger, he used the respectful second person plural in speaking to Ilia Ivanovitch, whilst the latter said "thou" to him. Dmitri Ivanovitch was tall, thin, and taciturn, a silent pipe-smoker. The lively Emilia Lvovna often said to him, "But why do you never talk, Mitienka?" To which he invariably answered, "It is not every one who is as talkative as you are, Emilia Lvovna." Yet they were on the best of terms. Dmitri Ivanovitch would have gone through fire for his sister-in-law, as she well knew. She had the utmost confidence in him, and depended upon his support in every difficult circumstance.

At Panassovka the men spent the greater part of the day, and often even of the night, in playing cards; games were organised between neighbours and relations, and that occupation was considered most important. Meals were prolonged indefinitely; everything was served in abundance and eaten with a connoisseur's appreciation, each dish being discussed. After the meal was over, the cook would make his daily appearance, and the next day's menu was drawn up by the whole party. After a siesta, gambling was resumed. Thus the days went by in the cult of good cheer and of cards, interspersed with conversations about horses and sometimes about politics.

By this time Ilia Ivanovitch was beginning to become bald and obese. It is difficult to define what[6] was his inner life; not even to his wife did he ever speak of it. As to his children, he petted them when they were small, but as they grew up, their intercourse with him was limited to kissing his hand morning and evening. He was not indifferent to their welfare, but left it entirely to his wife's active solicitude. The children were on very different terms with their mother; not only did she spoil them, but also always eagerly shared all their childish interests. Owing to that, and to her bright and affectionate disposition, they looked upon her as their intimate friend and confidante.

Masters and servants were on good terms, relations between them were even remarkably human, according to the ideas of the time, and in spite of certain customs inherent to serfdom. For instance, the younger maids were punished by having their faces slapped and their hair pulled. Even the kindly and peaceable Dmitri Ivanovitch would soundly box his valet's ears when he found him drunk. At that time such things were not thought cruel or humiliating, but looked upon as a paternal correction. The peasants had confidence in their "barin" (master) and consulted him or appealed to his generosity when in trouble.

Ilia Ivanovitch never opposed the free choice of his serfs in matrimony, a rare tolerance at that time. According to custom every betrothed couple came to salute him,

7

the young man in his Sunday clothes and a fine, bright-coloured scarf, the girl wearing an embroidered bodice and a head-dress of many-coloured ribbons. They knelt before him and bowed three times to the ground, then offered him sacramental loaves, hard and shaped like pine cones, on beautifully[7] worked diapers. Ilia Ivanovitch and Emilia Lvovna blessed the bride and bridegroom with "ikons," embraced them, and gave them a sum of money for the wedding.

The Metchnikoffs were liked by their peasants and looked upon as good masters.

[8]
CHAPTER II

Metchnikoff's brothers and sister — Childish characteristics.

The two elder children, Ivan and Leo, were educated at Petersburg, whilst Katia, the only daughter, was brought up at home. Like all other girls of noble family, she was educated with the object of being suitably married. She was a slender, pretty brunette, like her mother, but less beautiful. Though sensitive and intelligent, she interested herself in nothing but the reading of French novels. There was a great difference in age between Katia and her little brothers, whilst there were only two years between them. Kolia (Nicholas) was the old aunt's favourite, a fine, handsome boy with velvety black eyes; his slow and grave movements had earned for him the nickname of "Peaceful Papa."

The youngest of the family, Ilia (Elie), on the contrary, was full of life and spirits. Fair and slender, with silky hair and a diaphanous, pink and white complexion, he had small, grey-blue eyes, full of kindliness and sparkle. Very highly strung and impressionable, his temper was easily roused, and he was so restless that he went by the name of "quicksilver." He always wished to see everything, to know everything, and found his way everywhere. When, after a long silence, there was a sudden outburst of many voices around the card-tables, he would rush to the[9] drawing-room, saying, "Are they going to fight?" He ran about the house all day, following his mother as she attended to her various duties; he examined the provisions, tasted everything, and even went to the "diévitshia" to see what the maids were doing. He tried to sew or to embroider, exasperated everybody, and ended by being turned out. He would then look for something else to do, go to see whether the table was laid, inquire about the menu, and ask the queerest questions. He could only be kept quiet when his curiosity was awakened by the observation of some natural object such as an insect or a butterfly that he was trying to catch, or by watching the "grown-ups" at their card games. But, of all things, music fascinated him most, and he would remain for hours sitting by the piano listening without a movement. He was very much spoilt by his mother, who had a weakness for her Benjamin, and who also wished to make up for the very obvious preference shown for Kolia by the great-aunt.

Moreover, Ilia was a frail little boy and often suffered from his eyes; the doctor advised that he should not be allowed to cry or to rub his eyes, and, in order to avoid this, he was permitted to have his own way in everything. He was much too intelligent not to understand the advantage that the situation offered and was quick to profit by it. In the face of the least semblance of refusal or reproach, he would begin to rub his eyes and announce in a whining tone that he was going to cry. He was therefore very much spoilt and very capricious; his mother said he was "neurotic"; his sister, who often had differences with him, called him a "little beast." In reality, Ilia was very good-hearted, tender, and loving; he was[10] affectionate, especially with his mother, and could always be managed by an appeal to his feelings. But if he was sensitive to kindness, he was equally so to the least injustice. He could not forgive his great-aunt the predilection which

8

she exhibited on every occasion for Kolia; for instance, at table, she would choose tit-bits for him, and Ilia observed with bitterness that she always reserved the chicken's breast for her favourite. Every time a chicken was served, poor Ilia followed the dish round the table with anxious eyes, and she invariably placed the coveted morsel in his brother's plate.

When the day was over, Ilia was put into his little bed and told to "say his prayers and go to sleep." But he did not obey at once: after a thousand merry tricks, his eyelids would begin to close in spite of him; then he would make up his mind to kneel and say his prayers, folding his little hands: "Lord, keep and preserve father, mother, great——" But suddenly remembering the latter's injustice towards him, he would correct himself hastily, "No, not great-aunt, she is too unkind!" and continue, "My sister, my brothers, everybody, and myself, little Ilia." Still he did not go to sleep immediately; a nervous child, he was frightened of being alone; now and then he would lift his heavy lids to see if the maid was still there. Sometimes the latter, thinking he had gone to sleep, would leave the room on tiptoe. Ilia, seeing her no more, would start, raise his head and, stretching his thin neck, send an anxious look around the room, faintly lighted by a night-light. The vacillating flame threw trembling and dancing shadows. Seized with intense terror, he would hide his face in his pillow and scream with all his might. Avdotia[11] Maximovna would then rush to soothe him and soundly rate the servant girl, "Are you not ashamed to leave a noble child all alone?" Ilia would then go on sobbing for a little while, but, reassured after all, would presently sink into deep, childish sleep.

[12]
CHAPTER III

Journey to Slaviansk — The coach attacked by peasants.

In 1850 the children were taken to the baths of Slaviansk. On a warm summer day the heavy "berlin" coach, drawn by six horses with a postilion, rolled along the high road, across the steppes, followed at a distance by a "tarantass."[3]

In the spacious, antique coach, with its dusty hood, sat Emilia Lvovna, with her three children; the valet, Petrushka, dozed on the box, next to the coachman. The tarantass was occupied by Dmitri Ivanovitch and a cousin.

The heat was oppressive. At the start every one was excited; Emilia Lvovna was trying to remember if anything had been forgotten and was discussing with Katia the details of their installation at Slaviansk. The boys hung out of the windows, gazing at the horses, at the tarantass, and making all sorts of comments. Ilia was so restless and talkative that he was constantly being told, "Do be quiet! Keep still!"

By degrees, however, children and "grown-ups" began to feel drowsy, owing to the monotony of the road, the heat, and the swinging of the carriage. The tarantass had disappeared, for Dmitri Ivanovitch wished to visit an aunt whose house was not far from[13] the road. The outline of a forest was now seen on the horizon; it came nearer and nearer, and soon the coach stopped before the forest inn. Everybody woke up, the children were delighted to be able to run about and stretch their limbs. They begged their mother to let them go into the forest whilst the horses were resting, and obtained permission to go, but not too far, and with Petrushka.

They ate an appetising lunch at the inn and the children ran off at a gallop. Everything delighted them, the underwood, grass patches, ravines, and mysterious paths. But they had hardly entered the forest when they heard a sinister, confused rumour in the distance; they stopped to listen, and recognised the voices of a tumultuous crowd. The children's joyous excitement fell; frightened and docile, they hastened to return to the inn, from which Emilia Lvovna, looking anxiously out of a window, was making urgent signs to them to return. The coach was still standing without horses, and, a little farther off, the latter were surrounded by a crowd of peasants, of whom many were completely drunk. They shouted vociferously, and closely pressed the coachman and the postilion, threatening to confiscate the horses and detain the travellers if they were not given a ransom of a thousand roubles.

Terrified, the children clung to their distracted mother; Ilia felt her trembling, and his own little heart fluttered like a bird that has been caught. The drunken peasants appeared to him like monstrous ogres or brigands about to capture, perhaps kill, his family and himself; he could hardly keep back his tears. Already the peasants had bound the coachman and the postilion and were taking away the[14] horses. Clinging close to each other, the mother and children listened anxiously; they thought again and again that they could hear the bells of the tarantass. At last it appeared in the distance, and the children joyously whispered, "There they are!" They hastened to inform Dmitri Ivanovitch of what had happened. He at once went with his cousin towards the crowd, and negotiations were opened, but for a long time without result.

At last the cousin had a happy idea; he declared he would go back to his aunt's house in the neighbourhood and borrow the thousand roubles from her. The peasants consented to let him go alone, keeping the other travellers as hostages. After a time, which to the children seemed endless, the sound of the tarantass bells was again heard, accompanied this time by numerous heavy footsteps, and the vehicle reappeared, escorted by a company of soldiers commanded by two officers. Instead of going to his aunt's, the cousin had gone to a neighbouring military camp and was bringing assistance.

There was a sudden change of scene. Emilia Lvovna and Katia furtively made the sign of the cross. Ilia had let go of his mother's hand and was no longer clinging to her, but, stretching his head forward and opening his eyes wide, eagerly waited to see what was going to happen. "Now," he thought, "we shall not be captured; it is their turn; I am glad!" And, perhaps for the first time in his life, his little heart was moved by feelings of hatred.

In the meanwhile a repulsive scene was going on: a hand-to-hand struggle, invectives and screams. The peasants were securely bound. Men and women hastened from a neighbouring village; one of the[15] women slapped an officer's face. Furious, he ordered the soldiers to fill her mouth with earth; she was thrown on the ground; the new arrivals in their turn attacked the soldiers, and a regular battle raged.

Ilia was alarmed, shaken, and profoundly disgusted with that exhibition of brutality. The coachman and postilion, their bonds unloosed, hastened to put the horses in, and whilst reprisals were still going on, the family hurried away. They reached Slaviansk without further trouble, excitedly talking over their adventure. This episode was the first deep and definite impression which remained on little Ilia's mind; it struck him so much that he kept the memory of it during his whole life.

From that moment he held crowds, violence, and all manifestations of brute force in the utmost horror, whatever their cause might be.

[16]
CHAPTER IV

Departure for Kharkoff — Town life.

The following year was to be spent at Kharkoff. Katia was now seventeen and her marriage had to be contemplated.

10

The boys' life was still quite a childish one, made up chiefly of games and mischief. Kolia had been taught to read by the great-aunt; Ilia had learnt by himself, asking people now and then for the name of some letter. He was able to read fluently quite early.

The departure for Kharkoff was a great event, prepared long beforehand. The children, delighted at the prospect of a change, impatiently waited for the moment to start. At last every one was seated in the coaches and, saying to the coachman, "Off! God keep us," they started to drive along the high road through the steppes.

Life at Kharkoff was very much the same as at Panassovka, with social elements added. Moreover, the children's liberty was somewhat restricted. Already on the journey they were given to understand that, in a town, they could not go out alone, nor shout in the streets, nor point at people and things with their finger, and that they should have to make less noise, even in the house. For the first time they unconsciously realised that their family was not the centre of the universe, that there were many others[17] who also had to be taken into account. Ilia did not welcome this discovery.

The flat occupied by the Metchnikoffs was on the first floor, above that of the owner of the house. One day when the children were running about, making a fearful noise, some one came up to say that the landlady was ill and begged that the noise should cease. Ilia, interrupted in the midst of a game, became furiously angry; in his rage he seized a whistle, and stooping to a crack in the floor, whistled with all his might. It was only with much difficulty that he was induced to stop and to calm himself.[4]

The children's horizon soon widened; Dmitri Ivanovitch took them to the theatre and a new and fantastic world opened out to them. The very next day they attempted a performance of the play they had seen; soon, on Kolia's suggestion, they began to compose plays for themselves. Kolia wrote a drama entitled "Burning Tea," in which the hero having offered his friend tea that was too hot, the latter burnt his tongue; a duel ensued, etc., etc. Ilia hastened to follow his brother's example. He composed something in the same style, but even more absurd. Having realised that it was so, he gave up literature. That period was for him a series of disappointments which perhaps helped to lead him to the path he was ultimately to follow. His brother, following the "grown-ups'" example, played cards with other boys or with the maids. Ilia attempted to do the same, but his nervousness left him no self-control; he lost continually and games generally ended in quarrels and tears; he became disgusted with[18] cards for the rest of his life. Kolia was fond of muscular exercises, such as gymnastics, wrestling, etc. Ilia, younger and therefore weaker, was constantly humiliated, and his pride kept him away from physical amusements. Thus, by means of elimination, he became gradually isolated from surrounding influences. But, at that time, no new element had intervened in his daily life and he spent his existence in the gentle warmth of his mother's tenderness, absorbed in his childish games and studies.

[19]
CHAPTER V

Leo Metchnikoff's illness — Private tutors — Botanical studies — A memorable birthday.

In 1851, in the middle of the winter, the Metchnikoffs heard that Leo, their second son, was suffering from hip-disease, and the doctors advised that he should be taken away from Petersburg. Poor Emilia Lvovna was in great despair and shed many tears; her brother-in-law, Dmitri Ivanovitch, calmly announced that he was going to fetch Leo. He took his great fur coat, his fur cap and fur-lined boots, and started that very day for

Petersburg by coach. He took but the necessary time to go and to bring Leo back, only stopping at relays to change horses.

The boy was then thirteen years old, handsome, gifted, and intelligent; he walked with crutches, but his general health seemed good, and it was decided that he should work at home to prepare for the Lycée, under the tuition of students as tutors. Thus a new element was introduced into the family life.

In 1853 Leo had as a tutor a student named Hodounof, a very intelligent young man, who wished not merely to teach him but to impart to him the love of science. Leo was extremely gifted and worked with great facility, but he lacked concentration and was therefore somewhat superficial. This cooled his tutor's enthusiasm, whilst on the other hand he[20] became more and more interested in little Ilia. It was in the course of country walks that they were drawn together. Hodounof used to take Leo for walks in order to study the local flora, and Ilia came out with them, at first for the sake of the exercise. But soon he became interested in the flowers and showed so much taste for botany that he attracted Hodounof's notice; soon the tutor's interest became concentrated on the little boy and he gave him serious attention.

It was with a real enthusiasm that Ilia gathered and studied plants; he soon became thoroughly acquainted with the local flora. He thought himself very learned already and wrote memoirs on botany. Passionately fond of teaching, he used to offer all his pocket-money to his brothers and other children to induce them to hear lectures which he gave them. His vocation was fixed from that moment. He was then eight years old.

When the family returned to Kharkoff he spent all he had in buying books on natural history, which he read with passionate interest. These contained many things that he could not understand, but his curiosity was all the greater. When he was eleven years old his passion for natural history almost cost him his life. While fishing for hydra in a small pond he was so eager that he fell into the water and was only pulled out with great difficulty.

That particular day, his own and his father's name day, was nearly fatal to him, not only through water but through fire. It was a family custom to hold a great gathering of friends and relations at Panassovka on St. Elias's day. Preparations for the feast began days beforehand; the whole household was in a turmoil.

[21]

On that particular St. Elias's day, so many guests came to Panassovka that there was not enough room in the house to accommodate them all, and the children were transferred to a pavilion outside the house.

Whilst in the drawing-room people were talking and playing cards, the servants were holding rejoicings of their own. Towards night-time the majority of the coachmen and footmen brought by the guests were completely drunk; a cigarette imprudently thrown on some hay started a fire. Soon the stables were ablaze and many horses perished in the flames, in spite of every effort to save them. Presently the wind changed in the direction of the pavilion and the thatched roof caught fire. There was a rush to save the children, who were with much difficulty taken out through a window.

In spite of intense terror, Ilia's first thought was for his baby nephew, the son of his sister, who had then been married a year; he ran in affright all over the house searching for the child, and only became calm again after he had ascertained that it had been carried out into the garden.

Katia being married there was now no reason to spend the winter in the town. The father and mother therefore remained at Panassovka and Dmitri Ivanovitch took the boys to Kharkoff, where they entered the Lycée. They had been well prepared by their tutors,

and moreover spoke French and a little German, having had special teachers for these languages. Their French tutor, M. Garnier, was gay, boastful, and pretentious; his idea of teaching them French literature was to memorise Béranger's chansons. He was passionately fond of shooting and gave to that[22] sport as much time as he could, greatly to the detriment of his pupils' studies, for they were not allowed to accompany him for fear of an accident. Their mother, perhaps on account of her weak heart, was so nervous that they were discouraged from any sporting tastes. The German tutor also neglected the children: his favourite occupation consisted in drinking beer. On one occasion he gave so much to little Ilia that the boy conceived a lifelong distaste for beer. Ilia took advantage of his tutors' indifference to devote himself to his favourite study of natural history. His vocation was so obvious that it could not be mistaken. It seems a strange thing that a passion for science should have developed in so inappropriate an environment. Evidently the first impulse was given by Hodounof, but, if his influence stimulated this passion, it cannot have created it. This vocation probably had a deeper source, and in order to discover it we should perhaps look back into the antecedents of the Metchnikoff family.
[23]
CHAPTER VI

Ancestors of the Metchnikoff family — The Great Spatar — Leo Nevahovitch.
The Metchnikoff family made no show of family pride; one old aunt, however, was extremely proud of one of their ancestors, the Great "Spatar" (sword-bearer). The following is the account given of this ancestor by E. Picot, after a Moldavian chronicle.[5]
Few men led such an adventurous life or made themselves glorious through such varied gifts as did Nicholas Spatar Milescu.

His name is connected with the history of Moldavian, Greek, Russian, and Chinese literature. His origin, his talents, his crime, the mutilation he suffered, his audacious journey across the whole of Asia to reach Pekin, the valuable information which he gathered during his embassy at the Court of the "Son of Heaven," everything conspires to excite curiosity concerning him.

Spatar was born in Moldavia in 1625. While yet very young he went to Constantinople, where he studied theology, philosophy, history ancient and modern, Greek, Latin, Slavonic and Turkish. He afterwards went to Italy to study natural science and mathematics. On his return to Moldavia he soon became known for his erudition, acquired great[24] influence, and became much appreciated at Court. Owing to clever political intrigues he preserved the simultaneous favour of several enemy princes, one of whom, Stepanita, covered him with benefits and honours. Nevertheless, Spatar wrote to Constantine Bassarab, in Poland, advising him to come and to overthrow Stepanita's throne. He sent his letter inside a hollow cane; Constantine, however, did not wish to launch himself into such an adventure, and indignantly sent the hollow cane and the letter to Stepanita himself. At first the prince, naturally angry, thought of having Spatar executed; he spared his life for the sake of his talents, but condemned him to have the tip of his nose cut off. Spatar went to Germany, where, says the naïve chronicler, a doctor made his nose grow again. He came back to Moldavia for a short time and then went to Russia. Thanks to his knowledge of languages, he was made an interpreter at the Court of the Tsar Alexis Michailovitch, and was the first tutor of his son Peter the Great, whom he taught to read and to write.

In 1674 the Tsar Alexis Michailovitch entrusted Spatar with a mission in China, where he was to open negotiations with a view to commercial and political relations between Russia and China. In the course of his journey Spatar carefully collected all possible information concerning the countries he traversed. He thus gathered much interesting geographical knowledge and highly important data concerning the commercial value of Asiatic rivers, and specially the Amour river.

At Pekin, Spatar rapidly learnt the Chinese language, occupied for three years the post of ambassador[25] in China, and returned to Russia bringing back most valuable information and many rich presents given him by the Emperor of China.

All this had excited the jealousy of the Muscovite courtiers; they took advantage of the coincidence between the death of the Tsar and Spatar's return to deprive him of his treasures and to have him exiled to Siberia. But, when Peter the Great ascended the throne, Spatar succeeded in making a letter reach him relating his misfortunes, and the Tsar recalled him, gave him back his property, and showered honours upon him. Spatar again became interpreter of the Embassy; Peter consulted him in all Far-Eastern questions, and gave him confidential documents to translate into foreign languages.

Spatar's literary activity was vast and varied. He translated the Bible from the Greek into Roumanian; he wrote a chronicle on the origin of Roumania, articles on theology, a Greco-Latin-Russian dictionary, and a work entitled Arithmetic, in which he discussed, by means of numbers and figures, questions of Theology, Philosophy, and Ethics. He dealt in his writings with Art, Archæology, and History; described his Siberian travels, China and the Amour river, and made numerous translations of diplomatic documents. His erudition was such that his contemporaries appealed to his knowledge as they would have consulted an encyclopædia.

He had married a Muscovite and had several sons and grandsons. Three of his nephews came from Moldavia to join him and entered the Russian army. He died in 1714 at the age of 80. Such is the history of the "Great Spatar."

The following notice is to be found in Brockhaus[26] and Effrone's Encyclopædia: "The Metchnikoffs are a noble family, descended from a Moldavian Boyar, the Spatar (sword-bearer) Joury Stepanovitch,[6] who came to Russia with Prince Cantemir. Peter the Great gave this Boyar large land estates. His son took the name of Metchnikoff (Russian translation of Sword-bearer)."

The following generations included military men chiefly, one sailor, one mining engineer, one senator, but no scientific men.

On the mother's side, Elie Metchnikoff had no ancestor as remarkable or as romantic as the great Spatar. Yet his grandfather, Leo Nevahovitch, was a very intelligent and highly cultivated man. He had been Farmer-General for tobacco in Poland. A Jew by race, he took to heart the persecutions directed against his co-religionists and defended them in literary newspaper articles. Nevertheless he accepted indirect advice from Alexander I. and let himself be baptized. He adopted the Lutheran religion and his children were brought up in it.

At the beginning of the Polish Revolution in 1830, Nevahovitch was warned that his house was about to be sacked; the warning reached him as he was peacefully enjoying a theatrical performance. He hurried to prepare for departure and left Warsaw with his family for Petersburg, where he lived on his income. Having given up business, he took up literary work and translated German philosophical works, made friends in the literary world, and knew Pushkin and Kriloff. His children, Emilia Lvovna amongst others, inherited his intellectual gifts. One of his sons was a remarkable caricaturist and edited a caricature[27] newspaper which was very well known at the time. The Nevahovitch family produced no men of science. Metchnikoff himself considered that he had inherited his mother's disposition and turn of mind. In any case, his ancestors on both sides included talented individuals, from whom he may have inherited his gifts and his innate taste for science.

[28]
CHAPTER VII

The Kharkoff Lycée — Bogomoloff and Socialism — Atheism — Natural History studies — Private lodgings — Private lessons in histology from Professor Tschelkoff — A borrowed microscope — First article — Italian Opera — The gold medal.

In 1856 Dmitri Ivanovitch took the boys to Kharkoff in order to make them enter the Lycée. They passed their entrance examination quite satisfactorily; Kolia was admitted into the fifth class and Ilia into the one below it. They were day boarders and lived in the house of one of their former tutors.

This was at a time when the new and liberal reign of Alexander II. was giving birth to many hopes; the Lycées preserved but insignificant traces of the hard regime of Nicholas I. Previous narrow and doctrinal teaching was giving way to a current of realistic and rational ideas, physical and natural science had become the vogue, and professors were trying to come into touch with their pupils and to influence their intellectual development. The boys on their side were founding mutual instruction clubs, attending popular Sunday lectures, interesting themselves in social questions—in fact the revolutionary movement was beginning to strike root. Life in general was intense, aspirations exalted, and hopes radiant.

During his first school year Elie worked assiduously in all branches of the curriculum, and his[29] name soon appeared on the honours list. The Russian language teacher became his friend, and greatly contributed to his development by choosing for him books of general knowledge. Under this direction Elie read, among other things, Buckle's History of Civilisation, which had at that time a very great influence on the young Russian mind. According to the author's principal thesis, the progress of humanity depended chiefly upon that of positive science; this idea sunk deeply into the boy's mind and confirmed his scientific aspirations.

When he reached the fifth class he formed a friendship with one of his schoolfellows, Bogomoloff, who had great influence over Elie's ulterior development; he was the son of a colour manufacturer, and his elder brothers were studying chemistry at the Kharkoff University with a view to applying it to their industry. They had travelled abroad and had brought back novel ideas and books forbidden by the Russian censorship; they influenced their young brother, who in his turn initiated Elie. It was thus that the latter became acquainted with materialistic ideas and social theories; he read the Popular Star, the Bell of Herzin, and other publications prohibited in Russia. Little by little he lost the faith which he had held when under his mother's influence. Atheism, however, was to him more interesting than disappointing; it incited in him a state of general criticism. Ardently passionate in this as in all things, he preached atheism to others and received the nickname of "God is not." The course of teaching at the Lycée did not escape his criticism; when he had reached the fourth class he omitted those exercises which seemed to him devoid of interest. On the other hand, he plunged with[30] passion into the study of natural science, botany, and geology.

He had ceased to be a model student, but his scientific aspirations became stronger from day to day.

In order to cultivate foreign languages, the two brothers had been placed in a boarding-house where morals were strict and patriarchal, the food bad, and the director's sermons long and tedious. None of these things suited Elie. This regime, with the addition of dancing lessons, inspired him with the deepest aversion; he resolved to obtain from his parents permission to take furnished rooms for himself and his brother.

In spite of the current of political exaltation which was then universal in Russia, Elie was too deeply immersed in his studies to be carried away in that direction. He did at one time attend popular lectures and the political gatherings of the students, but he felt that science was his real vocation. He was so early and so completely absorbed by it that he was not interested in the great movement for the emancipation of the serfs. It is true that, at Panassovka, the question was not acute as elsewhere, the serfs being quite happy; however, the fact remains that it was his passion for science which kept him, in spite of his exalted ideas and ardent soul, apart from the noble movement for liberation.

In the third class he made friends with a group of students who were devoted to science and to intellectual culture. Elie, owing to his ardour and vivacity, played the part of a ferment in that little circle, each member of which was to make a special study of certain scientific branches in order that they[31] might together edit a new encyclopædia of human knowledge. He studied German so as to read in the original the classical materialistic writers, Vogt, Feuerbach, Buchner, Moleschott, etc. The Lycée lectures were relegated to the background. Nevertheless, owing to his great facility of assimilation, he was successful in every branch. Plans for his ulterior activities were soon definitely fixed.

At that time of intense intellectual effervescence in Russia, libraries were invaded by a number of translations of works on natural science. Elie absorbed them with avidity, and read amongst others a Russian translation of Bronn's book on the Classes and Orders of the Animal Kingdom. He saw for the first time in the plates of that work pictures of micro-organisms, amoebæ, Infusoria, Rhizopoda, etc. That world of lower beings impressed him so strongly that he resolved from that moment to devote himself to the study of them, that is, to the study of the primitive manifestations of life in its simplest forms.

He was then fifteen years old. The two brothers now obtained from their parents permission to live in furnished rooms, an independent arrangement which allowed each of them to satisfy his individual tastes. Apart from the Lycée, Kolia spent his time in playing cards and billiards and in other amusements, whilst Elie worked with ardour, his only recreations being music and debates on abstract subjects. When he entered the second class he had become completely specialised. In order to tackle serious scientific studies, he tried to come into touch with one of the University professors. The University of Kharkoff was still making use of ancient methods; teaching was given by means of manuals, with practical[32] application; but Elie, who did not know that, dreamt of finding in laboratories assistance and means of, at least, undertaking personal scientific work. He attended a lecture on comparative anatomy, and, in order not to appear too young, he wore his ordinary clothes instead of the Lycée uniform. After the lecture was over, he shyly approached the professor and begged to be allowed to study protoplasm under his direction. The professor received him coldly, and told him in a pedantic tone that he was in too much of a hurry, and that he should first of all finish his course at the Lycée and then get admitted into the University.

It was a disappointment for the eager boy; however, he did not lose heart but continued to attend divers University lectures, clinging to the hope that another professor might be more sympathetic. He was pleased with the lectures of a young physiologist, Tschelkoff by name, and decided to make another attempt. This time he was successful.

16

The professor received him kindly and consented to give him private lessons in histology. Then, fired with a passionate desire to produce something personal in medical science, and attracted by Virchow's cellular theory, he dreamt that he might create a general theory of his own in medicine. In order to increase his scientific knowledge, he undertook with his friend Zalensky the translation of Grove's work, The Unity of Physical Forces. The professor of chemistry and natural history willingly encouraged the two boys in this work, to which they gave up the whole of the school year. Elie wasted no opportunity of learning; during those lectures which did not interest him he used to read scientific books. One day that he was[33] doing so during catechism he did not notice that the priest, wishing to know what he was reading, had come up to him. The latter, however, was greatly impressed by the title of Radlkoffer's learned work on The Crystals of Proteic Substances; he returned the book without a word and never interfered with him again.

Through the assistance of some medical students, Elie obtained the loan of a microscope; he studied Infusoria and imagined that he had made divers discoveries; he hastened to write an article, and sent it to the only scientific Russian paper then in existence, the Bulletin of the Moscow Society of Naturalists. To his great joy his MS. was accepted, but before long the young scientist perceived that his deductions were erroneous, for he had mistaken phenomena of degenerescence for phenomena of development. He was able to stop the publication of this article, the first he ever wrote, and it never appeared.

Thanks to Tschelkoff, who lent him a microscope for the duration of the holidays, he was able to study the local fauna of inferior animals. At the beginning of his last year at the Lycée, he read a text-book of geology by a Kharkoff professor and, with juvenile assurance, wrote a critical analysis of it. Inserted in the Journal de Moscou, this was Elie's first publication; he was then sixteen years old. Encouraged by this success, he sent several other criticisms, but they were not accepted.

The last examinations were coming near: Elie wished to obtain the gold medal, not only out of pride, but in order to prove to his parents that he deserved their assistance in order to go abroad to continue his studies. He therefore provisionally suspended his[34] favourite pursuits and resumed the study of the long-neglected school programme. The last examinations took place in the spring of 1862. It happened to be the Italian Opera season and Elie could not resist the temptations offered him by music. In order to make up the time, he often had to work the whole night long at the cost of severe fatigue.

In spite of this complication, he passed his examinations brilliantly and obtained the gold medal. He now wished for nothing but to devote himself to scientific study.

[35]

CHAPTER VIII

An early love — A schoolfellow's sister — A pretty sister-in-law.

In spite of his precocious vocation, Elie was in no wise indifferent to his surroundings. His mind was sensitive and impressionable and his affections deep and tender, especially where his mother was concerned. He never undertook anything without consulting her, a sweet habit which he preserved even in his maturity.

It was already at the age of six that he received his first love impression: a lady came on a visit to Panassovka with her little girl of eight, a lovely curly-headed child, sweet and graceful, a living floweret. Ilia could not admire her enough, and was most lavish in his attentions, offering her flowers and fruit, inventing games to amuse her and trying by every means to make himself agreeable to her. The presence of this charming little girl caused him great joy and tender emotion; he wished that she might never go away.... But

17

the visit soon ended, and this first idyll was short-lived; new impressions were not long in replacing it. Nevertheless the picture of the pretty child was so deeply impressed in his mind that he never forgot her.

The second time he fell in love was when he was already at the Lycée; one of his schoolfellows had a very pretty sister whom Elie used to meet on half-holidays.[36] He admired her from afar, and tried to contrive opportunities of meeting her; she was the object of his dreams for the whole of one term.

But he was presently to be seized by a more serious feeling. When he was in the third class at the Lycée he came as usual to Panassovka for the summer holidays and found there a new inmate, his elder brother's young wife. Soon, to his own astonishment, he found that the image of his last winter's passion was being effaced by that of his sister-in-law. She, a pretty, fashionable girl, was bored with country life; she criticised the simple habits at Panassovka which formed a sharp contrast with her tastes; she soon became very unpopular and, feeling lonely and bored, tried to attract her young brother-in-law. Elie, at first a willing comrade, soon found himself harbouring a more tender feeling for his sister-in-law; she complained to him of the family's hostility, declared herself misunderstood, and easily excited the pity and sympathy of the sensitive boy. He became her ardent defender and went so far as to fight her battles, even with his mother, whom he reproached with fancied injustice. For nearly four years he remained under his sister-in-law's sentimental influence. He afterwards freed himself completely from it, but the fact remains that she was the first woman who inspired real sentiment in his youthful manhood.

[37]
CHAPTER IX

Journey to Germany — Leipzig — Würzburg — A hasty return.

During his later years at the Lycée, Elie had attended several courses at the Kharkoff University and had realised the inadequacy of the teaching and the impossibility of any personal research work in the laboratories. His greatest desire, therefore, was to go abroad to study. At that time, the German universities, being nearer, chiefly attracted Russian students. Their laboratories were widely opened to foreigners, and lectures were being given by a pleiad of celebrated professors.

In order to attain his object, Elie took care to secure his mother's support. It was not very difficult, for she believed in her son's scientific future and was anxious to help him; she succeeded in convincing his father and, by means of serious sacrifices, the necessary sum was procured. Elie, who was especially interested in the study of protoplasm, chose the University of Würzburg, where the celebrated zoologist Kölliker was lecturing. Thinking that in Germany the term began in September, as in Russia, he hastened to depart. The journey at that time was long and complicated; yet, in spite of much fatigue, Elie only stopped one day in Berlin and hurried to Leipzig, the centre of the book trade, in order to procure the necessary books. He reached Leipzig in[38] the evening and was greatly embarrassed, not knowing where to find a lodging. A young German in the station offered him a room in his own family's house and took him there. The next morning, very early, Elie ran out to buy his books and, in his haste, forgot to note the number of the house and the name of the street; it was with the utmost difficulty that he found the place again. Much disturbed by this misadventure, he hastened to start for Würzburg and, on arriving there, met with a great disappointment; all the professors were absent, this being the middle of the holidays, and the lectures were not to begin for six weeks. The poor boy, thus alone for the first time among strangers, felt completely lost. He was given the address of some Russian students and he hastily sought them out, full of joy and hope, only to be received coldly and distrustfully by his compatriots. After this discouraging reception, he sadly proceeded to look for a room, and having found one in the house of a disagreeable old couple, he brought his bag there. But, as he began to unpack it, he was seized with a feeling of such utter despair that he hastily put his luggage together again and announced to his elderly hosts that he was going. Surprised and indignant, they abused him so brutally that his distress only increased; he rushed to the station, took the first train, and returned to Panassovka without a stop. This hurried return disconcerted his family, but, seeing the state he was in, nobody reproached him. His mother had felt much anxiety on his account, and was in fact not sorry to keep him a little longer under her wing. Thus, in dismal failure, ended that first journey abroad, so ardently desired. The result might have been very different if Elie had reached Würzburg at[39] the right moment, or if the Russian students had been more friendly. Too young and too impressionable to bear absolute solitude, he could only have been saved by his favourite studies or by a friendly environment. His plans and fair dreams had been overthrown by a series of simple mishaps.

[40]
CHAPTER X

Kharkoff University — Physiology — The Vorticella — Controversy with Kühne— The Origin of Species — The Gastrotricha — University degree.

There was now no choice and he had to resign himself to the Kharkoff University. There is not much to relate about this period, which was but a fugitive episode in the course of Elie Metchnikoff, for the "Alma Mater" did not have upon him either the influence or the prestige which it generally exerts upon youth.

Whilst the stream of new ideas had already reached the Lycée, the University of Kharkoff had remained extremely conservative; this was owing to the fact that the Lycée professors were young men, whilst those of the University were elderly and old-fashioned. Officials rather than scientists, they were content with ancient methods, and lectured without practical work, from obsolete and ill-chosen manuals. A few of them drank, others neglected their work. In the Medical and Natural Science Faculties, only two agrégés were newly appointed, Tschelkoff, the physiologist we have already mentioned, and a chemist named Békétoff. These two were indeed scientists and master-minds, and it was only under their direction that any one did any serious work; the other lectures were pure formalities. Elie wished to go in for medical studies[41] but his mother dissuaded him. "You are too sensitive," she said, "you could not bear the constant sight of human suffering." At the same time, Tschelkoff suggested the Natural Science Faculty as being more appropriate to purely scientific activity. Elie accepted his opinion and began to study physiology under his direction. His great desire was to embark at once on personal research, and his teacher advised him to study the mobile stalk of a ciliated Infusorian, the Vorticella. The question was to determine whether this stalk presented any analogy with muscular tissue and whether it offered the same reactions. Elie set to work with ardour and found that the stalk of the Vorticella had no muscular character. His memoir on the subject appeared in 1863 in Müller's Archives. It provoked a severe, even brutal, answer from the celebrated physiologist Kühne which deeply grieved the young scientist and, stimulating his energy still further, incited him to repeat his experiments. He obtained the same results as the first time, and answered Kühne in a somewhat bitter manner, the latter's tone having stirred his combativity.

Meanwhile, Elie was yearning for independent and more general study. During his unsuccessful journey, he had acquired in Leipzig many recently published scientific books, and, among them, Darwin's Origin of Species. The theory of evolution deeply struck the boy's mind and his thoughts immediately turned in that direction. He said to himself that isolated forms which had found no place in definite animal or vegetable orders might perhaps serve as a bond between those orders and elucidate their genetic relationships. This leading idea made him choose for[42] his researches some very singular fresh-water creatures, partly like Rotifera and partly like certain worms of the Nematode group. He succeeded in establishing a new intermediate order which he named "Gastrotricha," and which was straightway accepted.

The whole of his first year at the University was given up to those special studies. As he was fully aware that the teaching of the University did not answer to his aspirations, he resolved to remain there as short a time as possible, and to get through the course of studies in two years instead of the four which were usual. In order to succeed in doing so, he provisionally gave up his scientific researches, attended the lectures as a free auditor, and spent the whole of the second year in cramming for the "candidate" examination, which answers to a Licentiate in Western universities. It happened again this time that the examinations coincided with the Opera season, but, though he indulged in his passion for music, he succeeded, by dint of a supreme effort, in passing them very brilliantly.

Having gone through the University at such an accelerated pace, he did not come into contact with other students, who, themselves chiefly preoccupied with politics, took little interest in a youth so exclusively absorbed in science. He therefore formed none of those attractive juvenile friendships which he had enjoyed at the Lycée. His hasty University studies necessarily left lacunæ in his general knowledge, a fact which he afterwards keenly deplored.

With the exception of Tschelkoff, his teachers had had no decisive influence on his career, and his two years at the University formed but a colourless episode in his life.

[43]
CHAPTER XI

Heligoland — Giessen Congress — Leuckart — Visit to Leo Metchnikoff at Geneva — Socialist gatherings — Metchnikoff's discovery appro-pri-ated by Leuckart — Naples — Kovalevsky — Comparative em-bry-ology — Embryonic layers — Bakounine and Setchénoff — Cholera at Naples — Göttingen — Anatomical studies — Munich; von Siebold — Music — Return to Naples — Intracellular digestion.

Elie still had his Licentiate thesis to prepare. In order to do so, he decided to spend two months in the island of Heligoland, of which the flora and fauna were very attractive to naturalists. In spite of his previous failure, his parents made no objection to his departure; they gave him the little money they could spare and Elie started, in 1864.

As soon as he arrived in Heligoland he became absorbed in his work. He proceeded with his idea of bringing light upon the genealogy of organisms through the study of isolated forms outside definite groups.[7]

His ardour in his work attracted the attention of several German scientists, one of whom introduced him to the celebrated botanist Cohn, who soon became interested in him. During the walks which they took together, they held scientific conversations full of interest for the youth. Cohn advised him to work under the celebrated zoologist Leuckart. Elie received this counsel with enthusiasm, but there was a great difficulty, which was the lack of money to prolong[44] his stay abroad. He did not wish to ask for more from his parents and decided on the following plan, which he expounded in the following letter to his mother, the constant confidante of all his aspirations:

Heligoland, Aug. 12, 1864.

Dear Mamma, ... I am thinking of staying here another month, after which I shall go (at least that is my desire) for ten days to Giessen, where there will be a General Congress of naturalists and physicians from the whole of Europe. This Congress tempts me so much that I want to do my utmost to attend it.

Besides all the scientific benefit that I shall reap from conversations with scientists, I can also study Professor Leuckart's rich collections. This would complete the studies which I am successfully pursuing at the seaside.

In order to realise my ardent wish to profit by such treasures, I must remain three weeks longer at Heligoland, travel to Giessen and live there for ten days; all that out of the money which was to keep me here until the 26 Aug. only.... Therefore, instead of living in the hotel, I have taken a room at a fisherman's, for half the price; instead of a dinner and coffee I eat what I can get and I only spend 90 centimes a day for my food. (Food is dear, as all the provisions come from Hamburg and from England.) Instead of changing my linen two or three times a week, I only do so once or twice, which allows me to spend less on laundry.

The money thus economised, together with the sum which I had put aside for my first installation at Petersburg, constitutes a sufficient capital to provide the following joys and advantages: 1°, I shall stay three weeks longer at the seaside, which will allow me to get on with my researches and to increase my collections; 2°, I shall attend the Congress; 3°, I shall be able to study Leuckart's collections and take advantage of his books and counsel.

I beseech you not to look upon this description of my present life as a complaint or a murmur; on the contrary I am delighted to procure so many advantages at so small a[45] cost; I am happy, too, to be able to assure you in all conscience that I am not wasting the money that you have found for me with so much care and affection. I only wish I could find myself oftener in the same conditions.

Please also believe that my health is in no way suffering from my work. I give you my word that until now I have not had a single headache.

Moreover, I do not think work is at all detrimental to health; I see here several German scientists who could fell an ox with their fist! Altogether I beseech you not to be anxious on my account; you have quite enough painful preoccupations without that, and I am in such excellent circumstances that there really is nothing to worry about. I kiss your hands many times.

Yours affectionately,

Elie Metchnikoff.

P.S.—Write to me oftener. Every word from you is so precious to me!

He did not tell his mother that he never had enough to eat. Neither did he wish Cohn and his other acquaintances at Heligoland to notice it, and he carefully concealed his style of living.

He went to Giessen for the opening of the Naturalists' Congress and read with success two papers dealing with his researches at Heligoland. Engelmann (who was to become well known as a physiologist) and he were the youngest members of the Congress, and their extreme youth attracted general attention. Elie at last made Leuckart's acquaintance; he was charmed by him and definitely decided to begin at once to work under his direction, and, as his stay abroad had thus to be prolonged, he asked and obtained a bursa from the Russian Ministry of Public Education.

The results of his researches at Heligoland had[46] led him to suppose that the Nematodes (of the worm type) formed an independent group; he now proposed to settle that question. Leuckart allowed him to work in his laboratory during his absence for the holidays; Elie immediately set to work and discovered a very curious and quite novel case of alternation of generations; hermaphrodite and parasitic Nematodes giving birth to a free bisexual generation.

Delighted with his discovery, he hastened to communicate it to Leuckart, who was incredulous at first but had to give way to evidence when Elie showed him all the intermediary stages. Still the German scientist was obviously annoyed that this discovery should have been made in his absence and independently from him. He proposed to the young man that they should continue researches in collaboration and publish a joint memoir. Elie accepted joyfully. In his ardour he worked too much, and fatigued his eyesight so that he was forced to limit his microscopical researches to a few hours a day, and Leuckart advised him to take a rest.

It happened that Elie's brother Leo had just settled in Geneva and invited him to stay with him; Elie started to join him. The brothers had not met for a long time. Leo had been travelling and had resided in many different places. He was an extraordinarily gifted man, impulsive, brilliant, and artistic, but restless and incapable of adhering to a steady course of action; he scattered his activities and did not therefore produce all that his rich nature was capable of. He had a remarkable gift for languages; he knew not only a number of European languages but also several Oriental languages, having been in the East, where he had occupied a post of agent in navigation and commerce.[47] He afterwards lived in Italy, took an active part in the Garibaldi movement and was wounded. A clever painter, he also had real literary talent; handsome, witty, agreeable, he was a most attractive personality. Elie had great affection for him.

He found him surrounded with young men and studying a map. They were discussing the acquisition of a piece of ground in Italy in order to found a socialistic community, and Leo, who knew the country, was to choose the locality. Elie was at once made acquainted with the political questions of the day; the young scientist was unfavourably impressed, for the whole reduced itself to party questions and dogmatic discussions founded on hollow grounds. Accustomed as he already was to positive scientific methods, vague and arbitrary theories could not satisfy him.

On the other hand, he was deeply impressed by the personality of the celebrated socialistic Russian writer, Herzen, who resided in Geneva at that time. The young revolutionaries considered him as too literary and too much of a theoretician; they themselves yearned for a direct-action policy. Leo Metchnikoff, however, admired him fervently. Meetings often took place in Herzen's rooms; he used to read to his guests with wonderful effect his yet unpublished manuscript Passé et pensées. A great and powerful figure, the superiority of his intelligence was almost crushing, while his sparkling wit and the nobility of his whole being endowed him with an incomparable and irresistible personal charm. Metchnikoff often said that no man had left a deeper impression on his life. As a politician, however, he had not the same prestige in his sight.

[48]

This sojourn in a revolutionary centre interested him much, but had the result of confirming his conviction that science was immeasurably superior to politics, and he congratulated himself on the path he had chosen. After he had rested, he started to return to Giessen and stopped at Heidelberg, a centre for Russian students who gathered around Helmholtz, Virchow, and Bunsen. He hurried to the library in order to see scientific periodicals; one of the first that came under his eyes was a number of the Göttingen News, containing a memoir by Leuckart on the Nematodes which they had studied together; Leuckart described, in his own name, their common researches and also those personal to the young man, whom he only mentioned incidentally. Elie was shocked and indignant. On his return to Giessen he tried to obtain an explanation from Leuckart but in vain; the latter eluded his questions and gave him no answer.[8]

In his despair, the youth confided in Claus, a professor of zoology whose acquaintance he had made at the Congress, who told him that Leuckart was in the habit of such dealings, and urged Elie, as an independent stranger, to reveal the fact. He pressed this with so much insistence that Elie ended in following his advice; he sent an article stating the case to Dubois-Reymond's journal. He then departed from Giessen without taking leave of Leuckart.

Having had a bursa of 1600 roubles a year granted him for two years by the Russian Ministry of Public Instruction, he was able to undertake a journey to the shores of the Mediterranean in order to pursue his researches.

[49]

He had heard of a very talented young zoologist, Alexander Kovalevsky, who also knew him by hearsay and had written him a letter full of enthusiasm concerning the rich Mediterranean fauna and the facilities for work in Italy. He therefore went to Naples on leaving Giessen. Though the journey in itself had but a secondary attraction for him, he had expected to receive a strong impression; but his imagination had painted such grandiose pictures of the country that he had to cross, that the reality disappointed him, and Italy, like Switzerland on a former occasion, fell very far short of his expectations. He stopped at Florence, which made but a poor impression on him. Museums fatigued him, for he saw a great deal too many works of art all at once without any previous preparation. Architecture and the plastic arts in general did not take any hold of him. During his rapid journey he only saw the country quite superficially and had no time to become impregnated with its beauty. He therefore hastened towards Naples, where his work and Kovalevsky attracted him far more.

He found in Kovalevsky a young man with shy but cordial manners and the clear sweet eyes of a pure child, obviously an idealist. He had for science an absolute cult, the sacred fire of the worshipper; no sacrifice was too great, no difficulty too repellent for his ardour. On a closer acquaintance, the small, timid young man proved to be a hard fighter where science was concerned. The two young men formed an excellent impression of each other, and a friendship was started between them which was to last a lifetime. Though very different from each other, they met on common ground, a passion for science. They[50] worked with the greatest energy, going together on zoological excursions, exchanging their ideas, discussing their aspirations; a similarity of tastes lent great attraction to their friendship.

At Giessen, Elie had read Fritz Müller's For Darwin, a book which had a decisive influence on the future direction of his researches. Fritz Müller, in his embryological works on certain crustaceans, had been the first to confirm in a concrete manner Darwin's evolutionist theories; he had thus demonstrated that it was chiefly in embryology that precious indications were to be found concerning the genealogy of organisms.[9] Under the influence of this work, Elie, who until now had limited himself to introductory researches, resolved to concentrate all his efforts on the comparative embryology of animals. He started to work in that direction, and his researches confirmed him more and more in the opinion that the key of animal evolution and genealogy was to be sought for in the most primitive stages, in those simple phases of development where no secondary element has yet been introduced from external conditions. In those primordial stages, essential characters, common to all, reveal the analogy and connections between animals from different groups.

Every animal begins by being unicellular, for the egg-cell, the reproducing cell, common to all, corresponds to a unicellular being. It is only after fecundation, when it has become an ovum, that this first cell evolves by dividing itself into consecutive segments, each of which is a new cell. This phenomenon is analogous with the multiplication of unicellular[51] beings through division; only, those segments of the ovum do not separate but constitute a whole under the aspect of a hollow sphere, called a blastula, which is the first manifestation of a multicellular being. This blastula is formed of superposed layers, each of which gives birth to specialised organs in the embryo. The outside layer, or ectoderm, produces teguments and the nervous system; the internal layer, or endoderm, gives birth to endothelial cells, the digestive and internal organs; between those two layers comes a third, intermediary layer, the mesoderm, from which the skeleton is developed and also the muscle and blood tissues.

The evolution of these layers in Vertebrates was well known, but very little so in Invertebrates, though it is only through the development of inferior forms that the origin and general evolution of living beings can be elucidated. That is why, during many years, the principal theme of Metchnikoff's researches was the comparative study of the embryonic layers of inferior animals and the ulterior fate of their constituting elements. By following this train of thought, he was able to demonstrate that the development of lower animals takes place on the same plan and follows the same laws as that of higher animals; thus, that there is a real communion between all living beings, which is the concrete confirmation of the theory of evolution.

By their work, Kovalevsky and Metchnikoff contributed to the foundation of Comparative Embryology. The comparative study of cells produced from the divers embryonic layers, and observations on the ulterior development of the functions of those cells, gradually led Metchnikoff to his theory of phagocytes[52] and to pathological biology. An uninterrupted thread can be followed right through his life-work, from the beginning until the end.

In spite of his absorbing work he took great interest in his surroundings, and during this first stay in Italy he became acquainted with two interesting personalities, Bakounine the anarchist and the celebrated physiologist Setchénoff. Both resided at Sorrento. Kovalevsky and Metchnikoff, who greatly desired to know them, decided to call on them, after much hesitation.

Bakounine, a giant with a leonine head and a thick mane of grey hair, struck them as being a fiery enthusiast but an intolerant sectarian, easily roused; for instance, any small and unimportant local meeting was enough for him to predict an imminent revolution in Russia. His theories were epitomised in these words, "We must not leave stone upon

24

stone"; but when asked what should be built up on those ruins he could only say, "We shall see later." Elie looked upon him as a force powerful by its fire and vitality, but thought his mind neither judicial nor profound.

Very different was the impression produced on him by Setchénoff. He carried great weight through the depth of his intelligence, his persuasive eloquence and general thoroughness. He was of a Mongol type and his features were plain, but his splendid eyes, deep and intelligent, shrewd and yet kindly, illumined his face with an unforgettable inward beauty. When Elie went to see him, it was with the uneasy feeling that his own knowledge of chemistry and physics was very restricted, having been very superficially acquired during his rapid passage through the University. In spite of this cause for bashfulness, a mental compact[53] and exchange of ideas was immediately established between the two, and a sympathy was born between them which developed into a lifelong friendship. Elie expatiated upon his plans for the study of the embryology of inferior animals from the evolution point of view, and received from the older scientist much encouragement, for which he never ceased to be grateful.

He worked a great deal during this first stay at Naples, in spite of periods of great fatigue. As a relaxation, he plunged into philosophical reading. After Kovalevsky's departure, he joined Bakounine's circle, the members of which took their meals in a restaurant which rejoiced in the sonorous name of Trattoria della Harmonia. In the autumn of the year 1865, a cholera epidemic broke out in Naples. Every one was nervous and depressed, and this general depression was increased still more by some of the customs of the country—continuous lugubrious church bells, funeral processions in which penitents took part, carrying smoking torches and wearing hoods over their heads with holes for their eyes, etc. Elie, on whom the epidemic had made a great impression, was even more disturbed by the death of one of the members of their little circle, a popular Englishwoman, liked by everybody. She had no fear of cholera and was bright and merry. But one day she did not come to the Trattoria della Harmonia; she had been struck by the scourge and was dead the next day.

Elie was so struck by her death that his nerves, already very tense, gave way and he left Naples, being, moreover, worn out with overwork.

He started for Göttingen, for he wanted to begin the study of Vertebrates under the direction of Professor[54] Keferstein. Keferstein straightway gave him a valuable lizard specimen to anatomise. Elie was not good at technique, on account of his nervous temperament; he used occasionally to lose his patience and his temper, to that point that he flung his material across the room. It happened so on this occasion; having completely wasted the valuable lizard, he conceived a still greater horror of technique and soon left Professor Keferstein for Henle, the celebrated anatomist. He worked with him for a short time at the histology of frogs' kidneys, a subject chosen by the Professor. Soon the young man realised that he was no longer capable of submitting to school discipline and resumed his independent researches. When he had to do with those problems which absorbed him he was always able to conquer his aversion for technique and to do what was required. He studied the embryology of the green-fly from the genealogical point of view, and went to Munich for the summer term in order to work with the celebrated zoologist von Siebold, a typical and venerable old German scientist. The latter was too old already to be troubled with pupils, and Elie studied his insect embryology independently; however, he visited the old man assiduously, and they had long scientific conversations. Their relations were always extremely cordial, and they even kept up a regular correspondence for many years.

During his stay in Germany, music was the young man's only recreation. He did not play any instrument; his parents, discouraged by the failure of their elder children, had not had him taught, and besides, his precocious vocation would have left him no time. Yet he certainly had a natural talent for music, which he passionately loved. He could only whistle, but[55] with that feeble means succeeded in reproducing complicated compositions. Having assiduously attended excellent concerts, he had made himself thoroughly acquainted with classical music, and Beethoven and Mozart always remained his favourite composers. His stay in Germany taught him to appreciate the great capacity for work of the scientists of that country; he admired the organisation of their laboratories, allowing every force, great or small, to be utilised and making useful collective work possible in those complicated researches which demand the collaboration of divers specialists. On the other hand, he felt a great aversion for the manners and customs of German students. Their corporations, duels, and long sittings in beer-houses were distasteful to him; he could not understand how these coarse "Burschen" could become transformed into cultivated intellectuals and respectable scientists. People to whom he expressed this wonder merely said, "Youth must have its fling...." Moreover, scientists themselves were not particularly courteous to each other. More than anywhere else personal questions held a foremost place, and kindliness was rare between colleagues.

After staying some time in Munich, Elie returned to Naples, war having broken out between Northern and Southern Germany. This time, in order to spend less on the journey, he took a steamer at Genoa, but with fatal results, for a storm was raging; he suffered a great deal, and, when he reached Naples, violent fits of giddiness made him incapable of doing any work at all for some time. Cholera reappeared, and the landlady of the rooms he shared with Kovalevsky died of it. Much depressed, the two started for Ischia, but Elie soon realised with terror that he was not yet well[56] enough to work; in order to recover quickly, he went to Cava, a pretty little place, renowned for its salubrious climate.

There he met Bakounine again, and they saw a good deal of each other in a friendly way. Bakounine nicknamed him "Mamma" because of his almost maternal attentions, a nickname which, for the same reason, was given him later, quite independently, by other intimates. Yet, though their relations were cordial and even affectionate, there was not really much in common between the two. Elie thought Bakounine's ideas superficial, and disliked his sectarian mentality; they ultimately drifted apart.

His health having gradually recovered owing to the rest, he returned to Naples in the autumn, after the epidemic had abated, and at last resumed his work.

Whilst studying the history of the development of Cephalopoda he found that they had embryonic layers similar to those of Vertebrates; this was the first time that the fact was established. It was extremely important, for it constituted a concrete and indisputable proof of the existence of a genetic connection between inferior and superior animals. Metchnikoff chose this subject for his thesis, and, having completed his researches, he returned to Russia in 1867.

By this time he had made great use of his three years' stay abroad. Though he had not showed himself a docile pupil, yet he had become initiated into the organisation of scientific work in Germany; he had carried out independent researches and had been able to choose with full knowledge the future path of investigations which he was to pursue for many years in the field of Comparative Embryology.

[57]

Already the observations he had made had in themselves a real importance. For instance, his studies in divers specimens of the worm type, a type which offers very heterogeneous forms, had permitted him to establish links of continuity between certain groups among them. Whilst studying those animals at Giessen in 1865, he had discovered the capital fact which proved to be the starting-point of all his future work—the intercellular digestion of an inferior worm, a land planarian, the Geodesmus bilineatus. He had compared this digestion with that of the superior Infusoria and had seen in it one more proof of the genetic connection between the type of the Protozoa and that of worms.

He did not then realise the full bearing of this observation, which really constituted the basis of his future phagocyte theory; this was only to appear eighteen years later.

He had also made researches on numerous specimens of insects and on the scorpion, establishing the fact that they all had embryonic layers; he concluded that he was "entitled to extend the theory of embryonic layers to Arthropoda."

Finally, he had discovered embryonic layers similar to those of the Vertebrates in inferior Invertebrates, the Cephalopoda (Sepiola). This established a link of continuity between the higher and lower animals.

[58]
CHAPTER XII

Petersburg — Baer prize — Return home — Friendship with Cienkovsky — Odessa — Naturalists' Congress at Petersburg — Departure from Odessa — Zoological Lecturer's Chair at Petersburg — Messina — Enforced rest — Reggio — Naples — Controversy with Kovalevsky — Visit to the B. family — Mlle. Fédorovitch — Educational questions — Difficulties of life in Petersburg.

During his stay abroad, Metchnikoff had successfully carried out several researches, and this allowed him to apply for a post of docent at the new University of Odessa, which he had chosen on account of its proximity with the sea and its marine fauna. Whilst awaiting the result he went to Petersburg in order to pass his thesis and to prepare himself to become a professor. He received a pleasant welcome, for his lively and sociable disposition had made him many friends. The brothers Kovalevsky, with whom he was already on friendly terms, offered him hospitality; he also made the acquaintance of Professor Békétoff, and soon became a member of his family circle.

He was well received everywhere, for his scientific precocity excited general interest. He was even elected magister[10] by the Faculty, without having to pass an examination, on account of the work he had done. He and Kovalevsky halved Baer's first prize, and they were invited and treated with the utmost kindness by Baer himself. Metchnikoff had certainly[59] entered upon a successful phase; his friends nicknamed him "the star." As soon as he was made a magister, he received his appointment at the Odessa University, and, the holidays drawing near, he was at last able to return to his home. Needless to say how joyfully and lovingly he was received by his family. He spent two months with them, utilising his leisure in preparing himself to teach.

In his hurry to arrive in Odessa in good time in order to take his bearings before starting his lectures, he went there much too soon and found nobody at the University; he then decided to go to the Crimea for some preliminary studies on the fauna of the Black Sea. Before long, he made the acquaintance of the celebrated botanist Cienkovsky, who invited him to stay in his villa. Though the scientist was already 46 years old and Elie only 22, they soon became fast friends. Cienkovsky was a man of great European culture; passionately fond of science as he was, his critical mind submitted everything to a close analysis. He took great interest in young Metchnikoff and showed him a marked predilection, but that did not prevent him from criticising him severely. He reproached him with a lack of self-control, and undertook the paternal task of civilising the impulsive, fiery, sometimes even violent young man. He preached to him tolerance towards the opinions of others, a strict self-discipline, and the absolute necessity of bowing to certain social conventions against which Elie blindly rebelled. Cienkovsky acquired great prestige in his young friend's eyes; years later, even, Metchnikoff took pleasure in quoting his axioms and in trying to conform with them.

He worked with ardour during his stay in the[60] Crimea; though the heat was great, 50° C. (122° F.) in the sun, he undertook zoological excursions and surprised every one by his endurance and energy.

At the end of the holidays, he returned to Odessa and began his professorate with much zeal and success. His lucid, living lectures stimulated his pupils, third-year students, who were all older than himself. Friendly relations soon reigned between them and their young lecturer; he organised practical studies, and his laboratory became a very active centre of work.

Thus everything was going well, and perhaps he might have remained at Odessa for a long time if it had not been for the following incident, due to his passionate and intolerant disposition. A Congress of Russian naturalists was to take place in Petersburg at the end of the year 1867. Elie eagerly wished to attend it as a delegate and took steps for that purpose; this brought him into conflict with his chief, who desired the mission for himself. Knowing that the old Professor had no real scientific interests, Elie thought himself justified in insisting, and counted upon Cienkovsky's support, but the latter was of opinion that the younger man should give way. Elie, becoming more and more excited, lost all sense of proportion and committed the grave error of telling his pupils about what he considered a serious injustice. The latter, out of sympathy for their young lecturer, hooted the old Professor, which naturally embittered the quarrel. However, all the agitation ended in both zoologists being sent to the Congress in the quality of delegates.

When he reached Petersburg, Elie hurried to the[61] house of his friends B——, who received him with open arms; it was a great joy to him to find himself in friendly surroundings after the recent strife. Impulsive and impressionable as he was, the disagreeable incidents he had traversed made him yearn to leave Odessa, a desire which was to be promptly realised. His communications had great success at the Congress; the President even invited him to read a paper at the general meeting; but, though strongly attracted by this proposal, which would have allowed the young scientist to expose his ideas on the comparative development of the embryonic layers, he refused it, considering that that complicated question was not yet sufficiently matured.

Nevertheless, the Congress had brought him into prominence and was the cause of his obtaining a Professorship of Zoology at Petersburg. Moreover, he had the additional good fortune of being given a scientific mission and went abroad to work until the autumn term.

He went to Naples in the spring of 1868, thinking to find Kovalevsky there, instead of which he found a letter from his friend awaiting him. The latter had had to go to Messina for urgent embryological work and begged Elie to look after his wife and new-born child. Metchnikoff did so most willingly until he was able to send them off to Messina. He himself followed soon after, for Kovalevsky wrote him that zoological specimens and conditions of work were far better at Messina than Naples. This time, Metchnikoff undertook the study of Sponges and Echinodermata. The two friends worked unceasingly, but Elie's sight was too weak for such excessive fatigue; he was again obliged to interrupt his studies for a while, and during[62] that period of enforced rest he felt for the first time the need of a sentimental affection in his life.

He dreamed of a helpmeet who would conform with his tastes. At Petersburg he had become very fond of Professor B.'s young daughters, the eldest of whom was about thirteen years old, and he wondered if he could not train one of those little girls to become the realisation of his ideal. He was too active by nature, however, to linger very long over reveries or over a prolonged rest; he therefore undertook a short journey through Reggio and Calabria, on his way towards Naples.

His eyesight being now restored, he began work again as soon as he arrived. This period, however, was not a pleasant one: to begin with, he obtained in the study of Ascidia a result which differed considerably from that obtained by Kovalevsky,[11] and this scientific controversy grieved and preoccupied them both. Besides, Elie's nerves suffered from his constant anxiety about his eyes, the tropical heat and the noisy life of Naples. Incessant serenades used to keep him awake at night, and, on one occasion, his exasperation reached such a point that he poured a bucket of water over the head of some persistent musicians. Tired with all these things, he left Naples for Trieste, where he carried out successful researches into the transformations of Echinodermata, from the point of view of Comparative Embryology and genetic connections between inferior animals.

Having obtained results which interested him, he returned to Russia and joined the B. family in the[63] country, near Moscow. Their young friend Mlle. Fédorovitch, whom he had already met in Petersburg, was staying with them, and she and Elie became very good friends. His affection for the B. children led him to ponder over general educational questions. He was struck for the first time by the lack of harmony in human nature, which was due, he thought, to the considerable difference between the organism of the child and that of the adult, a difference which does not exist in animals to the same degree.[12] As soon as he returned to Petersburg he tried to study this subject, and made comparisons between the brain of a man and that of a dog at various ages, but without result.

He was not long in realising that the conditions of work in his new post were extremely unsatisfactory. He had no proper laboratory and had to work between two specimen cases in a non-heated zoological museum; there was no room for practical work. All his enthusiasm, all his aspirations towards scientific activity and rational teaching struck against indifference, lack of organisation, and lack of means. He protested with his usual vehemence, but could obtain nothing; being equally unable to adapt himself to his uncongenial surroundings, he found himself getting more and more discontented and unnerved. Moreover, his everyday life was most uncomfortable, for he wished to do without servants, on principle and in order to economise, and to do his household work himself; but he soon tired of taking the necessary care of his rooms, which became a regular chaos. He left off preparing his own meals and went out for them to an inferior[64] restaurant in the neighbourhood. Yet, in spite of all his efforts and privations, he never seemed to make both ends meet. He resigned himself to giving lessons at the School of Mines in order to increase his resources; the school was a long way off, he had to walk the distance in the coldest weather in order to lecture to students who did not interest him. The work wearied him without giving him any moral compensation. Altogether, the life in Petersburg, on which he had founded great hopes, brought him nothing but disappointments and made him become more and more pessimistic and misanthropical.

[65]
CHAPTER XIII

29

Slight illness — Engagement to Mlle. Fédorovitch — Marriage — Illness of the bride — Pecuniary difficulties — Spezzia — Montreux — Work in Petersburg University — The Riviera — Cœlomata and Acœlomata — St. Vaast — Panassovka — Madeira — Mertens — Teneriffe — Return to Odessa — Bad news, hurried journey to Madeira — Death of his wife — Return through Spain — Attempted suicide — Ephemeridæ.

It was only in the house of his friends the B.'s that Elie felt at his ease. He was devotedly fond of their children, whom he used to take for walks on Sundays and to the theatre now and then; he was always ready to read to them and to indulge them in every possible way.

He continued to entertain the dream of marrying one of them some day, and was particularly interested in the eldest, a girl of thirteen, intelligent, gifted, and lively; however, as he knew her better, he realised the incompatibility of their respective tempers, an incompatibility which brought about frequent disputes. These were generally smoothed down by a mutual friend, Mlle. Fédorovitch, who invariably showed Elie a marked and cordial sympathy. He became ill at this juncture and she nursed him with a devotion which brought them together even more, as will be seen from the following letter to his mother:

Dear Mother—I have just had an inflammation of the throat which lasted two weeks; it is quite gone now and I would not even have mentioned it to you if it had not been connected with what follows.

[66]

When I fell ill, the B.'s, knowing me to be alone and uncared for, brought me to their house. During my stay with them, I acquired the conviction that my darling little girls did not love me, especially the eldest, who interested me even more than her three sisters.... The dreams I told you of have vanished!

It was a grief to me, for, apart from my scientific interests, I cherished them more than anything. I have no acquaintances and do not require any, but I long to have some one with me to whom I could become attached and who could share my pleasures and leisure.

My grief would have been greater still if I had not seen that Ludmilla Fédorovitch, whom I mentioned to you this summer, showed me much sympathy in all my troubles.

We were already very good friends, and have now drawn nearer together; who knows? perhaps the 800 roubles which are going to be added to my salary will be very useful.

I will keep you informed of everything, dear Mother, for I am sure of your sympathy; I love you better than the whole world and I have full confidence in you.

Au revoir, dear Mother, I kiss your hands.—Your

Elie Metchnikoff.

Mlle. Fédorovitch became ill in her turn; the sympathy which Elie showed her on this occasion brought them still nearer to each other, and he soon decided to marry her.

He informed his mother of this; much alarmed, she tried to dissuade him, for she feared that by marrying a girl in delicate health, her son would be assuming too heavy a task in his difficult circumstances.

He answered as follows:

I received your letter to-day, dear Mother. It grieves me very much. My project inspires you with doubt, you counsel prudence and, though you say you believe me to be reasonable, yet you fear that I am acting on an impulse. If I really am reasonable, why fear a blind impulse? On the[67] other hand, if I am blindly carried away, it is not likely that I shall listen to reason.

I did tell you that I had great affection for the B. girls, and it was true. But did I ever tell you that they had the same for me? You are mistaken in thinking that I did not like Ludmilla Fédorovitch at first. I was not in love with her but we were very good friends, and whilst I did not consider her as my feminine ideal, I was sure of her absolutely honest, loyal, and kindly disposition. The very fact that I knew Ludmilla for a long time before I thought of marrying her, should prove to you that there is some chance of my being neither blind nor partial.

Her love for me is beyond doubt, as you will see when you know her.

I also am very fond of her, and that is a solid basis for future happiness.

Yet I will not answer for it that we shall spend our life like a pair of turtledoves. A rosy, boundless beatitude forms no part of my conception of the distant future.

Yet I do not see the necessity of waiting till I become a thorough misanthrope, and I am already inclined that way.

Please do not believe that, if I do not dream of a rosy happiness it is that I feel none at all; that is not the case; I am in a happy medium.

I like Ludmilla and I feel comfortable with her; but at the same time I preserve the faculty of feeling every trouble and worry in life. I do not at all think that it is enough to love in order to be happy. Therefore I have begun to take steps to obtain a Professor's chair, and I am very desirous of being successful in that financial operation.

Soon after that, he wrote the following letter to his mother:

Dear Mother—In my last letter I had already spoken to you of Ludmilla Fédorovitch. I can now give you information about her which will surely interest you.

She is not bad-looking, but that is all. She has fine hair; her complexion is not pretty. We are about the same[68] age, she is a little over 23. She was born at Orenburg; then she lived for a long time with her family at Kiahta (Siberia), after which she was abroad for nearly two years and finally settled in Moscow. Ludmilla, or Lussia, was, as you remember, a very zealous intermediary between me and the B. girls to whom I was so attached.

She loved me already then, though she said to herself that I had too much affection for the B. children ever to return her feelings.

31

And she was perfectly right, as long as my affection for those children lasted.

But, when it ceased, I naturally took more notice of Lussia's sympathy for me, and I am not surprised that I have acquired much affection for her.

She has faults which must seem graver to me than to you, but what is to be done?

Fortunately she herself sees them. The greatest of her faults is a too great placidity, a lack of vivacity and initiative; she adapts herself too easily to her surroundings. But, being placid, she is also firm; she can bear a great deal whilst preserving complete self-control. She is extremely kind and good-natured; I have not yet found a vulgar trait in her character.

I have told you of her faults, you must therefore not think me partial if I find qualities in her.

The fact is—and I cannot forget it—that always, when I had any kind of trouble, she soothed me by her attitude towards me.

Even though I have dark previsions for the future (as you know, I am not given to seeing life through rose-coloured glasses), I cannot help thinking that by living with Lussia I should become calmer, at least for a fairly long time.

I should cease to suffer from the misanthropy which has invaded me lately.

I intend to have no children—it is an embryologist who is speaking. On the contrary, I want to preserve the utmost liberty. Nevertheless, one must conform with certain legal conventions, which will probably take place in January.

[69]

Lussia has no fortune, but we shall be entirely guaranteed by the increase in my salary.

It is very regrettable that the event should be retarded by the customary formalities; in any case it will certainly end by taking place.

I beg you to write to me, dear mother that I love, anything that comes into your head à propos of my affair.

Rejoice that I am now very happy and wish that it may last.

I ask the same of Papa, whom I beg you to salute from me. I embrace you, dear Mamma, and I remain your very affectionate son,

E. Metchnikoff.

As Elie learnt to know his fiancée better, he became more and more attached to her. Their happiness seemed likely to be complete, but a cruel Fate had decided otherwise.

32

The girl's health was not improving: her supposed bronchitis was assuming a chronic character. Yet the marriage was not postponed, and the bride had to be carried to the church in a chair for the ceremony, being too breathless and too weak to walk so far.

Elie did his utmost to procure comforts for his wife, and hoped that she could still be saved by care and a rational treatment. It was the beginning of an hourly struggle against disease and poverty; his means being insufficient, he tried to eke them out by writing translations. His eyesight weakened again from overwork, and it was with atropin in his eyes that he sat up night after night, translating. There was but one well-lighted room in his flat, and he turned it into a small laboratory for the use of his pupils; his own researches he had to give up, his time being entirely taken up by teaching and translations.

He hid his precarious position from his parents in order not to add to their heavy expenses nor to[70] confirm their previsions concerning his marriage. His wife's illness, the impossibility of carrying on scientific work, the lack of friendly sympathy to which he thought himself entitled, all this weighed on him, making him bitter, suspicious, and distrustful; he thought himself persecuted. The situation became intolerable and, in spite of his pride, he forced himself to apply for a subsidy to take his wife abroad and to go on with his researches. Having obtained it in 1869, he immediately left Petersburg, which he now hated.

Youth is elastic: the young couple started full of joy, gay as children, and ready to forget all their trials. Alas, it was not for long: having halted at Vilna in order that the patient should have a rest, she had an attack of hæmorrhage of the lungs, to the great alarm of her husband, who nevertheless did his best to reassure her. They continued the journey as soon as her condition allowed it, only to be interrupted by another relapse. At last they reached Spezzia, chosen on account of the climate and the marine fauna.

Little by little, Ludmilla Metchnikoff's health improved and her husband was able to resume work. He studied aquatic animals in view of the genealogy of inferior groups, and, amongst others, studied the Tornaria, which was believed to be the larva of the star-fish. However, to his astonishment, he ascertained that, in spite of great similarity, it was not the larva of an Echinoderm, but that of one of the Balanoglossi, of the worm type. This fact established a link between the Echinodermata and worms, a very important result from the point of view of the continuity of animal types.

Metchnikoff felt his courage returning and also[71] his natural high spirits. His wife, who was a clever draughtswoman, helped him with the drawings for his memoir, and both felt happy and contented; this stay at Spezzia was a real oasis in their life.

When the heat became excessive they went to Reichenhall, a summer resort prescribed by the doctor. There, Metchnikoff completed his previous researches on the development of the scorpion, and finally established the fact that this animal possesses the three embryonic layers which correspond to those of the Vertebrates.

As his young wife's health was still too precarious to allow her to spend the winter in Russia, Metchnikoff, obliged to return to Petersburg, installed her at Montreux and asked his sister-in-law, Mlle. Fédorovitch, to stay with her. The enforced separation deeply grieved the young couple, whose only consolation was daily correspondence.

Metchnikoff resumed a life of hard work; he was now an agrégé at the Petersburg University and had to leave the School of Mines; this diminished his resources, but at the same time he obtained an extra salary of 800 roubles as Extraordinary Professor. His position in the University was nevertheless very difficult, for his situation was coveted by different parties with which he had nothing to do. They wanted it for one of their adherents. His devoted friend Setchénoff, Professor of Physiology, then thought of proposing him to the Faculty of Medicine as a Lecturer in Zoology, and whilst

33

Metchnikoff awaited the result of his efforts, he obtained leave to go to the seaside to do research work.

He joined his wife and took her to San Remo and to Villafranca. Her health had improved and[72] she was even able to take part in his work. He was engaged in studying Medusæ and Siphonophora, animals which interested him, not only from the point of view of the origin of embryonic layers, but also from that of general morphology, for he was still pursuing the problem of genetic links between animals. He had already been able to prove the presence of embryonic layers in many inferior animals; moreover, he had found, while studying the metamorphoses of Echinodermata, the proof that the structural plan, hitherto considered immutable, could become transformed in course of development. Thus the bilateral plan of the larva of Echinoderma becomes a radial plan in the adult. The structural plan therefore is not an absolutely differentiating character, since specimens of the same type can show a different plan according to their stage of development. One of the genetic questions still unsolved was that of the body cavity. Always present in higher animals, it is totally absent in certain lower groups, such as Sponges, Polypi, and Medusæ. It was being questioned whether their dissimilar morphological characters did not correspond with a duality of origin separating animals which possessed a body cavity (Cœlomata) from those which did not (Acœlomata).

Kovalevsky, it is true, had observed that the body cavity of many animals (Amphioxus, Sagitta, Brachiopoda) took its origin in the lateral sacs of the digestive cavity, sacs which detach themselves from it in order to form the body cavity. But, in order to establish a genetic connection between those animals that have a body cavity and those which are devoid of it, it was necessary to show the homology of corresponding organs in both groups.

[73]

Through his researches on the development of Cœlomata (Echinodermata) on the one hand and Acœlomata (Ctenophora and Medusæ) on the other, Metchnikoff succeeded in proving that the lateral sacs of the digestive cavity which give birth to the body cavity of the Cœlomata (Echinodermata) correspond to the canals and vaso-digestive sacs of the Acœlomata (Ctenophora and Medusæ). The difference consists in that the latter do not detach themselves in order to form a body cavity, which is therefore lacking.

The result of his researches satisfied Metchnikoff; moreover, he began to feel again hopeful of his wife's recovery. The only dark spot was that Setchénoff's efforts had failed. Metchnikoff was not appointed by the Faculty of Medicine, for it was found advisable to replace the Chair of Zoology by one on Venereal Diseases. On the other hand, he was nominated for the Odessa University, supported by Cienkovsky and unanimously elected.

As he only had to go to his new post in the autumn, he went for the summer to St. Vaast in Normandy to study Lucernaria; unfortunately the stay was not a success; the weather was cold and the sea very rough, which made the Lucernaria impossible to find. Life conditions were very difficult, all the male population being at sea and the women being in the fields. In order not to waste this journey he studied Ascidians, and found that he had previously been mistaken at Naples when he thought that the nervous system of those animals originated from the lower embryonic layer. Kovalevsky had been right in affirming the contrary, and Elie hastened to write to tell him so.

St. Vaast, open to every wind, was not favourable[74] to the patient, and Metchnikoff had to take her away. They went to Russia to stay with her parents and then to Panassovka. The doctors having advised a course of treatment by "koumiss," or fermented mare's milk prepared in a special way by the Tartars, Elie engaged a Tartar servant specially for that purpose, but in vain. In spite of every treatment, his wife's health was steadily growing worse. The cold at St. Vaast had been followed by such a dry heat in Russia that, in order to procure a little coolness for the patient, they had to spread wet sheets around her. She constantly had high temperatures and frequent attacks of hæmorrhage. It was obvious that she must leave Russia, and Metchnikoff, obliged to rejoin his post at Odessa, asked Mlle. Fédorovitch to go with her to Montreux.

The separation was all the harder that all hope of recovery was beginning to wane. The patient, however, had been told of the magical effect of Madeira in cases of tuberculosis, and she clung to the idea as to a plank of safety. Elie resolved to take her there. He set to work with renewed ardour in order to obtain the sum necessary for the journey; in spite of all his self-denial, his normal resources would not have sufficed, and he had recourse to translations and literary articles. He had a theme ready, which he developed in a paper called Education from the Anthropological Point of View—in fact a preliminary sketch of his ideas on the disharmonies in human nature. In it, he analysed the disharmonies due to the great difference of development between the child and the adult: whilst the young of animals are very rapidly able to imitate the adults and to live like them, the man-child is incapable of it. His brain, especially in[75] civilised races, demands a long period of development in order to equal that of the adult, whilst certain instincts in the organism mature, on the contrary, long before their function is possible. Moreover, a child's sensibility is extremely developed whilst his will is by no means so. These causes provoke suffering and a series of regrettable consequences.

Apart from frenzied efforts and unceasing labour, Metchnikoff was going through a painful moral crisis, due to the impossibility of making his conduct accord with his convictions. Party intrigues continued to be rife at the Odessa University: Poles were being persecuted by Nationalists; one professor was refused admission on account of his Polish nationality, and Cienkovsky resigned by way of protest. Metchnikoff shared his views and longed to follow his example, but was prevented by his lack of means and felt it deeply. It also went against his conscience to ask for leave as frequently as his wife's condition made it necessary.

She wished to see her parents once again before going to Madeira, and he took her to Russia for the last time: she never saw her family again.

At last they were able to start. The long journey was very fatiguing, the sea voyage was rough, but, when she landed in Madeira, the patient thought herself saved. The very next morning Metchnikoff started feverishly on a voyage of discovery. Nature on the island was extremely beautiful; alone the sight of numerous sick people reminded him of suffering and death. The words "a flower-decked grave" haunted his mind, and a growing despondency warned him that he had nothing to expect from this luxuriant spot. From the aspect of the rocky coast, beaten by the[76] waves, he realised that the beach fauna must be very poor; his only refuge, research work, was likely to be denied him.

He was advised to hire a small house, which would be cheaper than a boarding-house, and he did find a pretty furnished villa with a garden; it was beyond his means, but a young Russian named Mertens, who had been a fellow-traveller, proposed to share it with them. The arrangement proved highly satisfactory, and Mertens, at first merely an agreeable neighbour, became a close friend.

Before leaving for Madeira, Metchnikoff had obtained a scientific mission and a subsidy from the Society of Natural Science Lovers of Moscow, and felt it a moral obligation to obtain some results. The scantiness of the marine fauna was a bitter disappointment; he had to fall back upon what little he found, and embarked on the study, hitherto unknown, of the embryology of Myriapoda. But this research work

35

brought him a new source of torment instead of satisfaction: he could not master the technique, which proved to be very difficult, and this irritated him; his failures disappointed him, made him vexed with himself; his nerves, already strung to the highest point by suffering and anxiety, made the disappointment unbearable. On the other hand, the external aspect of life formed a striking contrast with the state of his mind. A wealth of natural beauty, all flowers and perfumes, in an incomparable site, congenial surroundings and home comforts formed the frame for these two young lives, of which one was waning whilst the other was spent in a useless struggle to save it.

Metchnikoff's natural pessimism was growing under the influence of these painful circumstances. His[77] conception of life was a sombre one; he said to himself that the "disharmonies" of human nature must infallibly end in a general decadence of humanity. He set forth his reflections in an article entitled The Time for Marriage, in which he discussed the following concrete fact: With the progress of civilisation and culture, the time for marriage recedes gradually, whereas puberty remains as early as before; the result is that the time between puberty and marriage is becoming longer and longer, and constitutes a growing period in which there is no harmony. The statistics of suicides prove that there is a close connection between them and the period of disharmonies.

Whilst he worked, his wife tried to make use of her leisure: she interested herself in poor children, sketched flowers, read novels ... life flowed peacefully in spite of the underlying drama.

Yet the thought that he was not fulfilling his obligations was intolerable to Metchnikoff. He thought of resigning and founding a small book-shop at Madeira in order to be independent and not obliged to leave his wife, but lack of funds made this plan impossible. In his search for new resources, he went to Teneriffe to look for a subject for an article. He met with several disappointments on this trip; yet he saw the Villa Orotava, with its celebrated giant dragon-tree, which had already then been brought down by a storm. He also visited the Caves of the Guancios, the primitive inhabitants of the Canary Islands. Having gathered the necessary observations, he hastened to return to Madeira, where months passed without bringing any change.

The book-shop idea was abandoned as being impracticable and Metchnikoff had to return to Odessa,[78] asking his sister-in-law to come to Madeira in his place. When she had arrived, he confided the two girls to Mertens and to the care of the devoted Dr. Goldschmidt, and went away conscious of the uselessness of his efforts and more deeply pessimistic than ever.

When he reached Odessa, in October 1872, he found there his friend Setchénoff, whom he had previously proposed for a Physiology Lecturer's chair, and whose affection was a great comfort to him at this sad time. The correspondence between him and his wife during that period is full of an infinite tenderness, as if they felt the supreme separation coming near, and yearned to express their mutual love.

At the end of January 1873, between two classes, Metchnikoff received a letter from his sister-in-law telling him to come in haste if he wished to find his wife still living. He delivered his lecture like an automaton, then went to obtain his leave and hurried off. He accomplished the whole journey without a break. On arriving at Madeira he found his wife so changed that he scarcely knew her, and it was only through sheer force of will that he kept his alarm from her. She suffered so much that she had to be given morphia constantly and could no longer leave her bed.

Metchnikoff himself was in very poor health; his eyes were so sensitive from overwork that he had to remain in the dark, only going into the garden at dusk to observe spiders and snails. Time was progressing slowly and miserably, and bringing nothing but anxiety as to the means to support this sad existence. Metchnikoff had hoped to receive the Baer prize for a zoological work, but did not obtain it: it was refused on the pretext that his memoir[79] had been presented in manuscript instead of being printed. In reality, the German party had wished to give it to a fellow-German.

A friend of his, who sent him the bad news, offered to lend him 300 roubles, and Metchnikoff accepted; he could now think of nothing but holding out till the end.

One morning the patient's condition suddenly became much worse. The doctor was sent for in a hurry and declared that it was now a question of a few hours.... When Metchnikoff went back to his wife he found her with eyes wide open and so full of mortal anguish and utter despair that he could bear it no longer and went out hastily, not to show her his dismay.

This was his last impression; he never saw her again.

Only half conscious, he walked up and down the drawing-room, opening and closing books without seeing them, his mind full of disconnected pictures; he wondered to himself how his family would hear the news. Time passed without his realising it. Then his sister-in-law came to tell him that all was over. This was on the 20th April 1873.

Metchnikoff's feelings were complex: a mixture of crushing despair and of relief at the thought that the terrible agony was at last ended.... During the whole of the sad first night he sat with his sister-in-law in a distant room, talking of those things which are only mentioned in moments such as these. When Dr. Goldschmidt came in the morning to offer Metchnikoff his sympathy and help he found him apparently almost calm. Metchnikoff asked him to make a post-mortem examination of the deceased and to look after her sister. A Scottish minister[80] came to bring religious comfort and to exhort him to look there for consolation. Metchnikoff thanked him, but firmly assured him that it was not possible to him.

The funeral took place two days later; he did not attend it and did not see the corpse. Immediately after the funeral he left Madeira with his sister-in-law. Being no longer anxious to economise, he took with him a sick young Russian who wished to see his mother again and could not afford the journey.

After the catastrophe, Metchnikoff felt incapable of thinking of the future, his life seemed cut off at one blow; he destroyed his papers and reserved a phial of morphia, without any settled intention. They journeyed back through Spain; it was during the Carlist insurrection, and several episodes on the way distracted their attention. Elie and his sister-in-law reached Geneva, where they found Leo Metchnikoff and several relations, among whom he seems to have recovered himself. He even related some of their travelling experiences, meetings with Carlists, frontier incidents, etc., with some spirit. But his apparent calm concealed black despair.

He said to himself: "Why live? My private life is ended; my eyes are going; when I am blind I can no longer work, then why live?" Seeing no issue to his situation, he absorbed the morphia. He did not know that too strong a dose, by provoking vomiting, eliminates the poison. Such was the case with him. He fell into a sort of torpor, of extraordinary comfort and absolute rest; in spite of this comatose state he remained conscious and felt no fear of death. When he became himself again, it was with a feeling of dismay. He said to himself that[81] only a grave illness could save him, either by ending in death or by awaking the vital instinct in him. In order to attain his object, he took a very hot bath and then exposed himself to cold. As he was coming back by the Rhone bridge, he suddenly saw a cloud of winged insects flying around the flame of a lantern. They were Phryganidæ, but in the distance he took them for Ephemeridæ, and the sight of them suggested the following reflection: "How can the theory of natural selection be applied to these insects? They do not feed and only live a few hours; they are therefore not subject to the struggle for existence, they do not have time to adapt themselves to surrounding conditions."

His thoughts turned towards Science; he was saved; the link with life was re-established.

[82]
CHAPTER XIV

Anthropological expedition to the Kalmuk steppes — Affection of the eyes — Second expedition to the steppes — The eggs of the Geophilus.

After the misfortune which had befallen him Metchnikoff placed his only hope in work, and the condition of his eyes was therefore for him a source of great preoccupation. He applied to the Petersburg Geographical Society for an anthropological mission in order to undertake researches less trying to his eyesight than microscopical work.

As he went deeper into anthropology, he was struck by the fact that this science lacked a leading thread and was guided by no general idea but reduced to mere measurements, very precise and detailed, it is true. Metchnikoff wondered whether it would not be advisable to apply to anthropology the methods used in embryology and to establish an analogy between the diverse human races and the different ages of the individual. In order to solve this problem he had thought at first of visiting the Samoyedes as being the most primitive of the aboriginal peoples of Russia. But the project was not realisable and he determined to visit, at his own expense, the Kalmuks of the Astrakhan steppes, also a primitive Mongol race.

Before his departure he went to see his family and that of his late wife. Long afterwards his sister-in-law, Mlle. Fédorovitch, wrote me the following account of that interview:

[83]
He was still suffering from an inflammation of the eyes. This man, whom I cannot picture to myself without a microscope or a book, was, at that sad period of his life, reduced to complete inactivity. We had always been struck with his power of becoming absorbed in scientific reading, even during meals; it inconvenienced no one, for he heard at the same time the conversation that was going on and even took part in it from time to time. Now, the day after his arrival, I came to call him to tea and found him seated in his darkened room with scissors in his hands and the floor around him littered with small pieces of paper ... such was the occupation to which he was reduced.

He told me that, if I liked, he would come to live in Moscow and devote his life and his work to our family. I refused and told him why; my refusal grieved him, but I was right. Besides a feeling of generosity, his offer was actuated by a desire for an immediate object in life. Soon after that, he started for the Kalmuk steppes in order to undertake anthropological researches. I was often haunted by the thought of his sad figure in the midst of the steppes.

The journey was difficult and fatiguing. Metchnikoff did not know the Kalmuk language and had to depend on interpreters. From the very first he was painfully impressed by the brutality of the Russian officials towards the natives. At every halt the Kalmuks declared that they had no horses; the Cossack who convoyed Metchnikoff would then begin to swear and to play with his "nagaika" or leather-thonged whip, and the required horses appeared as by magic. After a while Metchnikoff became used to such scenes and looked upon them as a custom of the country. He found it more difficult to put up with the indescribable dirt, the smell of mutton fat which impregnated the food, and the continual barking of dogs during the night, details which destroyed the charm and poetry of primitive life. In spite of these[84] unfavourable conditions, Metchnikoff worked indefatigably. The physical measurements of the Kalmuks led him to conclude that the development of the Mongol race was arrested in comparison with that of the Caucasian race; he found that all the relative proportions of the diverse parts of the Kalmuk skeleton corresponded with that of youth in the Caucasian race: a large head, a long torso, short legs, absolutely the relative dimensions of our children. This conclusion was further confirmed by the structure of the eyelid in the Kalmuks, of which the fold (epicanthus) in the adult corresponds with that of the fold of the eyelid in our children.

These interesting results somewhat raised Metchnikoff's moral, the more so that his eyesight began to improve; he returned to Odessa but found that he was still unable to use a microscope. He therefore decided to go back to the steppes in order to proceed with his researches, and, this time, began his journey by the Stavropol province. The steppes there are very fine, with tall, luxuriant grasses and a profusion of flowers filling the pure atmosphere with perfume; the infinite space and absolute calm offer a peculiar and powerful charm. But the population is depressed and apathetic, as is the case with that of the Astrakhan steppes. The reason must be that the Kalmuks consume milk which has undergone alcoholic fermentation, and that provokes a slight but chronic intoxication. Yet a few among them are extremely intelligent and of fairly high culture. Thus, in the course of his ethnographical researches Metchnikoff came across a priest (bakshâ) who imparted to him such instructive facts on the principles of the Buddhist religion and on the organisation of its clergy that he[85] even planned to go with him to Thibet, where no stranger can penetrate without the help of an adept. This plan, however, was never executed.

After he had collected numerous anthropological data, Metchnikoff went again to the Astrakhan steppes in order to verify and to complete his observations of the preceding year. Whilst traversing some oases where the Russians were making experiments in artificial forestry, he had the pleasant surprise of finding some Myriapoda (Geophilus) bearing a number of eggs. The history of the development of those creatures was still unknown—a notable lacuna in embryology. Delighted at the idea of filling it, Metchnikoff did not hesitate to undertake a long and difficult extra journey and repaired to Astrakhan, taking with him his precious material, in order to fetch the necessary apparatus for his researches. But during the long journey several eggs perished and he had to return to the oasis with a borrowed microscope to study other eggs on the spot. In spite of very difficult conditions and of the persistent weakness of his eyesight, he succeeded in filling the lacuna in the embryology of the Geophilus.

He had at the same time collected very interesting anthropological data. His hypothesis as to the necessity of applying to anthropology the comparative methods of embryology was fully justified, for, thanks to that process, he was able to establish a definite correlation between the Mongol race and the adolescence of the Caucasian race. He presented a report on the subject to the Anthropological Society of Moscow, but, his attention being afterwards turned in other directions, he never came back to this subject.

[86]
CHAPTER XV

"As to thee, Hector, thou art to me as a father and a revered mother and a brother, and thou art my husband."—The Iliad.

Studies on childhood — The family in the upper flat — Lessons in zoology — Second marriage — Private life — Visit and death of Lvovna Nevahovna — Conjugal affection.

Metchnikoff's anthropological researches led him to the study of childhood, which in its turn suggested reflections on questions of Pedagogy. His eyesight was still weak and his hunger for activity very great; in order to satisfy it, he gave lessons in a Lycée and public lectures in the Odessa University. Though time was passing, Metchnikoff could not get used to his solitude; he spent his active kindness on his friends and all around him, whilst living like an ascetic and giving away all that he could spare. But nothing could quench his thirst for a family life and affectionate intimacy.

My family at that time lived in the same house as he did, on the floor above him; we were eight children, our ages ranging from one to sixteen years. We were noisy neighbours and we incommoded Metchnikoff, who was awakened every morning by the noise in our kitchen, where meat was being minced for the children. One fine day he could stand it no longer and went upstairs to ask if this nuisance could not be stopped; my father promised that he would[87] see that it ceased. We were all seated round the tea-table when he came in, and, seeing a stranger, my sister and I hurriedly collected our lesson books, and hastened to leave the room. We did not even have time to distinguish Metchnikoff's features, but were struck by his paleness. Shortly after that incident we met him at the house of a mutual friend. He had already seen us from his window as we went off to the Lycée, and it used to amuse him to see us bravely stepping over a large pool of water which was permanent in the street.

One of his pupils was a professor in our Lycée, and Elie had the opportunity of informing himself concerning our studies. Having heard that I was interested in natural science, it occurred to him to offer to give me lessons in zoology. I was delighted. He asked and obtained permission from my parents, and we eagerly set to work. Elie, being strongly attracted by me, returned to his former idea of training a girl according to his own ideas and afterwards making her his wife. He might have realised his programme of completing my education first and marrying me afterwards if he had not been prevented by the complete lack of accord between his ideas and those of my father. It was the eternal conflict of two generations, "fathers and children." My father was an excellent man, of great nobility of character, but he was a type of the old Russian patrician school and belonged to a different epoch, with different opinions and customs. This caused inevitable and frequent disagreements, and Elie decided to ask for my hand without further delay.

My mother was much younger than my father, and her sympathies were all with the young generation.[88] She was an idealist, gentle, intelligent and artistic, and, in her youth, had painted and played the violoncello, but a very early marriage and numerous children had forced her to give up the practice of art, to her lifelong regret. Great sympathy arose between her and Elie; she supported him in everything and became for him a tenderly attached friend. He explained to her his theories on marriage, and then confided to her his feelings towards me. My extreme youth troubled her very much, but Elie endeavoured to reassure her, saying that he fully understood the rashness of his projects, but that he was ready to suffer all the consequences; in fact, he declared, if he did not succeed in making me happy, he would have the strength to help me to create another existence for myself. I had not suspected my Professor's feelings towards me, and was deeply moved when I was told of them; it seemed to me impossible to understand that this superior, this learned man could wish to marry a little girl like myself! I thought with terror that he must be mistaken about me; I felt as if I were going up for an examination without any previous study. However, I had a great affection and admiration for Elie; I was attracted by his whole personality, which produced a strong impression upon others as well as upon myself. This is how Setchénoff describes him, in his own autobiography:

Elie Metchnikoff was the soul of our circle. Of all the young men I have known in my life, young Metchnikoff was the most attractive with his lively intelligence, inexhaustible wit and abundant knowledge of all things. He was, in Science, as serious and as productive (he had already done much in zoology and acquired a great name in that branch) as he was full of life and varied interest in a circle of friends.

[89]

Moreover, my young imagination was impressed by his sad history and by his interesting appearance, at that time not unlike a figure of Christ; his pale face was illumined by the light in his kindly eyes, which at times looked absolutely inspired. My whole heart went out to him, but I was not yet ripe for matrimony and was somewhat thrown off my balance by the unexpectedness of the event. Fearing that I was not up to his level, I used to try beforehand to find worthy subjects of conversation in order that he should not feel bored in my society, but everything I thought of seemed to me so clumsy and stupid that I rejected one subject after another until he came and found me at a loss. He could not understand how deeply I was troubled, and cannot have been satisfied with my attitude, which really was that of a zealous pupil.

Our marriage took place in February 1875; it was a very cold winter and the ground was covered with a thick coating of glistening snow. A few hours before the ceremony my brothers came with a little hand sledge to fetch me for a last ride. "Come quick," they said, "this evening you will be a grown-up lady, and you can't play with us any more!" I agreed, and we rushed out to the snowy carpet which covered the great yard of our house. In the midst of our mad race my mother appeared at the window; she had been looking for me everywhere and was much disturbed. "My dear child! what are you thinking of? It is late, you have hardly time to dress and to do your hair!" "One more turn, mother! It is the last time, think of it!" Other childish emotions awaited me; my wedding-dress was the first long dress I had ever worn, and I feared to stumble as I walked. Then, too, I was frightened at the idea of[90] entering the church under the eyes of all the guests. My little brother tried to reassure me by offering to hold my hand, and my mother made me drink some chocolate to give me courage.

Elie was awaiting us at the entrance; my shyness increased when I heard people whispering around us, "Why, she is a mere child!" The ceremony took place in the evening, after which Elie wrapped me carefully in a long warm cloak and we set off, the sledge gliding like the wind, towards our new home. In spite of the day's emotions, I rose very early the next morning in order to work at my zoology exercises and to give my husband a pleasant surprise. He was now free to superintend my education, a very difficult and delicate task when having to do with a mind as unprepared for life as mine was.

The scientific methods which Metchnikoff applied to everything might have constituted a grave error at this delicate psychological moment; yet, in many ways, he showed himself a strangely clear-sighted educator. He made it a principle to give me entire liberty whilst directing me through the logic of his arguments. It is with deep gratitude that I realise how he, so superior to me, took care not to stifle my fragile

41

individuality but to respect it and to encourage it to develop. Like all Russian young people of the time, I was very enthusiastic concerning political and social questions that I was not mature enough to understand, and my father forbade us to frequent political circles with which he had no sympathy, fearing that we might be influenced by them. Elie, on the contrary, left me full liberty, though he himself disapproved of my tendencies. He considered that political and social questions belonged to the realm of[91] practical experience, in which young people were lacking, as also in practical preparation. He never prevented me from making myself acquainted with the social movement, but submitted it to close analysis and criticism; it is owing to this very efficacious method that I did not become one of the numerous political victims of that time.

Elie took a lively and warm interest in everything which concerned me. Not having had time to pass my final examinations from the Lycée before my marriage, I was now obliged to go up before a special board for the whole curriculum. He helped me to prepare this, even the catechism, with the utmost keenness and gaiety, enlivening the driest subjects by means of interesting and instructive reading. I was glad to continue my biological studies under his direction after I had passed my examinations. Not only did he give a general interest, a leading thread, to every particular subject, but he also knew how to develop independent work. For instance, he made me compare representative examples of divers groups by practical study in order to let me deduce for myself their characteristics and their generic connections.

And it was not my education only which interested him; he associated me with every detail of his life and initiated me into his thoughts and his work; we read together a great deal, he had an excellent delivery and liked reading aloud.

He thoroughly enjoyed giving me pleasure; we often went to concerts and theatres, and beautiful music or dramatic scenes moved him even to tears. Musical themes haunted him, and he would whistle them softly to himself even at his work. Without[92] caring for luxury, he was glad to contribute to the simple embellishment of our home because he knew I appreciated it. When we travelled, always with scientific research as an object, he never failed to point out every interesting feature that we happened to pass. He had a peculiar talent for making a journey instructive as well as attractive; his eagerness, infectious gaiety, inquisitive mind, and remarkable organising faculty made of him an incomparable guide and companion.

We worked together for many years; it was both delightful and profitable to work with him, for he opened out his ideas unreservedly and made one share his enthusiasm and his interest in investigations; he could create an atmosphere of intimate union in the search for truth which allowed the humblest worker to feel himself a collaborator in an exalted task.

Though I always took a strong interest in scientific questions, Art was the real passion of my life. But, imbued as I was with the narrow, utilitarian views which surrounded my youth, I had looked upon Art as a luxury which should not be indulged in at a time when the poorer classes could not read and write. When at last I became emancipated from this fallacy, my husband did his best to encourage my artistic development though he himself did not appreciate plastic art. Form and colour in themselves or in harmony did not appeal to him; he took much more interest in a subject than in the way it was treated; he liked psychological or realistic work, landscapes, "genre" pictures, but classical, Renaissance, or Impressionist works bored him. In spite of the divergence of our tastes in that connection, he never ceased[93] to encourage me or to take an active interest in my work; often and often he accompanied me to picture

42

galleries, making sincere and somewhat pathetic efforts to appreciate the beauty of great masterpieces.

Next to music he enjoyed Nature most, perhaps because it offered him an inexhaustible source of scientific observation. His wearied nerves caused him to seek for soothing impressions, and calm, quiet ponds were what he preferred, with their reeds and aquatic plants, among which he loved to discover tiny beings, hidden under the leaves and below the surface of the water.

Teaching and public work took up nearly the whole of his time; his leisure was devoted to home life and to an intimate circle of friends with whom he was bound by a common scientific fervour and by a University life. He kept up those friendships even after life had scattered them. His active kindness made him a centre of attraction to his relations and we were always very much surrounded. After his father died, in 1878, his mother and two of her grandchildren came to live with us. She was at that time sixty-four years of age and had the appearance of an old lady; she did not follow the fashion but wore her white hair simply parted and framing her face; alone her fine dark eyes had preserved their youthful sparkle and bore witness to her former beauty. She had a bright and cheerful disposition and a charming kindliness to every one; her desire for activity was unfortunately thwarted by the state of her health.

Elie showed his mother a tender solicitude which manifested itself in the smallest details; for instance, he who detested cards would play Patience with her; or he would drive her round the markets, which[94] interested her like the good housekeeper she was. When he came in from the laboratory he never failed to go to her to ask her for details of her health; he talked to her playfully and affectionately, making her laugh, telling her the incidents of the day. She continued to be interested in everything, especially that which concerned her dear Elie, the "consolation of her life," as she called him.

In spite of his affection for his mother, he bore her almost sudden death very stoically, knowing as he did that the grave heart disease from which she suffered was bound to cause her increasing pain.

My family became his, and the relations between him and my father became such that the latter, feeling ill and nearing his end, made him our guardian. Until the last my mother preserved for my husband a tender friendship which he fully returned. For years he bore the burden and responsibilities of the family. With my young brothers and sisters he kept up a tone of merry affection; always indulgent with them, he was anxious to neglect nothing that could be useful. Though ever led by the desire to procure happiness around him, it sometimes happened that he made a mistake in his appreciation and failed to reach his goal. The human soul is a riddle, life is complicated, and we ought not always to judge by results but by motives.... As far as I am personally concerned, his affection, kindness, and solicitude have always been unbounded. If during early years a few misunderstandings arose between us, they were due to my youthful obstinacy or to his nervous sensitiveness. We had our trials, but our friendship and deep affection emerged from them stronger and purer than ever. At a certain time, Elie, believing that happiness[95] called me elsewhere, offered me my liberty, urging that I had a moral right to it. The nobility of his attitude was the best safeguard.... As years went on, our lives became more and more united; we lived in deep communion of souls, for we had reached that stage of mutual comprehension when darkness flees and all is light.

[96]
CHAPTER XVI

Metchnikoff at the age of thirty — Lecturing in Odessa University, from 1873 to 1882 — Internal difficulties — Assassination of the Tsar, Alexander II. — Further troubles in the University — Resignation — Bad health: cardiac symptoms — Relapsing fever — Choroiditis — Studies on Ephemeridæ — Further studies on intracellular digestion — The Parenchymella — Holidays in the country — Experiments on agricultural pests.

Elie Metchnikoff was now thirty years old, and his personality was fully characterised though it had not yet reached the culminating point of its development.

His dominating point was his passionate vocation; his worship of Science and of Reason made of him an inspired apostle. He had the faults and qualities of a rich and powerful nature. Vibrating through all the fibres of his being, he shed life and light around him. His temper was violent and passionate; he could bear no attack on the ideas which were dear to him, and became combative as soon as he thought them threatened. His was a wrestler's temperament; obstacles exasperated his energy and he went straight for them, pursuing his object with an invincible tenacity; he never gave up a problem, however difficult, and never hesitated to face any sacrifice or any privation if he thought them necessary.

A strange contradiction with this iron will was offered by occasional disconcerting impulses, like that which caused the failure of his first journey abroad, or by sudden attacks of fury for insignificant reasons[97] such as an unexpected noise in the street, a cat mewing or a dog barking, or angry impatience when he could not solve a frivolous puzzle, etc. This impulsive disposition gradually calmed down as he grew older, and ultimately very nearly disappeared.

In his personal relations also he was apt to lose his temper, but a reaction very soon followed the outburst, and his efforts to be forgiven when he felt guilty were very touching. On the other hand, he did not easily forget an offence, though no desire for revenge ever soiled his soul, and his gratitude for kindness was absolutely indestructible.

He harboured pessimistic theories to that extent that he looked upon the procreation of other lives as a crime on the part of a conscious being; his physical and moral sensitiveness was intense. And yet he had inherited from his mother a natural gaiety and delightful elasticity which always ended by gaining the upper hand. He was fond of joking; his wit was occasionally somewhat cutting, but that was entirely due to the appropriateness of his remarks; he never hurt people's feelings intentionally. He sometimes gave offence by a professional habit of using personal and concrete instances by way of arguments, but he applied the process to himself as well; it was the objective method, nothing more, and those who knew him well never doubted it.

His benevolence was most active and never insipid, though marked by an almost feminine sensibility. He was an incomparable companion and friend, and had the gift of smoothing difficulties and inspiring courage, security, and confidence. He took the greatest interest in others and easily came down to their level, always finding points in common, [98]"an opportunity for the study of human documents," he said. Thus he conversed simply and sympathetically with the humble as with the great, with the young as with the old. It was no mere intellectual interest that he bore them, but he put his whole heart into it, which made him extremely easy to approach. And yet he never departed from absolute freedom of speech, sometimes mixed with harshness. Truth and sincerity, for him, came above everything; he carried the courage of his opinions to the highest degree, even if it was likely to shock his hearers or to do him harm. He jealously guarded his independence and nothing could force him to act against his convictions. Full of enthusiasm, always interesting, he enlivened all around him. His ideas and his activity

44

were in constant effervescence; no serious question left him indifferent; he read everything, knew about almost everything, and willingly informed others; his vibrating expansiveness made him a centre of attraction in his private life as in the laboratory or in any other sphere of activity.

From 1873 to 1882 his energies were chiefly absorbed by teaching and by the inner life of the University of Odessa, into which he threw himself with his usual enthusiasm. His lectures were full of life, always bringing out general ideas to throw light upon the most arid facts; he made use of these as an architect utilises coarse materials in order to erect a harmonious edifice. His creative power endowed his lectures with an æsthetic character in spite of their extreme simplicity; not that he concerned himself much about form, but because of his wealth of ideas and the logical way in which he developed them, starting from the simple and reaching the[99] complex in a harmonious synthesis. His own enthusiasm established a living bond between him and his audience.

He was on excellent terms with the students, though he made no bid for popularity. Not only did he give no encouragement to the prevailing tendency of the young men towards politics, but he endeavoured on the contrary to bring them back to their studies; he tried to prove to them that social problems demand knowledge and a serious practical preparation. Otherwise, said he, social life would be as medicine was before it entered into the path of science, and when any middle-aged woman, any bone-setter, was allowed to practise therapeutics. At the same time, students found in him willing protection in the persecutions directed against them, and earnest help in their work when they showed the least interest in it; he would eagerly welcome the smallest spark of the "sacred fire."

Owing to the absolute independence of his ideas and conduct he had great influence on young men, and this caused him to be looked upon in administrative spheres as a "Red"—almost an agitator. In reality he was struggling against the inertia and reactionary forces which were shackling the normal development of culture and science in Russia. He called himself a "progressive evolutionist," for he considered that alone a deep and conscious evolution could give stable results and lead to real progress. He thought that Revolution, and especially Terrorism, merely provoked a reaction which might be long-lived, and that, as long as the people were not sufficiently educated, a revolution might easily result in the transfer of despotism from one party to another. Socialistic doctrines did not satisfy him; according[100] to him, they did not leave sufficient scope to personal initiative and to the development of individuality, two factors which he considered as essential to every progress.

He looked upon scientific work as his mission, and avoided politics because he did not think himself competent to deal with them. But scientific activity being closely limited by the state of the University, which was badly oppressed at that time by reactionary powers, he was led to take part in the defence of the University's right to autonomy. He brought all his energies into the struggle, though trying to keep from party tactics and to act purely in the interests of science. For instance, he would vote either for a Radical or a Conservative without sharing the opinions of either, but merely guided by their scientific value.

At the beginning of his scientific career at Odessa he led a very active campaign in favour of the teaching of Natural Science. He urged that, in order to teach properly, Natural History professors should themselves have made independent researches on living fauna and flora, and tried to introduce a series of measures to allow biologists special holidays and missions to desirable places, at the proper seasons, for research purposes. "There is no doubt," he said, "that scientific activity would be much increased if the proposed measures were adopted. Then, before long, our young scientists would not need to go to study in German universities, but could go abroad already prepared to undertake independent research." The Commission which examined his report demanded certain modifications, [101]"because of the Imperial injunction to be very strict in granting travelling permits to professors." Metchnikoff somewhat altered the text, which, after being adopted by the University Council, was rejected by the Ministry and remained without effect. Thus was every independent suggestion stifled, even when it had but a purely scientific object.

Soon the situation of the Odessa University became even more difficult. Between 1875 and 1880 reaction increased considerably, and the inner life of the University became very unfavourable to any scientific activity. Already before that it was teeming with intrigues, the Professors of Ukrainian origin being hostile to the "Muscovites." Yet it was still possible to remain apart from these local intrigues, until political reaction, filtering into the University, created in it the deepest divisions. The hostility of parties was now based on political opinions, either "Reactionary" or "Liberal." The students were being more and more carried away by this movement and no longer took any interest in their studies.

All these conditions made normal teaching and scientific work impossible, and Metchnikoff, seeing that politics from above and from below now swallowed up everything, tried to take refuge in his laboratory but in vain; even there he could no longer find the necessary calm, and only during the holidays could he really work.

Thus passed the years until March 1, 1881, when the crime which ended the days of Alexander II. was followed by a great reactionary movement. The authorities, seeing conspiracies and plots everywhere, persecuted without cause all the elements which were ticketed as "dangerous." Though the University still preserved its autonomy, this was entirely fictitious,[102] for the Ministry thwarted every desire for independence; the nomination of professors elected by the University Council was only ratified by the Ministry if they were reactionaries, without any regard for their scientific value. Soon the Chairs were occupied by ignorant men of doubtful morality.

The life and honour of the University became endangered, and Metchnikoff found himself obliged to take part in the struggle; he did so with vehemence and energy; the independence of the University was involved, and, as long as he could hope to save it, he struggled. At the meetings of the Council and of the Faculty he never failed to give vent to his critical opinions with a vehement frankness which earned him in the University the reputation of an "enfant terrible." In the meanwhile every resolution passed by the Council, if not reactionary in character, was systematically quashed by the Ministry, which thus paralysed every means of action, and Metchnikoff found himself faced with the alternative of submitting or handing in his resignation. He decided for the latter: his convictions were involved, and moreover his health could not withstand the continual agitation and strain on his nerves.

As we could not afford to live in independence, he applied for a vacant post of entomologist in the zemstvo[13] of Poltava, and at the same time wrote out his resignation, holding it in readiness for an opportunity which was not long in coming.

The Conservative party in the Faculty arose against a Liberal professor who had accepted a very clever thesis in which the Reactionaries perceived Socialist tendencies. The Dean of the Faculty proposed that[103] all such theses should be refused, and the Faculty approved. This was the signal for a storm in the University, the Dean was hooted by the students, and many of them were threatened with being expelled. The Curator desired the more influential professors, of whom Metchnikoff was one, to intervene with the students in order to bring disorder to an end, and the professors consented, on condition that the offending Dean should resign. The Curator promised that he should be asked to do so, and order was immediately restored; but the Dean remained and many students were severely and unjustly punished. Metchnikoff thereupon produced his resignation, which was promptly accepted, and thus his University career came to an end.

Besides his University lectures, he gave public lectures on Natural History which were attended by a number of female students, for women at that time were only admitted to the Faculty of Medicine, and these lectures were extremely useful to them. Metchnikoff, though he did not believe that women could accomplish creative work in science, was strongly in favour of higher education for women, considering it as necessary to their general intellectual development. Genius, he thought, was peculiar to the male sex, no woman having created anything "of genius" even in domains which had always been accessible to them, such as music, literature, and the applied arts. The very rare exceptions, to his mind, only proved the rule; yet he did not draw the conclusion that woman was in any sense inferior to man. He merely held that her gifts are different from those of men.

Metchnikoff's health had been seriously shaken[104] by the emotions and annoyances of university life. Already in 1877, after political intrigues at the University, he had felt the first symptoms of cardiac trouble, which were the beginning of a long period of ill-health. He consulted Bamberger, a great Viennese physician, who, however, found nothing serious, and merely forbade him the use of wine and tobacco, to neither of which was he addicted.

His health suffered further through the violent anxiety which he went through in 1880 whilst I lay dangerously ill with typhoid fever, contracted in Naples. Though worn out with devoted nursing, he tried to make up the time lost to research and over-worked himself, with the result that cardiac trouble was followed by fits of giddiness and unconquerable insomnia. He fell into such a state of neurasthenia that, in 1881, he resolved in a moment of depression to do away with his life.

In order to spare his family the sorrow of an obvious suicide, he inoculated himself with relapsing fever, choosing this disease in order to ascertain at the same time whether it could be inoculated through the blood. The answer was in the affirmative: he became very seriously ill. His condition was aggravated by anxiety concerning the University; for he was sufficiently conscious to be aware of the events which were taking place in Russia. The murder of Alexander II. caused him to foresee a political reaction of the most terrible type; already, a reactionary Rector had been appointed. Metchnikoff developed intense jaundice and had a serious relapse with alarming cardiac weakness; during the crisis he had a very distinct prevision of approaching death. This semi-conscious state was accompanied by a feeling of great happiness;[105] he imagined that he had solved all human ethical questions. Much later, this fact led him to suppose that death could actually be attended by agreeable sensations.

His robust nature, however, triumphed over all these grave complications, and, during his convalescence, he was filled with a joy of living such as he had never experienced before; from that moment his moral and physical balance was completely restored. There was one unpleasant sequel to his illness, an acute affection of the sight (choroiditis), but it fortunately disappeared without leaving any traces, and, in fact, he never suffered again from his eyes, in spite of his constant use of the microscope.

After his recovery he had a renascence of vital intensity; the life instinct developed in him in a high degree; his health became flourishing, his energy and power for work greater than ever, and the pessimism of his youth began to pale before the optimistic dawn of his maturity. However, the relapsing fever had very probably increased, if not started, the cardiac trouble which eventually caused his death.

During the time when Metchnikoff was forbidden the use of the microscope on account of his eye weakness, he studied Ephemeridæ from the point of view of natural selection. He wished to elucidate the manner in which this selection operates during the very short life of those insects: the rudimentary structure of their buccal organs does not allow them to feed themselves, and they have no time to adapt themselves to external conditions.

During the 1875 holidays, at Gmunden and on the Danube, he observed the nuptial flight of the mayflies, a phenomenon which constitutes their short[106] adult existence, preceded by a long period in the larval state. Thousands of these diaphanous, ephemeral insects swarm above the water in a compact cloud; now and then, dead Ephemeridæ fall like snow-flakes, and that is the final and tragic completion of the nuptial flight. Metchnikoff wished to unveil the mechanism of this sudden death, evidently due to a physiological cause; but he obtained no definite results either that year or the following, when he continued his observations in the Caucasus. He realised that the life of these insects was too short to allow him to solve the problems which interested him, and, his eyes now being cured, he went back to his studies on the origin of multicellular beings or metazoa.

He studied the development of inferior sponges and ascertained that they possess the three embryonic layers which correspond to those of other animal types, but that these layers have not the same degree of independence or differentiation. He found that in certain inferior sponges the mesoderm develops before the endoderm and gives birth to it. These two layers, born one from the other, manifest common primordial characters. Therefore he was in no wise surprised to discover that, in these inferior sponges, the amœboid and mobile cells of the mesoderm fulfil digestive functions equally with, and even more than those of the endoderm; in fact, with primitive beings, functional characters are not more strictly delimitated than morphological characters. It is only a more advanced differentiation which separates them.

He connected these new facts with that which he had observed in 1865 in one of the lower worms, the earth planarian Geodesmus bilineatus. This worm is actually without a digestive cavity, for the latter is[107] entirely filled by parenchymatous cells inside which digestion takes place.

By their primitive structure, lower sponges and worms come near the higher Infusoria, to which they are even more closely related by this intercellular digestion which is common to them.

This led Metchnikoff to ask himself whether this was not, generally speaking, the primitive mode of digestion. He carried out numerous researches on this point during the following years, and found the same intercellular digestion in other lower worms, such as the Mesostoma and aquatic planarians, and afterwards in some lower Cœlentera and some Echinoderma. He was thus enabled to establish definitely that the primitive mode of digestion was really intercellular, for the lower multicellular animals either do not possess any digestive cavity or else their digestive cavity develops late, as for instance with lower jelly-fish or with hydropolypi. Even when the cavity is developed in these inferior animals, the digestive functions are fulfilled by the mesodermic cells.

The question as to what are the ancestral forms of multicellular animals cannot be solved through direct observation, for there is a lacuna between them and unicellular beings, a lacuna which is due to the disappearance of intermediary forms. It can only be filled by hypotheses, based upon the embryology of those animals which, in their embryonic development, repeat the inferior forms from which they are derived, thus reflecting the general evolution of living beings. It was therefore to the embryology of lower multicellular beings that Metchnikoff turned, in order to endeavour to reconstitute their origin and to show the link between them and unicellular beings.

[108]

We know that the ovule or primitive genital cell of every animal may be compared to a unicellular organism. After fertilisation the egg undergoes consecutive divisions or segmentation; each segment constitutes a new cell, and their aggregation forms a hollow sphere called a blastula, which is similar to a colony of unicellular beings. The blastula differentiates itself into embryonic layers, the ectoderm, endoderm, and mesoderm already mentioned.

In the majority of animals the origin of the first two layers, ectoderm and endoderm, is due to the invagination of one of the poles of the blastula; the invaginated part of the walls forms the internal layer, the endoderm, and lines the cavity produced by invagination; this cavity thus becomes a digestive cavity. This stage of development, called gastrula, is similar to a cup with a double wall, of which the outer is the ectoderm and the inner the endoderm.

This stage, discovered by Kovalevsky, is to be found in the evolution of most animals and corresponds to the adult stage of some of them. It was consequently considered as the primitive type of multicellular beings.

Haeckel founded thereupon his theory of the gastræa, according to which the common ancestor of animals was a lower animal, now disappeared, and similar to that stage of development. He therefore gave to this hypothetical animal the name of gastræa.

Metchnikoff, however, discovered among primitive multicellular animals, such as sponges, hydroids, and lower medusæ, a stage of development still more simple than the gastrula; this stage is without a[109] digestive cavity and only assumes the gastrula form in its ulterior evolution. He also made the remarkable discovery that, in the most primitive multicellular animals, the endoderm is formed, not by means of invagination, but by the migration of a number of flagellated cells from one pole of the wall of the blastula into the central cavity. These cells draw in their flagellum, become amœboid and mobile, multiply by division, fill the cavity of the blastula, and become capable of digesting. They originate the digestive cells of the complete organism and give birth to the mesoderm, which explains how the latter comes to contain a number of devouring cells even though these do not constitute digestive organs properly so called. Metchnikoff gave to that stage the name of parenchymella, for the migrating cells constitute the endoderm in the condition of a parenchyma.

The invariable presence of this stage in the simplest multicellular animals, the primitive amœboid state of the endodermic cells, cases of ulterior transformation of the parenchymella into the gastrula form in certain animals, the absence of a differentiated digestive cavity,—all that proved, according to Metchnikoff, that the parenchymella is more primitive than the gastrula, and is therefore entitled to be considered the prototype of multicellular beings.

He saw a confirmation of this in the fact that primitive adult animals also have no digestive cavity but merely an intracellular digestion (sponges, turbellaria).

He concluded that the common ancestor of multicellular beings was a being constituted by an agglomeration of cells without a digestive cavity, but endowed with intracellular digestion, like that of the[110] "parenchymula" stage of development. He therefore gave to that hypothetical ancestor the name of parenchymella.

49

Later, in 1886, he definitely formulated his theory of the genesis of multicellular beings, and having already stated the phagocyte theory, he substituted for the name parenchymella that of phagocytella, which indicated at the same time the primitive mode of digestion of that hypothetical ancestor.

Reduced to its simplest form, it presented, according to Metchnikoff, a certain analogy with a colony composed of unicellular beings of two kinds: the first, flagellated, forming the external layer, and the others, amœboid, occupying the centre of the colony and capable of digesting.

It may be interesting to mention here that, in this hypothetical description, Metchnikoff foresaw the existence of similar, but real, beings discovered a year later by Saville Kent, namely, the flagellated colonies of Protospongia.

Thus the link between the unicellular and the multicellular beings could be constituted through the intermediary of flagellated colonies on the one hand and, on the other hand, of beings similar to a phagocytella. The indivisible colony became the multicellular individual.

While studying the genealogy of beings, Metchnikoff continued his researches on intracellular digestion. In 1879, at Naples and at Messina, he was able to establish the fact that the mesodermic cells of many larvæ of Echinodermata and Cœlenterata, endowed with a digestive tube, nevertheless contained strange bodies. Therefore, even complicated organisms with a differentiated digestive system could still[111] contain at the same time some primitive cells with an autonomous digestion.

All these researches on the unity of the origin of multicellular beings and their morphological elements, and also those concerning intracellular digestion, were gradually preparing Metchnikoff's mind for the conception of the phagocyte theory.

We spent the summer of 1880 with my family in the country. The cereals were invaded by a harmful beetle, the Anisoplia austriaca, which was devastating the country. Metchnikoff took the study of this scourge to heart and tried to find a remedy. He had, the preceding year, observed a dead fly enveloped with a sort of fungus which had evidently been the cause of its death. Hence he conceived the idea that it might be possible to combat harmful insects by provoking epidemics among them. He now returned to this idea; on dead bodies of Anisoplia he found a small fungus, the muscardine, which was invading the insects by means of filaments, and he succeeded in infecting healthy beetles.

At first he confined himself to laboratory experiments; then a great landowner, Count Bobrinsky, placed experimental fields at his disposal. As the acquired results were very encouraging, Metchnikoff, forced to leave the neighbourhood, left a young entomologist in charge of the application of his method. So far as he himself was concerned, this study proved the starting-point of his researches on infectious diseases.

[112]
CHAPTER XVII

Death of his father- and mother-in-law — Management of country estates — Agitation and difficulties — Departure for Messina with young brothers- and sisters-in-law.

In the spring of 1881, Metchnikoff having recovered from relapsing fever, we went to stay with my parents at Kieff and found my father dying. He entrusted Elie with the care of the family, and they came to live with us at Odessa. But, the following year, we had the misfortune to lose my mother also. From that moment my husband took upon himself the responsibility of the whole family.

Our resources came from landed property, and he, who had never concerned himself with rural questions, had to make himself acquainted with them. In this he was greatly helped by a neighbour, Count Bobrinsky, through whose influence he came to abandon the purely theoretical opinions he had hitherto held concerning agrarian questions. He had considered communal property as a desirable agrarian system: Count Bobrinsky showed him that it was not so, at any rate in Little Russia.

Metchnikoff came to the country with the keenest desire to make himself useful. First of all he devoted the gratuity which he had received on leaving the University, to a school which my sister and myself desired to open in our family property. But we were[113] met by administrative opposition which nearly wrecked our plan, under the pretext that it was intended for political propaganda. And though cordial relations were established from the first between Metchnikoff and the peasantry, many complications were unavoidable, due to the general agrarian situation, to the insufficiency of the peasants' allotments, and to their primitive methods of cultivation.

My father, whose property was in the province of Kieff, had inherited another domain in that of Kherson; Metchnikoff therefore had to manage both estates and to adapt himself to their very different respective circumstances. The majority of the farmers in Little Russia at that time were Jews and were beginning to be persecuted both by the Government and by the peasants; Elie was constantly obliged to intervene. In the province of Kherson, it was a tradition with the peasants that the land should belong to them, and they imagined that this could be brought about by the simple elimination of the farmers. Therefore they inflicted constant vexations upon the latter, allowing cattle to pasture in their crops, pulling up their beetroots, etc. Metchnikoff attempted in vain to re-establish peace by means of compromise; he persuaded a farmer to sub-let part of the land to the peasants, but this had to be given up, for the latter did not carry out their engagements. Relations between the farmers and the peasants were getting worse and worse, and Metchnikoff, foreseeing a catastrophe, warned the local administration that the situation was getting very grave and would lead to irreparable consequences. He was merely told that preventive measures would be useless; hereupon the[114] peasants brutally murdered a keeper who was turning the cattle away from the crops. Then at last the administration awoke, arrested the murderers, and twelve men were exiled to Siberia.

All this caused Metchnikoff the deepest anxiety, the more so that he was absolutely incapable of altering the situation. As soon as it became possible, he sold to the peasants that portion of the land which belonged to us personally; until then, the property had been common to the whole family, of which the younger members were not yet of age. This, however, was not a general solution, and these moral preoccupations, as well as the heavy responsibility incumbent upon him, kept him from his scientific work. He was therefore very pleased to hand over the management of the property to one of my brothers who had just completed his studies in a Higher Agricultural School, and, in spite of difficult conditions, Elie had the satisfaction of giving up everything in good order.

Thanks to my parents' inheritance, he was able to abandon his share of the Panassovka patrimony to the children of his brother and to live henceforth independently. He wished to pursue researches on the shores of the Mediterranean: therefore, in the autumn of the year 1882, we went to Messina with my two sisters and my three young brothers. The children were no trouble to Elie, who loved them; on the contrary, he enjoyed organising the journey and arranging all sorts of pleasures for them. The children, accustomed to his kindly indulgence, always came to "the Prophet" for everything they wanted.[14]

[115]

CHAPTER XVIII

Messina — Inception of the phagocyte theory — Encouragement from Virchow and Kleinenberg — First paper on phagocytosis at the Odessa Congress in 1883 — The question of Immunity — Article in Virchow's Archiv, 1884.

At Messina, we settled in a suburb, the Ringo, on the quay of the Straits, in a small flat with a garden and a splendid view over the sea. We did not have much room, and the laboratory had to be installed in the drawing-room, but, on the other hand, Elie only had to cross the quay in order to find the fisherman who provided him with the material needed for his researches and with whom we frequently went sailing.

Metchnikoff loved Messina, with its rich marine fauna and beautiful scenery. The splendid view of the sea and the calm outline of the Calabrian coast across the Straits delighted him. He enjoyed it all the more after the many excitements of life at the University, and eagerly gave himself up to his researches. Often, in later years, he delighted to recall memories of that period, the more so that this was connected with the principal phase of scientific activity which led to the formation of his phagocyte theory. After the earthquake in 1908, he wrote a few pages on Messina and ended his article by the following lines:

Thus it was in Messina that the great event of my scientific life took place. A zoologist until then, I suddenly[116] became a pathologist. I entered into a new road in which my later activity was to be exerted.

It is with warm feeling that I evoke that distant past and with tenderness that I think of Messina, of which the terrible fate has deeply moved my heart.

They say that Messina will be rebuilt in the same place but in a different way. Houses will be constructed of light materials, they will be low, and the streets broad....

The town will be a new Messina, not "my Messina," not that with which so many dear memories are associated in my mind....

Metchnikoff continued to study intracellular digestion and the origin of the intestine. He foresaw that the solution of those problems would lead to general results of great importance. The study of medusæ and of their mesodermic digestion confirmed him more and more in the conviction that the mesoderm was a vestige of elements with a primitive digestive function. In lower beings, such as sponges, this function takes place without being differentiated, whilst with other Cœlentera and with some Echinoderma the endoderm gives birth to a digestive cavity; yet, the mobile cells of the mesoderm preserve their faculty of intracellular digestion. As he studied these phenomena more closely, he ascertained that mesodermic cells accumulated around grains of carmine introduced into the organism.

All this prepared the ground for the phagocyte theory, of which he himself described the inception in the following words:

I was resting from the shock of the events which provoked my resignation from the University and indulging enthusiastically in researches in the splendid setting of the Straits of Messina.

One day when the whole family had gone to a circus to see[117] some extraordinary performing apes, I remained alone with my microscope, observing the life in the mobile cells of a transparent star-fish larva, when a new thought suddenly flashed across my brain. It struck me that similar cells might serve in the defence of the organism against intruders. Feeling that there was in this something of surpassing interest, I felt so excited that I began striding up and down the room and even went to the seashore in order to collect my thoughts.

I said to myself that, if my supposition was true, a splinter introduced into the body of a star-fish larva, devoid of blood-vessels or of a nervous system, should soon be surrounded by mobile cells as is to be observed in a man who runs a splinter into his finger. This was no sooner said than done.

There was a small garden to our dwelling, in which we had a few days previously organised a "Christmas tree" for the children on a little tangerine tree; I fetched from it a few rose thorns and introduced them at once under the skin of some beautiful star-fish larvæ as transparent as water.

I was too excited to sleep that night in the expectation of the result of my experiment, and very early the next morning I ascertained that it had fully succeeded.

That experiment formed the basis of the phagocyte theory, to the development of which I devoted the next twenty-five years of my life.

This very simple experiment struck Metchnikoff by its intimate similarity with the phenomenon which takes place in the formation of pus, the diapedesis[15] of inflammation in man and the higher animals. The white blood corpuscles, or leucocytes, which constitute pus, are mobile mesodermic cells. But, while with higher animals the phenomenon is complicated by the existence of blood-vessels and a nervous system, in a star-fish larva, devoid of those organs, the same phenomenon is reduced to the accumulation[118] of mobile cells around the splinter. This proves that the essence of inflammation consists in the reaction of the mobile cells, whilst vascular and nervous intervention has but a secondary significance. Therefore, if the phenomenon is considered in its simplest expression, inflammation is merely a reaction of the mesodermic cells against an external agent.

Metchnikoff then reasoned as follows: In man, microbes are usually the cause which provokes inflammation; therefore it is against those intruders that the mobile mesodermic cells have to strive. These mobile cells must destroy the microbes by digesting them and thus bring about a cure.

Inflammation is thus a curative reaction of the organism, and morbid symptoms are no other than the signs of the struggle between the mesodermic cells and the microbes.

In order to verify these conjectures, he started studying the englobing of microbes by mesodermic cells in larvæ and in other marine invertebrates which he inoculated.

At that time, a well-known German scientist, Kleinenberg, was Professor of Zoology at Messina. Metchnikoff imparted his ideas to him and showed him his experiments. Kleinenberg encouraged him very much; he looked upon his theory as "an Hippocratic thought" and advised him to publish it at once.

Metchnikoff was also greatly encouraged by Virchow, who happened to pass through Messina and came to see his preparations and his experiments, which seemed to him conclusive. However, Virchow advised him to proceed with the greatest prudence in their interpretation, as, he said, the theory of[119] inflammation admitted in contemporary medicine was exactly contrary to Metchnikoff's. It was believed that the leucocytes, far from destroying microbes, spread them by carrying them and by forming a medium favourable to their growth.

Metchnikoff always preserved a deep gratitude towards Virchow and Kleinenberg for the moral support which they gave him at that time.

When the hot weather came, we left Messina for Riva, a delicious summer resort on the shores of the Lake of Garda. There, Metchnikoff wrote his first memoir on the reaction of inflammation and on the digestion of microbes by the mesodermic cells of lower invertebrates. On the way back to Russia through Vienna, he went to see the Professor of Zoology, Claus; he found other colleagues with him and expounded his theory to them. They were much interested, and he asked them for a Greek translation of the words "devouring cells," and that is how they were given the name of phagocytes.

Claus asked him for his memoir for the Review which he edited and in which it appeared soon afterwards, in 1883.[16] The new-born "phagocyte theory" was thus very well received by naturalists and by Virchow, the father of cellular pathology.

Having returned to Russia, we went to the country, where Elie had to attend to family business; nevertheless, he continued his researches in every leisure moment. He had observed in Echinoderma that, during the transformation of their larvæ, the parts becoming atrophied were englobed by mesodermic[120] mobile cells. In those observations he was delighted to have found an example of physiological inflammation, i.e. one which presented itself in normal and non-morbid conditions. He thought he might observe it also during the metamorphosis of the tadpole into a frog, whilst the tail was being atrophied. But he found that, instead of the leucocytes of the blood, certain cells from the muscular tissue were those which devoured the enfeebled elements of the tail; he thus learnt that phagocytes might be, not only the white blood corpuscles, but other cells of mesodermic origin.[17]

In autumn 1883 he read his first paper on phagocytosis to a congress of physicians and naturalists at Odessa.[18] He compared the phagocytes to an army hurling itself upon the enemy and looked upon the phagocytic reaction as a defensive force of the organism.

In that paper itself and from that moment onwards, the trend of his ideas towards optimism becomes visible. By discovering the phagocytic reaction of the organism, he made a first breach in his philosophy of human nature, hitherto so pessimistic; he discovered within it a salutary element which could be utilised by science to combat its discords. He began to have some faith in the power of knowledge, not only for this struggle, but also for the establishment of a rational conception of life in general. Thus he said in his paper to the Odessa Congress:

The theoretical study of Natural History problems (in the largest sense of the word) alone can provide a critical[121] method for the comprehension of truth and lead to a definite conception of life, or at least allow us to approach one.

And yet, until then, the theory of phagocytosis as a curative force of the organism was but a hypothesis, for he had not yet observed spontaneous phagocytosis in diseases and did not know pathogenic microbes. He therefore sought to study them in lower animals, whose simple structure made the observation easier. He found some small, transparent, fresh-water crustaceans, called daphniæ, which were diseased and easy to place alive under a microscope. These crustaceans are often infected by a parasite fungus (Monospora bicuspidata), of which the spores, shaped like sharp needles, are introduced with food into the digestive tube, traverse the walls of it, and thus penetrate into the general cavity of the body. They are immediately attacked by mobile phagocytes, which either singly or in groups englobe them; if the phagocytes succeed in digesting the spores, the daphnia recovers; in the contrary case, the spores germinate and develop into small fungi which invade the organism and kill it. The recovery or death of the daphnia depends therefore on the issue of the struggle.[19] This observation gave final confirmation to the hypothesis of the curative forces of the organism.

Metchnikoff was not content with observing lower animals but wished to study the reaction of the organism of mammals in infectious diseases. At that time, the best-known microbe was the bacillus of anthrax. He therefore chose that for his researches and ascertained that phagocytosis varied with the virulence of the microbes; thus, while phagocytes did[122] not attack virulent bacteria, they attacked and rapidly digested attenuated bacteria. Moreover, he observed a very active phagocytosis in refractory animals and the reverse in sensitive ones.

He thus came face to face with the question of immunity.

He approached it by a comparative examination of the reaction of the organism of vaccinated rabbits and of non-vaccinated ones, and ascertained that an active phagocytosis was only manifested in a previously vaccinated organism. Metchnikoff explained these facts by the theory that the phagocytes became accustomed, gradually, through vaccination, to strive against more and more virulent microbes.

From that moment, immunity appeared to him as being no other than this progressive hardening. He published his researches in 1884 in Virchow's Archiv, and impatiently awaited medical reviews, hoping to find some answer, but the memoir passed unnoticed; the full significance of it had not been grasped.

[123]

CHAPTER XIX

Ill-health of his wife and sister-in-law — Journey to Tangiers through Spain — Villefranche — Baumgarten criticises the phagocyte theory.

In 1884, Metchnikoff's work was interrupted by the ill-health of my eldest sister and of myself; physicians considered that we had weak lungs and advised that we should spend the winter in the South. Elie, full of anxiety, hastened to take us there.

My younger brothers were now old enough to remain at school in our absence so as to go on with their studies; we therefore started with my two sisters. As cholera was raging in Italy, we went to Spain, hoping to find a place with a mild climate and conditions favourable to my husband's work. But we traversed the whole country without finding the right combination, and, as we had come too far to go back, we decided to spend the winter on the African coast, at Tangiers, close to Gibraltar where we were.

Metchnikoff had not much taste for sight-seeing, but, with his inquisitive and observing mind, liked to understand what he saw, and never failed to acquaint himself with the history of the countries which we traversed and which, with his ever-ready solicitude, he wanted us to see. We therefore saw every interesting town on our route through Spain. In the evenings we read together works on the history and art of the[124] country, and in the day-time we went for long rambles in order to examine all that there was to see. The history of the country, full of the sombre fanaticism which is reflected in its art, the austere aridity of the central plateau of the land, the reserved temper of the population—none of that found any echo in the vibrating, sunlight-loving soul of Metchnikoff.

Gentle Italy, her exuberant life and highly-cultured past, charmed him much more. He was consequently better pleased with Southern Spain, which is more similar to Italy. He was greatly impressed by the grandiose site and luminous atmosphere of Granada and the Alhambra and by the superb gardens of Malaga, with their tropical plants and avenues of palm trees.

At Gibraltar, he was greatly interested as a zoologist in the only monkeys (Macaques or Barbary apes) which have remained wild in Europe; he never tired of watching their habits whilst those amusing creatures jumped from tree to tree above our heads.

He had ample leisure to do so, for a frightful tempest kept us at Gibraltar, preventing the crossing of the Straits. As Metchnikoff was very anxious to set to work, we took the first steamship which ventured out, but the sea was still running so high that our ship was damaged and we had to go back. A panic took possession of the passengers, during which my sisters and I were struck by the calmness of Elie, who did not seem to realise the danger. After a delay of a few days, we were at last able to cross.

Our first impression of Tangiers, an Arab port of a thoroughly Oriental type, was extremely vivid. The city lay before us with its tall minarets and flat roofs, shining white under the burning sun. The[125] steamer dropped anchor some distance from the landing stage, and we were taken ashore on small boats, immediately to be surrounded by a motley crowd with faces varying from the pale olive of the pure Arab to the coal-black of the negro. All these people, in brilliant and picturesque garments, were shouting, gesticulating, fighting for the possession of passengers and their luggage, dragging them into the boats or carrying them on their backs, themselves standing up to their waists in water.

That feverish agitation, noise, and glaring sunlight introduced us suddenly to new and violent sensations.

Already at Gibraltar, Metchnikoff had made arrangements with a Spanish-speaking Arab from Tangiers who undertook our installation. He provided us with a very primitive dwelling, himself serving as our guide, cook, and general factotum.

We hastened to look for zoological material: alas, the sea was almost a desert. After a long search we only found a few rare sea-urchins, and Metchnikoff had to content himself with this meagre fauna during the whole of the winter. He resigned himself to the study of the embryology of sea-urchins in order to fill a few lacunæ in his previous researches. As he could not work much for lack of materials, he came with us for long excursions, during which he used to improvise interminable and very amusing tales with which to entertain my little sister.

At the beginning of our stay we were greatly interested by the life and customs of the country. The picturesque and varied crowd, the dignified and biblical types of Arabs, the bronzed Berbers, negroes, fanatical sects of Aïssawas, snake-charmers, the jousts,[126] and mad races of cavalry across the sandy beach; opium smokers; mysterious silhouettes of veiled women; the call to prayer from the tall minarets—all that strange and exotic life fascinated us. But after a time the wild customs, continual shouting on the occasion of every ceremony, vendettas, cruel fanaticism, and also the absolute lack of intellectual resources, began to tell on our nerves. Inactivity weighed heavily upon Metchnikoff; nevertheless, he bore his ill-luck with his usual courage and gaiety, finding great consolation in the excellent influence that the climate of Tangiers had upon all our healths.

At last, in the spring, we started for Villefranche, where he immediately set to work with success upon the embryology of jelly-fish; an important monograph on that subject was published by him in 1886. In it he gave definite form to his theory of the phagocytella and the genetic relationships of animals and of their primitive organs, a theory already mentioned above (p. 110).

56

From Villefranche we went to Trieste, where Metchnikoff studied star-fish and filled the lacunæ in his researches on the origin of the mesoderm.

In a medical review which he read at Trieste, he found the first account of his phagocyte theory; it was an unfavourable and hostile criticism by a German scientist of the name of Baumgarten, endeavouring to prove that Metchnikoff's deductions were inadmissible. This grieved and pained him very much, but he immediately recovered himself and strongly determined to study the medical side of the question in order to prove on that ground that his theory was well-founded.

[127]

CHAPTER XX

A Bacteriological Institute in Odessa — Unsatisfactory conditions — Experiments on erysipelas and on relapsing fever.

The results of Pasteur's antirabic inoculations were published in 1885. The Municipality of Odessa, desirous of founding a bacteriological station in that town, sent Dr. Gamaléia to Paris to study the new method. Metchnikoff was appointed Scientific Director of the new institution, and Drs. Gamaléia and Bardach, former pupils of his, were entrusted with the preparation of vaccines and preventive inoculations. The Institute, opened in 1886, was founded at the expense of the Municipality of Odessa and of the Zemstvo of the Kherson Province.

Metchnikoff himself describes as follows the short time he spent in that Institute:

... Having given up my State work, I placed myself at the service of the city and the Zemstvo.

Absorbed as I was by the scientific part of the work, I confided to my young colleagues the practical part, i.e. the vaccinations and the perfection of vaccines.

It was to be supposed that all would go very well.

Work in the new Institute began with ardour. But, very soon, a strong opposition manifested itself against it.

The medical administration began to make incursions into the Institute, with a view to finding some infractions of the regulations.

Medical society was hostile to every work which issued[128] from the laboratory. The institutions which had subscribed funds for the Institute were demanding practical results, while all necessary work towards that object was met by every sort of obstacle.

For instance, in order to destroy certain voles, very harmful to the cereals of Southern Russia, we proposed to make experiments as to infecting those rodents with the microbe of chicken cholera. Laboratory experiments were begun with that object. But, one day, I received an order from the Prefect peremptorily forbidding those experiments. This measure had been taken at the instigation of local physicians; having seen in a Petersburg newspaper an article by some one who had not a notion of bacteriology, they had assured the Prefect that chicken cholera could turn into Asiatic cholera.

I had to appeal to the General Governor, who ended by countermanding the Prefect's order; nevertheless this incident was not without regrettable consequences concerning the ulterior activities of the Institute.

Apart from all that, a deep scission took place between the members, though they were so few, of the Institute itself, and this had fatal consequences.

The men who were in charge of the practical work ceased to work in concert; I could not take their place, being overwhelmed with scientific researches, besides which, holding no medical degree, I was not qualified to perform vaccinations on human beings.

Under those conditions, I understood that in my quality as a theoretician, I should do well to retire, leaving the laboratory to practitioners who, bearing full responsibility, would fill the part better.

During his stay at the Odessa Bacteriological Institute, Metchnikoff had busied himself with infectious diseases in order to answer the first objections to his theory. He began by the microbes of erysipelas and showed that the phenomena of the disease, as well as those of recovery, were in full accord with the postulates of the phagocyte theory.
[129]
And then he studied relapsing fever in order to answer Baumgarten's objections, affirming that there was no phagocytic reaction in that disease, though it almost invariably ended in recovery. Experiments on man not being possible, Metchnikoff procured some monkeys, which he inoculated with relapsing fever, and ascertained that Baumgarten's error was due to the fact that he had only looked for phagocytosis in the patient's blood, whilst it really took place in the spleen.

These researches on erysipelas and relapsing fever were published in Virchow's Archives in 1887. Besides this scientific work, he was also giving lectures on bacteriology to some physicians, and was in full productive activity when external opposition and the discord among his collaborators in the Institute itself forced upon him the conviction that he could remain there no longer.

At that very moment the Prince of Oldenburg, having founded a Bacteriological Institute at Petersburg, invited Metchnikoff to take charge of it. He had to refuse, fearing the Northern climate for my health, and knowing from experience that it was impossible for a layman to manage an Institute with a medical staff. Yet he could not do without a laboratory. Seeing no possibility of having one in Russia, he decided to look abroad for a refuge and a laboratory.

"Having learnt from experience at Odessa," he wrote, "how difficult was the struggle against an opposition coming from all sides and devoid of reasonable causes, I preferred to go abroad to look for a peaceful shelter for my scientific researches."

We were no longer held back by family considerations;[130] our links with Russia had gradually loosened. He had resigned from the University, discord reigned at the Odessa Bacteriological Institute, conditions of life in Russia were very unfavourable to scientific activity; in a word, "obstacles from above, from below, and from all sides,"—as Metchnikoff expressed it,—gradually led to his resolution to leave his native country.
[131]
CHAPTER XXI

Hygiene Congress in Vienna — Wiesbaden — Munich — Paris and Pasteur — Berlin and Koch — Failure of anthrax vaccination of sheep — Decision to leave Russia.

In 1887 we went to Vienna, where a Congress of Hygienists was held, in which, for the first time, bacteriologists took part. Metchnikoff thus had the opportunity of becoming acquainted with many of them and to make inquiries concerning bacteriological laboratories. Professor Hueppe, of Wiesbaden, very kindly invited him to come to work in his own. The idea pleased Metchnikoff, who thought that a peaceful little University town would be very favourable to his work. But he found that his situation would be very difficult at Wiesbaden on account of the lack of harmony between the different laboratories in the town; he therefore gave up the project which had seemed to him so tempting.

By this time many objections had been raised against the phagocyte theory, and, Emmerich having attacked him very violently, Metchnikoff went to Munich to have an explanation with him. This gave him the opportunity of realising that Munich, like Wiesbaden, was not a place where he would care to settle.

He had a great desire to know Pasteur and his collaborators, who had just been playing such an[132] important scientific part, and, finding ourselves within easy reach of Paris, we repaired thither, without the slightest idea of settling there. This is how Metchnikoff himself described his first interview with Pasteur:

On arriving at the laboratory destined for the antirabic vaccinations, I saw an old man, rather undersized, with a left hemiplegia, very piercing grey eyes, a short beard and moustache and slightly grey hair, covered by a black skull-cap. His pale and sickly complexion and tired look betokened a man who was not likely to live many more years. He received me very kindly, and immediately spoke to me of the question which interested me most, the struggle of the organism against microbes.

"I at once placed myself on your side," he told me, "for I have for many years been struck by the struggle between the divers micro-organisms which I have had occasion to observe. I believe you are on the right road."

Pasteur at that time was chiefly occupied with antirabic vaccinations and with the building of a new Institute in the rue Dutot. Seeing the vast dimensions of the edifice and learning that the scientific staff was not large, Metchnikoff asked Pasteur if he might hope to work in one of the laboratories in an honorary capacity. Pasteur not only acceded to this request but offered him a whole laboratory. He was most kind, invited us to his home and introduced Metchnikoff to his collaborators, who produced an excellent impression on my husband.

Though all this made him incline more and more towards the Pasteur Institute, he still dreaded life in a large and noisy city, thinking that a peaceful little University town would be more favourable to his work. Therefore, before making a final decision, he desired to visit a few more bacteriological laboratories.

[133]

On our way back we passed through Berlin, where Metchnikoff wished to see Professor Koch and to show him some interesting specimens of phagocytosis. The great savant received him very coldly. For a long time, while examining specimens of the spleen in relapsing fever, he refused to recognise in them an example of phagocytosis. Though he was at last obliged to bow to evidence, he yet remained unfavourable to the phagocyte theory, and all his assistants followed his example. Metchnikoff was much surprised and

59

grieved by this hostility towards his ideas, notwithstanding that they were based on well-established facts. We hastened to leave Berlin.

Many years later, when phagocytosis was generally admitted, even in Germany, Professor Koch and many other German scientists welcomed Metchnikoff very kindly, which somewhat counterbalanced the unpleasantness of early memories. But, at that time, the contrast between our impression of Paris and of Germany was so great that all hesitation was at an end: the choice was made.

On returning to Odessa, Metchnikoff began to prepare his resignation and his departure. Yet he still had time to make some researches on phagocytosis in tuberculosis, in reply to the objections which rained upon his theory.

In the spring, he handed over the direction of the Institute to Dr. Gamaléia and took leave; we went to the country for a while before our final departure. During that time, Drs. Gamaléia and Bardach were making anthrax vaccinations on a large scale in a vast private property in the province of Kherson. When we were settled in our country home, Metchnikoff received a telegram announcing that the first[134] anthrax vaccine had killed many thousand sheep. Though, as a matter of fact, his personal responsibility was not involved, the blow was a terrible one; he hastened back to Odessa to elucidate the cause of the catastrophe. But it remained obscure....

This painful episode was the last drop which made the cup brim over; it strengthened Metchnikoff in his resolve to leave Russia.

[135]
CHAPTER XXII

The Pasteur Institute — Dreams realised — Metchnikoff at fifty — Growing optimism — Attenuated sensitiveness — The Sèvres villa — Daily routine.

Having decided to settle in France, we hastened to make ourselves acquainted with contemporary French literature, thinking to find in it a reflection of the soul and manners of the nation. But the realistic literature of the time, in spite of the great artistic worth of many of the authors, gave us an erroneous idea of life in France, of which it represented but one of many aspects. It was therefore with apprehension that we asked ourselves if we should ever be able to adapt ourselves to the new conditions, and whether our isolation would not be great.

We arrived in Paris on the 15th of October 1888, and we lodged at a small hotel in the Latin quarter, not far from the rue d'Ulm where the old Pasteur Institute stood, the new one not being completed. There was but little room in the laboratory, and Metchnikoff felt rather uneasy, fearing that he was in the way. But the new Institute soon was sufficiently advanced for him to settle there.

He was given two rooms on the second floor; I served as his assistant; he was perfectly happy at being at last able to give himself up in peace to his work. Soon, young physicians came to work under[136] his direction. Their number having increased, he was given a whole floor in which to instal them, two rooms on that floor being reserved for his own use. He occupied these rooms until the end of his life.

His dreams were at last realised. This is from a narration of the causes which led to his departure from Russia, in his own words:

Thus it was in Paris that I succeeded at last in practising pure Science apart from all politics or any public function. That dream could not have been realised in Russia because of obstacles from above, from below, and from all sides. One might think that the hour of science in Russia has not yet struck. I do not believe that. I think, on the contrary, that scientific work is indispensable to Russia, and I wish from my heart that future conditions may become more favourable than in the time of which I have spoken in the above lines.

Soon he was able to appreciate the great French qualities: humanitarian manners, tolerance, and gentleness, real freedom of thought, loyal and courteous intercourse, all of which made life easy and agreeable. And most precious of all were the true friendships which he contracted with his colleagues and his pupils. Indeed the Institut Pasteur and France became for him a second Motherland, and when in later years he was invited to other countries with more liberal conditions, he habitually replied that only for one place would he leave the Pasteur Institute, "the neighbouring cemetery of Montparnasse."

However, after his death, the Pasteur Institute which he had so loved continued to give him hospitality and harboured his ashes....

[137]

Pasteur himself ever was most kind and helpful to Metchnikoff. During the first years, when his health still allowed it, he used often to come to the laboratory, questioning Metchnikoff on his researches with much interest and always warmly encouraging him. He even attended assiduously his course of lectures on inflammation. After his state of health no longer allowed him to go out, Metchnikoff used to visit him every day, and tried to cheer him by talking to him of current researches.

MM. Duclaux and Roux became his closest friends; they were at first brought together by scientific interests and by questions concerning the Institute; but, gradually, personal sympathy grew up between them, binding them by that solid bond which is made up of daily occurrences, inducing respect, confidence, and affection. Moreover, Metchnikoff felt the deepest gratitude towards Pasteur and his collaborators, who had given him the possibility of working in so favourable an atmosphere.

From the very first, Pasteur sympathised with the phagocyte theory; the other members of the Institute thought it too biological, almost vitalistic. But when they had made themselves thoroughly cognisant with it, they also adopted it. Thus, having found in the Pasteur Institute not only favourable working conditions but also moral support, Metchnikoff became deeply attached to it, and the interests of "the House" became his.

In 1915, on the occasion of Metchnikoff's seventieth anniversary, M. Roux, in a Jubilee speech, gave of him and of his work the following appreciation which describes, better than anything I could say, what his part was in the Pasteur Institute:

[138]

In Paris as in Petrograd, as in Odessa, you have become a leader of thought, and you have kindled in this Institute a scientific focus which has radiated afar.

Your laboratory is more alive than any in the house; workers come to it in crowds. There, the bacteriological events of the day are discussed, interesting preparations examined, ideas sought for that may help an experimenter to solve difficulties in which he has become involved. It is to you that one comes to ask for a control experiment on a newly observed fact, for a criticism of a discovery that does not always survive the test.

Moreover, as you read everything, every one comes to you for information, for an account of a newly published memoir which there is no time to read. It is much more convenient than to consult the library and also much safer, for errors of translation and interpretation are avoided.

Your erudition is so vast and so accurate that it is made use of by the whole house. How many times have I not availed myself of it? One never fears to take advantage of it, for no scientific question ever finds you indifferent. Your ardour warms the indolent and gives confidence to the sceptical.

You are an incomparable collaborator as I know, I who have had the good fortune of being associated with your researches on several occasions. Indeed, you did nearly all the work!

More even than your science, your kindliness attracts; who amongst us has not experienced it? I have had a touching proof of it when, many times, you have nursed me as if I were your own child. You are so happy in doing good that you even feel gratitude towards those whom you serve.

This is such an intimate gathering that I may be allowed to say quite openly that it is so painful to you not to give that you prefer being exploited rather than close your hand.

The Pasteur Institute owes you much; you have brought to it the prestige of your renown, and by your work and that of your pupils you have greatly contributed to its glory. You[139] have given a noble example of disinterestedness by refusing any salary in those years when the budget was balanced with difficulty and by preferring to the glorious and lucrative situations that were offered to you the modest life of this house. Still a Russian by nationality, you have become French by your choice, and you contracted a Franco-Russian alliance with the Pasteur Institute long before the diplomats thought of it.

At the beginning the members of the Pasteur Institute were few, and the association bore a quasi-family character, Pasteurians often being compared with a monastic order, united by the worship of science. The progressive growth of the Institute inevitably destroyed its character of intimacy, but it remained a precious scientific focus, and this is what Metchnikoff said of it in 1913, à propos of the twenty-fifth anniversary of its foundation:
If we weigh the for and against of the Pasteur Institute, it is indisputable that the first surpasses the second by a great deal. I do not think another institution exists that is equally favourable to work. Innumerable proofs have been adduced to attest this in the twenty-five years that our House has existed.

It was especially the development of pure scientific research in the Institute which interested Metchnikoff; he continually considered means of contributing towards it; he thought it necessary to attract active scientific forces regardless of their origin, to institute generous scientific "scholarships," and to stimulate by every means scientific activity and spirit.
As the rapid development of bacteriology necessitated having recourse to chemistry, physics, and physiology, he considered it indispensable to organise collective work in which specialists in these divers branches should take part, thus collaborating to the[140] solution of the same problem. Later he was able to realise this project, up to a certain point, in his own laboratory, when studying intestinal flora.
He thought it would be useful to extend this method, as far as possible, to researches such as that on tuberculosis and on cancer, such researches being complicated and protracted and demanding co-ordinate efforts and an organisation that should

prevent the repetition of individual first steps. A clinic attached to the Pasteur Institute and adapted to scientific researches seemed to him indispensable.

He also considered that the experimental study of those human diseases which can only be inoculated in anthropoid apes should be carried out through the breeding of those animals in the colonies, for infantile diseases demand very young apes as subjects for experiments, and they cannot be brought to Europe in sufficient numbers without great loss. A mission of workers might carry out experiments on the spot.

He thought the popularisation of science a very useful thing and wished the Pasteur Institute to participate in it by appropriate courses of public lectures. He attached great importance to the penetration into ordinary life of results acquired by science, for the struggle against disease consists chiefly in prophylactic and hygienic measures which can only be applied by a well-informed public. For that reason he was always willing to be interviewed on scientific questions by journalists and, indeed, by any one, however ignorant. In order to instruct the public he often wrote popular articles on questions of hygiene and medicine.

Science in general never was a dead letter for him; his most abstract conceptions were always narrowly[141] bound to life; he saw one through the other and considered that they should serve each other.

Apart from scientific researches, he took part in the courses given at the Pasteur Institute. He prepared his lectures with infinite care, and, in spite of his long experience, he never could give them without some nervousness, especially during the last years of his life. He used even to write down the first sentences and to read them out in order to give himself time to recover; but very soon his self-control would return, and he would proceed with animation and lucidity; his lectures were living and suggestive.

I have mentioned above Roux's masterly appreciation of his influence at the Pasteur Institute. The following was written to me, a year after Metchnikoff's death, by one of his closest disciples and collaborators, and describes in a vivid manner the deep feelings with which he inspired his pupils:

"You say that you love to think that he continues to live in others. Could it have been otherwise? A character as powerful as his is capable of influencing and illuminating the life, not of one individual, but of a whole generation. I look upon it as the greatest good fortune of my life that I was able to spend my best years in his orbit and to impregnate my mind with his spirit, not his scientific spirit, but that which he manifested in facing life and humanity.

"This bond has become so much part of myself that my first impulse is always to act in the way he would have approved. I even feel the need to share with others what I received from him. I do not know whether it will be given to me to solve certain problems posed by him, but I have the conviction that his spirit, in its purity, will be preserved among us. He will ever live in those who worked by his side, and in those who will come to work in his laboratory. It cannot be otherwise."

[142]
Metchnikoff on his part never remained indifferent to his pupils. His solicitude towards them was warm, sometimes paternal, always ready and active. Many of his pupils remained his friends and collaborators for years afterwards. His fiery and exclusive temperament, however, made him take up a very different attitude in exceptional cases, when he found himself in front of one who persisted in a path which Metchnikoff himself considered the wrong path, or before an action which he thought disloyal or work done

without conscience. Then he became beside himself, and positively dangerous to those who had exposed themselves to the paroxysm of his indignation.

Fortunately such cases were rare; as a general rule, the atmosphere of his laboratory was impregnated with scientific spirit and ardour; all forces in it converged towards the same goal, being bound together by a community of aspirations and activity of which he was the soul.

The first period of his life in France was taken up by the strengthening and development of the phagocyte theory and by an eager struggle in its defence. He displayed in it his full energy as a scientist and a fighter, and this was perhaps the most agitated, the most tense period of his life.

When at last his theory was securely established and began to be accepted, he continued his researches with the same passionate ardour but in an atmosphere of peace. It was joy and bliss to him to be able to work apart from other preoccupations, and the years of his life between fifty and sixty were the happiest he ever had.

The state of his soul and his ideas had considerably[143] evolved in the course of years; the great moral and physical sensitiveness which had so often made him miserable in his youth had decreased and he had become much less impulsive. Unpleasant sensations no longer caused him so much suffering; he could bear the mewing of a cat or the barking of a dog; personal vexations no longer made him take such a horror of life as to wish to be rid of it: he now merely tried to conquer them.

At first this change operated less upon his ideas than upon his sensations and sentiments. Accustomed as he was to analyse his emotions, he realised the development within himself of a new sense of appreciation; less sensitive now to extreme impressions, he had become more so to ordinary ones. For instance, though less enchanted by music, and less irritated by discordant noises, he enjoyed absolute calm more fully. Now indifferent to rich food, which he formerly used to enjoy, he appreciated simple fare, bread and pure water. He did not seek for picturesque sites but took infinite pleasure in watching the growth of grass or the bursting of a bud. The first halting steps or the smile of an infant charmed and delighted him.

Demanding less from life, he now appreciated it as it was, and experienced the joy of mere living. The instinct, the sense of life had been born in him. He now saw Life and Nature under a different aspect from that which they had borne for him in his youth, for he had gradually acquired more balance; he had become adapted.

In their turn, his ideas evolved towards a more optimistic conception of life. His reflections, freed from the yoke of his juvenile sensitiveness, tended towards[144] the possibility of a correction of the disharmonies of human nature through knowledge and will. This evolution had taken years. "In order to understand the meaning of life," he said, "it is necessary to live a long time, without which one finds oneself in the position of a congenitally blind man before whom the beauties of colour are spread out."

During the twenty-eight years that he lived in France, nearly all his time was devoted to the laboratory. Whilst the Institute was still in its beginning, work there was calm and collected; but, as its growing renown attracted many people, this quietude decreased considerably. Metchnikoff felt this, but could not bring himself to refuse to admit those who came; he compensated himself by peaceful Sundays and holidays.

For a long time we inhabited the neighbourhood of the Institute and spent the summers at Sèvres; in 1898 we bought a small villa there with a sum of money which we inherited from an aunt. In 1905 we settled there altogether, for Metchnikoff, confined in the laboratory all day, felt the need of fresh air; the daily walk that he was obliged to take to reach the house and the absolute calm, away from the noise of the city, suited him; he even fancied that the hill on which the house was built provided him with a wholesome exercise for his heart.

The return to Sèvres, which he greatly liked, was to him a daily source of pleasure. I can see him now, hastily coming out of the train, his pockets full of papers and brochures which he read in the train and parcels in his hands, for he loved to bring home little presents. A kindly smile illumined his face and he[145] never failed to express the pleasure he felt at coming home. "How pure the air is! How green the grass! What peace! You see, if I did not go to Paris to work I should not be so alive to the charm of Sèvres and the pleasure of rest." He used to come home at seven and do no more work; it was his daily rest. He then gave himself up to complete relaxation, joked, related the incidents of the day, spoke of his researches, planned experiments for the next day, read aloud part of the evening and then listened to music, not only because he liked it, but also because he wanted to "switch on to another line," i.e. rest his mind completely.

He was an incomparable companion, always alive and communicative, generously giving out the treasures of his heart and his intelligence. He liked a simple life; all artifice, all convention displeased him. He disliked luxury in his person to that extent that he never consented to possess a gold watch nor any object with no particular use. His only luxury was to gratify others. He enjoyed peaceful family life and a circle of intimate friends. Yet, appreciating as he did all serious manifestations of life, he was glad to have the opportunity of meeting people who were interesting either in themselves or for the knowledge which they could impart.

In Life as in Science he found precepts to help the evolution of his moral and philosophical ideas, which he placed in their turn at Life's service. If he could not solve a problem, he at least pointed out its importance.

His attentive penetration of things in themselves, coupled with a creative imagination, was the force which enabled him to open out new prospects and new paths.

[146]

On looking back upon his own life, he used to say that the period spent at the Pasteur Institute had been the happiest, the most favourable to his scientific work; he therefore remained deeply attached to it until the end of his life.

[147]

CHAPTER XXIII

Opposition to the phagocyte theory — Scientific controversies — Experiments in support of the phagocyte theory — Behring and antitoxins — The London Congress — Inflammation.

As long as Metchnikoff was but a zoologist, the scientific atmosphere around him remained calm and serene. But everything changed suddenly when he entered the domain of pathology with his theory of phagocytes and phagocytosis.

Here was the realm of secular traditions, deeply rooted, and of theories generally admitted but resting on no biological basis. Attacks and objections against his theories came following upon each other with a rush, only to be compared with the racing clouds of a stormy sky or the hurrying waves of a tempestuous sea. An epic struggle began for Metchnikoff which was to last for twenty-five years, until the moment when the phagocyte theory, his child now grown up, emerged victoriously. To each attack, to each objection, he answered by fresh experiments, fresh observations annihilating objections; his theory was assuming a wider and wider scope, becoming more solid, more convincing.... But only his intimates knew how much the struggle cost him in vital force, what sleepless nights, due to continuous cerebral tension and to the effort to conceive some new and irrefragable experiment, what alternations of hope[148] and depression.... In an ardent, stormy life such as this, each year counted for many.

As soon as he arrived at the Pasteur Institute he undertook active researches with the object of developing and defending the phagocyte theory.

By experiments on the rouget of pigs he refuted the objections of Emmerich, who affirmed that, in that disease, the destruction of the microbes was not due to phagocytes. By experiments on the anthrax of pigeons he answered the attacks of Baumgarten and his pupils. To Behring, who affirmed that immunity was due to the bactericidal power of the serum, he replied by a series of experiments on the anthrax of rats.

By all these researches Metchnikoff proved that recovery and immunity depended on the absorption and digestion of living, virulent microbes by phagocytes. Natural or artificial vaccination by attenuated microbes allows the phagocytes to become gradually accustomed to digest more virulent ones, and this confers immunity upon the organism. That phenomenon is comparable to that by which we can accustom ourselves gradually to doses of poison which would be very harmful if taken at the start (arsenic, opium, nicotine, etc.).

Little by little, the accuracy of Metchnikoff's observations began to be realised, and, moreover, other scientists supported him by their personal investigations. The part played by phagocytosis was becoming more and more evident and the question was ripening in France and in England, but in Germany it still met with great opposition.

At the Berlin Congress in 1890 the theory was received very favourably by Lister, whilst Koch[149] attacked it, trying to prove that phagocytes played no part in immunity, which, according to him, depended upon the chemical properties of the blood.

Soon after that, Behring discovered antitoxins, and this seemed to favour the chemical or humoral theory of immunity. According to the latter, microbes and their poisons were rendered harmless by the chemical properties of the blood serum, properties similar to those of disinfecting substances.

In spite of his firm conviction of the solidity of the phagocyte theory, this discovery was a shock to Metchnikoff, for it was in apparent contradiction with the cellular theory of immunity. He hastened to undertake a series of researches; his overflowing eagerness infected his whole circle, every one taking the warmest interest in the progress of his experiments.

This was just as preparations were being made to take part in the London Congress, where the question of immunity was to be debated and had indeed been placed at the head of the programme. Many papers were being prepared, and a veritable tourney of opinions was to take place at this Congress.

Metchnikoff had already been to England once, in the spring of 1891, on the occasion of his reception as an Honorary Doctor by the University of Cambridge. This gave him the opportunity of making closer acquaintance with the English, who inspired him with great sympathy; years only increased this feeling. He appreciated the originality of their earnest and generalising spirit, their loyalty and energy; he was grateful to them for the attentive and favourable attitude with which his scientific work and himself had been received.

[150]

He was therefore delighted that this Congress, which was to be the scene of his final struggle against his contradictors, should take place in England and not in Germany, a country hostile to his ideas.

In view of the importance of the coming debate, a series of fresh experiments was made. This time Metchnikoff undertook them not only in person, but also in collaboration with M. Roux and with some students. The whole laboratory was in a state of effervescence.

The principal papers to be read at the Congress on the question of immunity were those of Messrs. Roux and Büchner, the first entirely in favour of the phagocyte theory and the second supporting the humoral theory.

Metchnikoff read an epitome of his researches and of his answers to attacks on his theory. Towards the end of the Congress the latter had visibly acquired the suffrage of numerous scientists. Roux wrote to me from London concerning my husband's paper:

Metchnikoff is busy showing his preparations and, besides, he would not tell you how great is his triumph. He spoke with such passion that he carried everybody with him. I believe that, this evening, the phagocyte theory is the richer by many friends.

Thus the researches made in recent years and the results of the London Congress allowed us to consider the phagocyte theory of immunity as being solidly established.

Yet, Behring's discovery of antitoxins still hung over it like a sword of Damocles; it was imperative that the respective parts played by antitoxins and by phagocytes should be elucidated. With that[151] object in view, Metchnikoff undertook new researches and succeeded in ascertaining once for all the narrow link between immunity and the function of the phagocytes which probably elaborate the antitoxins as a product of their digestion of vaccinal toxins. He drew this conclusion from the fact that, in a rabbit vaccinated against hog-cholera, the exudate devoid of phagocytes[20] is neither bactericidal, nor antitoxic, nor attenuating, while it is so if it contains phagocytes. Therefore a relation of causality exists between cells and the acquired properties of humors. And the resistance of the animal is in visible correlation with the degree of phagocytosis which is manifested by it.

These results having been established, it seemed as if the last rampart of the humoral theory had been taken by storm.

In the meanwhile the persistent and bitter opposition of physicians to the phagocyte theory made a great impression on Metchnikoff, and, while stimulating his energy in defence of his ideas, it maintained him in a state of nervous excitement and even depressed him.

He asked himself why this obstinate opposition to a doctrine based on well-established facts, easily tested and observed throughout the whole animal kingdom? To him, a naturalist, it seemed clear and simple and all the more admissible that it was confirmed by the generality of its application to all living beings.

But, he thought, perhaps the real cause of the attitude of the contradictors lies in the very fact that medical science only concerns itself with the pathological phenomena of higher animals, leaving[152] their evolution entirely out of account, as well as their starting-point in lower animals—whilst it is the very simplicity of the latter which allows us to penetrate to the origin of the phenomena.

Perhaps a general plan of the whole, in the shape of a comparative study, embracing the whole animal scale, would throw light over the generality of phagocytic phenomena and would make their continuity understood through normal and pathological biology. He determined to make this effort. In order to place in a fresh light the biological evolution of phagocytosis phenomena in disease, he chose one of the principal manifestations of pathological phagocytosis, inflammation, and, in 1891, gave a series of lectures on this subject which he afterwards published in a volume. According to his usual method, he began by the most primitive beings, taking as a starting-point the lower organisms which do not yet possess differentiated functions, and whose normal digestion is, if necessary, used as a means of defence against noxious agents. Then, by a comparative study in every grade of the animal kingdom, he proved that the same mode of struggle and defence persists in the mesodermic cells, the phagocytes in all animals in general. In all of them, thanks to a special sensitiveness, Chimiotaxis, phagocytes move towards the intruder, to englobe it and digest it if they can. This reaction for defence by the organism takes place in beings endowed with a vascular system by the migration of the blood-phagocytes which traverse the walls of the blood-vessels in order to betake themselves to the invaded point.

In higher animals, all the symptoms which accompany this phenomenon of defence and which constitute[153] the classical picture of inflammation (a heightened temperature, pain, redness, tumefaction) are due to the complexity of the organism; but the essence, the primum movens of inflammation, with them also, is a digestive action of the phagocytes upon the noxious agent, therefore a salutary reaction of the organism, essentially similar to the normal digestion of inferior beings. Metchnikoff adduced numerous examples giving evidence of the genetic link which exists between inflammation and normal intracellular digestion, and while establishing the evolution of the former on biological and experimental bases, he showed at the same time the close connection which binds normal biology and pathological biology.

This series of lectures formed a volume which appeared in 1892 under the title of Leçons sur la pathologie comparée de l'inflammation, a book which contributed to the acceptation of the phagocyte theory and which showed the importance of Natural History applied to Medicine.

[154]
CHAPTER XXIV

Cholera — Experiments on himself and others — Illness of M. Jupille — Death of an epileptic subject — Insufficient results.

The acute period of the struggle in defence of the phagocyte theory now seemed to have come to an end and Metchnikoff turned his thoughts towards a new field of ideas.

Having elucidated the essence of inflammation, he wished to study the origin of another pathological symptom, i.e. the rise in temperature which constitutes a feverish condition. To that end he undertook a succession of experiments on cold-blooded animals; he injected microbes into crocodiles and serpents, hoping thus to provoke a rise in their temperature. But those experiments did not give the results expected.

In the meanwhile (1892) cholera had made its appearance in France; the specificity of the cholera vibrio was not finally established at that time. The observations made by Pettenkoffer on the immunity of certain regions, despite the presence of the cholera vibrio in the water, and the experiments made upon himself by that scientist, seemed to plead against the specificity of the cholera vibrio; but other facts spoke in its favour. Desirous of solving this question, Metchnikoff went to a cholera centre in Brittany in order to fetch the necessary materials. Having done so, he attempted to produce cholera in divers kinds of animals, but without success.

[155]
As he failed to solve the problem of the specificity of the cholera vibrio on animals, he resolved to experiment upon himself and consumed a culture of cholera vibriones. He did not contract cholera, which made him doubt the specificity of the vibrio, and therefore he consented to repeat the experiment on one of his workers (M. Latapie) who offered to submit to it: the result was the same. He then did not hesitate to accept the offer of a second volunteer (M. Jupille). The preceding results having led him to suppose

that the cholera vibrio became attenuated in vitro and might perhaps serve as a vaccine against cholera, he gave a culture of long standing to the young volunteer.

To his astonishment and despair, Jupille began to manifest the typical symptoms of cholera, and a doctor who was particularly conversant with the clinical chart of the disease declared the case a severe one because of the nervous symptoms which accompanied it.

Metchnikoff was in mortal anxiety, and even said to himself that he could not survive a fatal issue. Fortunately the patient recovered, and this terrifying experiment proved indisputably the specificity of the cholera vibrio. Yet the irregularity of its action showed that in certain cases conditions existed which prevented the inception of the disease, and Metchnikoff supposed that this might be due to the action of the different intestinal micro-organisms.

In order to simplify the question, he began by making experiments outside the organism. He sowed the cholera vibrio with divers other microbes and saw that some of them facilitated its culture whilst others prevented it. Similar experiments within the organism of animals gave no conclusive results; the[156] simultaneous ingestion of the cholera vibrio and of favourable microbes did not induce cholera.

The flora of the intestines, complex as it is, probably played a part on which it was difficult to throw any light. Yet Metchnikoff did not give up the idea of producing a vaccine against this disease with attenuated microbes, or, if not, to prevent its inception by preventive microbes. His thesis was strengthened when one of his pupils, Dr. Sanarelli, discovered a series of choleriform bacilli in the absence of any cholera epidemic, one of those microbes being found at Versailles, a town which had remained immune during every cholera epidemic.

Metchnikoff thought that this microbe, or some choleriform bacillus, similar though not specific, probably served as a natural vaccine against cholera in those localities which were spared by the epidemic though the cholera vibrio was brought there. This was a question that could only be solved by experiment.

At the time when he had himself absorbed a cholera culture, Metchnikoff admitted the risk of catching the disease; still, his eagerness to solve the problem had silenced in him all other considerations and feelings opposed to his irresistible desire to attempt the experiment. This "psychosis," as he himself called it later, recurred now, in spite of all the emotions he had gone through on the previous occasion, and he decided once again to experiment on man. It is true that he now only had to deal with choleriform microbes from Versailles which he believed to be quite harmless as they came from the water of a locality free from cholera. He therefore ingested some of the Versailles choleriform vibriones and gave some to several other people. Contrary to expectation, one[157] of the latter, an incurable epileptic, showed some symptoms of cholera, but recovered. But as, a short time later, this patient died from a cause which remained obscure, Metchnikoff thought that possibly the experiment might have had something to do with it, and finally resolved to perform no other experiments on human beings.

How could that unforeseen result be explained? Metchnikoff supposed that the intestine of the subject contained favourable microbes which had exalted the virulence of the bacillus, in itself weak and innocuous. If it were so, then certain intestinal microbes would influence the inception of diseases and the action of the micro-organisms would vary according to the society in which they found themselves. As such problems could only be solved through experiment, he again energetically sought for a means of conferring cholera upon animals. After many failures and difficulties, it occurred to him to try new-born animals whose intestinal flora, not yet developed, could not interfere with the swarming of the ingested bacilli. He chose young suckling rabbits for his experiments and, with the aid of favourable microbes, he succeeded at last in giving them characteristic cholera, through ingestion; thus it became possible to study intestinal cholera on these animals.

However, numerous researches on the prevention of cholera by means of divers microbes gave no results sufficiently conclusive to permit their application to human beings. The problem was rendered extremely complicated and difficult by the many and varied influences of numerous intestinal microbes and the inconstancy of microbian species in the same individual.

[158]

CHAPTER XXV

Pfeiffer's experiments, 1895 — The Buda-Pest Congress — Extracellular destruction of microbes — Reaction of the organism against toxins — Dr. Besredka's researches — Macrophages — The Moscow Congress, 1897 — Bordet's experiments.

Metchnikoff had scarcely recovered from all the emotions caused by his experiments on cholera, which he was still studying, when, in 1894, a work appeared by a well-known German scientist, Pfeiffer, bringing out new facts in favour of the extracellular destruction of microbes.

Whilst studying the influence of the blood serum within the organism and not outside it as his predecessors had done, he had found that cholera vibriones, injected into the peritoneum of a guinea-pig vaccinated against cholera, were nearly all killed in a few minutes and that they then presented the form of motionless granules in the peritoneal liquid. This granular degenescence, said Pfeiffer, took place apart from the phagocytes and therefore without their intervention. Metchnikoff repeated the experiment at once and ascertained that it was perfectly accurate.

The complexity of biological phenomena being very great, he fully admitted the possibility of other means of defence in the organism besides that of the phagocytic reaction. However, this new fact disagreed so much with his own observation, and[159] seemed so isolated, that Metchnikoff supposed an error of interpretation must have been made and tried to throw light upon it. He spent sleepless nights seeking the conclusive experiment which might explain Pfeiffer's phenomenon.

His excitement was all the greater that he was very soon going to the International Congress at Buda-Pest, where he intended to expose the results of his new researches, and he feared that he should not have time to make all the experiments which he required in support of his arguments. However, the general impression of the Congress was clearly favourable to the phagocyte theory. This is how M. Roux picturesquely described the scene at Metchnikoff's Jubilee in 1915:

"I can see you now at the Buda-Pest Congress in 1894, disputing with your antagonists; with your fiery face, sparkling eyes, and dishevelled hair, you looked like the Dæmon of Science, but your words, your irresistible arguments raised the applause of your audience.

"The new facts, which had at first sight seemed to contradict the phagocyte theory, now entered into harmony with it. It was found to be sufficiently comprehensive to reconcile the holders of the humoral theory with the partisans of the cellular theory."

This is how Metchnikoff had reconciled the apparent disagreement of Pfeiffer's phenomenon with the phagocyte doctrine: he demonstrated, by a series of experiments, that the extracellular destruction of the cholera vibriones in the peritoneum of a guinea-

70

pig vaccinated against cholera, did in no wise depend on the chemical properties of the blood serum, but was simply due to the digestive juices which had escaped from the inside of the leucocytes, damaged by the[160] intraperitoneal injection. Those digestive juices, or cytases, poured into the peritoneal liquid were what killed the injected cholera vibriones and transformed them into "Pfeiffer's granulations." On the other hand, if by means of various precautions the phagocytes were left unmolested, the extracellular destruction did not take place and the vibriones were digested within the phagocytes.

Metchnikoff used other experiments to prove that the bactericidal property of blood juices did not exist without intervention from the phagocytes. For instance, in a guinea-pig vaccinated against cholera, the bacilli are not destroyed if they are injected into parts of the organism that are devoid of pre-existing phagocytes, such as in the subcutaneous tissue, in the anterior chamber of the eye or in an aseptically-obtained œdema. On the other hand, if, in the same medium, some exudate is injected containing damaged leucocytes from which the digestive juice is leaking, the vibriones introduced are destroyed. The same results are obtained in vitro.

All these experiments proved that the extracellular destruction of the cholera vibrio was accomplished by the digestive juices which had passed from the phagocytes into the humors and not at all through a special property of those humors. Once again the phagocyte theory rose triumphant from the test.

After having finally proved that it is by means of its phagocytes that the organism fights microbes, Metchnikoff wished to find out whether it was by the same process that it struggled with their poisons, or toxins. This problem, far more difficult to solve, took him many years' study. Whilst every phase of the phagocytes' struggle against microbes can be[161] followed with the eyes, it is impossible to do so where poisons are concerned, since they are invisible; it is necessary to proceed by a different road.

Faithful to his method of taking as a starting-point the simplest expression of the phenomenon to be studied, Metchnikoff began by lower beings. Unicellular organisms, such as myxomycetes, amœbæ, and infusoria, sometimes manifest a natural immunity to certain poisons. It is also possible to endow them with artificial immunity by accustoming them gradually to substances which, ingested straight away, would infallibly have killed them. Such phenomena, seen in unicellular beings, could only be ascribed to the reaction of the cell itself. Therefore Metchnikoff supposed a priori that the phagocytes, being similar primitive cells of multicellular beings, would also react against poisons. And, in fact, he ascertained that the number of phagocytes in a rabbit's blood diminished considerably under the influence of a fatal dose of arsenic, whilst it increased under the influence of small doses of the poison, to which it was possible to accustom the animal.

Dr. Besredka, a disciple of Metchnikoff, made some very interesting researches, which entirely confirmed the share of the phagocytes in the reaction against sulphides of arsenic. He had chosen the trisulphide, a very slightly soluble salt of an orange colour, in order to find it again easily within the organism. After having injected non-fatal doses of it into the peritoneal cavity, he obtained an exudate in which all the orange granules of the salt were to be found included within those leucocytes which have a large, non-lobed nucleus—the macrophages. These cells gradually digested the salt they had englobed, which[162] ended by disappearing entirely within them, and the rabbit remained safe and sound. On the other hand, it died if the same doses of the same salt had been protected from the leucocytes by an elderberry bag, or when the leucocytes had been attracted elsewhere by a previous injection of carmine for instance. Those experiments removed all doubts as to the share of the phagocytes in the destruction of mineral poisons.

71

Certain experiments on microbian poisons spoke in the same sense. Thus MM. Roux and Borrel had observed that the diphtheritic toxin, which is inoffensive to rats even in large doses, kills that animal if a small quantity of it is introduced into the brain, the probable explanation being that, in cases of subcutaneous injections, the poison, "phagocyted" on the way, was destroyed before it reached the nerve cells.

Thus experiments seemed to plead in favour of the view that the part played by phagocytosis is not limited to the struggle against microbes, but also extends to the defence against poisons and toxins.

After having studied the mode of destruction of these, Metchnikoff wished to elucidate the origin of the counter-poisons, the specific antitoxins discovered by Behring in the humors of immunised organisms, a question of which the study was even more difficult.

Metchnikoff began by asking himself whether the microbes themselves did not produce antitoxins in order to defend themselves against enemy micro-organisms. He made many experiments but only obtained negative results, and concluded that the antitoxins must be manufactured by the organism itself.

[163]

The origin of this property must be more recent than that of the phagocytic reaction, for it does not exist in plants or in inferior animals. It was only from superior cold-blooded vertebrates, such as the crocodile—and that only in artificial conditions—and upwards, that Metchnikoff succeeded in finding a specific antitoxic power in the humors.

He ascertained that the vaccination of animals by toxins conferred, after a time, antitoxic powers to the blood and humors which contained leucocytes. He concluded therefrom that the presence of antitoxins depended on that of the phagocytes. Experiments on divers higher animals having proved that, in them also, antitoxins were localised in humors containing phagocytes, Metchnikoff concluded that the antitoxins were manufactured by the cells themselves. As toxins are absorbed and digested chiefly by macrophages, it is probable that it is the latter also which manufacture specific antitoxins, or the final product of the digestion of corresponding toxins. Metchnikoff could only propound this idea as an hypothesis, for the complexity and difficulty of a material demonstration did not yet allow of a definite solution of the problem. However, certain observations on toxins and antitoxins pleaded in favour of this thesis.

For instance, working in collaboration with MM. Roux and Salimbeni, he had found that it is by soluble poisons that the cholera vibrions harm the organism or kill it, but that small doses of the same poisons are vaccines and make the blood of the vaccinated animal antitoxic. On the other hand, a microbian vaccination is preventive against microbes only but not against toxins and the blood does not become antitoxic. This is explained by the fact that[164] it is not the same cells which digest cholera microbes and cholera toxins: the microphages digest the vibriones whilst the macrophages digest the poisons and, probably, manufacture as products of this digestion, the corresponding antibody, the cholera antitoxins.

On the contrary, in cases of the inclusion of microbes by macrophages, as, for instance, in plague, the blood acquires an antitoxic power by injection of the microbes themselves and not by their toxins, as was demonstrated by M. Roux and his collaborators. The same fact was observed by Metchnikoff on the alligator, in whom also microbes are digested by macrophages. In those cases, when microbes and toxins are digested by the same cells, the latter manufacture antibodies against both.

72

These facts rendered legitimate the supposition of the macrophagic origin of antitoxins.

In 1897 an International Congress took place in Moscow. Metchnikoff read a paper on the phagocytic reaction against toxins and another dealing with the whole of the knowledge acquired concerning human plague. He ended this by a plea in favour of Science, so often accused of having contributed nothing to the solution of the most important human problems, particularly ethical ones, and of having, on the contrary, sanctioned the law of Might by tabulating the laws of the struggle for existence. Metchnikoff objected that, far from doing so, Science, by revealing the laws of Nature, applied to humanity the benefits derived from them, whilst striving to counterbalance their cruel or harmful effects. The struggle against plague and other diseases was a[165] concrete example of this, for here medical science opposed itself to the cruelty of "natural selection." He wound up his speech by the following words, "Just as, in order to satisfy his æsthetic tastes, Man revolts against the laws of Nature which creates races of sterile and fragile flowers, he does not hesitate to defend the weak against the laws of natural selection. Science has been faithful to her mission and to her generous traditions. Let her, then, progress unhindered."

Metchnikoff's friend and companion, M. Nocard, wrote to me concerning Metchnikoff's paper:

Do not believe a word that Metchnikoff tells you. He had tremendous success. The somewhat free form of his paper contributed to its success, as it only made his conviction and enthusiasm more apparent. Thus the Sibyl on her tripod.

Metchnikoff had at this period a very talented disciple, M. I. Bordet, who opened a new path by a series of researches of the greatest importance. He found, among other things, that "the figured elements" can be destroyed outside the cells, in the humors. Thus, if red blood corpuscles from one animal are injected into an animal of a different kind, these globules are destroyed, not within the phagocytes, but outside them, in the ambient humors. Metchnikoff studied this phenomenon and proved that the explanation was the same that he had previously given of Pfeiffer's phenomenon in the case of cholera vibrions. In Bordet's experiments, the leucocytes which were already existing in the humors were also damaged by the experimental shock; but, if this was carefully avoided, the phagocytes, remaining intact, englobed[166] and digested the injected red corpuscles and no phenomenon similar to Pfeiffer's took place.

These observations led Metchnikoff to a thorough study of the destruction of cellular elements by the phagocytes. He had already observed that, whilst the struggle with microbes is chiefly undertaken by small leucocytes with a lobed nucleus—the microphages—it is the great leucocytes with a single large nucleus—the so-called macrophages—which undertake the destruction of cells, "figured" elements, as well as that of toxins. The macrophages are to be found not only in the blood but also in different organs such as the liver, spleen, kidneys, etc.; they seize upon living cells by means of mobile protoplasmic prolongations with which they draw them in and end by ingesting them completely. Not only do they thus absorb foreign cellular elements such as red corpuscles, spermatozoa, etc., but also all the weakened cells of the organism itself.

This weakening may be due to normal phenomena such as the metamorphosis of insects or tadpoles, when certain organs, as they weaken, become useless or inactive. But, oftener, this weakening is due to pathological causes, as in morbid atrophies or poisoning by microbian toxins. In any case, the enfeeblement of cells exposes them to be devoured by macrophages, which brings about the atrophy of the cells or even of the organs which contain them.

These observations suggested to Metchnikoff the idea that senile atrophy might be due to the same mechanism, and his thoughts turned towards the problem of the causes of old age.

But, before undertaking researches in a new direction, he wished to conclude those he had been[167] pursuing for twenty years on the phenomenon of phagocytosis. He therefore started to complete his investigations on immunity in order to epitomise them and to give a definite form to his doctrine on that subject.

[168]

CHAPTER XXVI

1900. Immunity — Natural Immunity — Artificial Immunity.

For centuries the question of immunity has occupied the human mind because the prevention of disease has ever been one of the greatest preoccupations of Man. Savages had already observed that man can become refractory to the venom of serpents, either through a slight bite or by the application of certain preparations of that venom on scarified skin. It was also a popular and very ancient notion that the contact of a slightly scratched hand with the pustules of cow-pox conferred immunity against human small-pox. It was on this observation that Jenner founded his method of antivariolic vaccination. The latter, in its turn, suggested to Pasteur the idea of attempting antimicrobian vaccinations. Having ascertained that old cultures of chicken cholera, previously very virulent, had become harmless, he wondered whether they had become a vaccine and proved by experiment that they had. That led him to the principle of the attenuation of viruses and to that of vaccination by attenuated microbes. Thus the problem of the mechanism of immunity was stated.

The first theories propounded on the subject concerned the humors. Pasteur supposed that immunity was due to the absorption, by the vaccinating microbes, of certain nutritive substances in the humors,[169] which, not being renewed for some time, were missed by the microbes afterwards introduced into the organism, which therefore could not develop completely. Chauveau, on the other hand, thought that, in cases of immunity, the humors contained substances which were unfavourable to microbes. Those theories explained particular facts, but were not applicable to the generality of cases.

Other theories,[21] whilst attributing an active part to the organism itself, failed to account for the mechanism of immunity in general. This was due to the fact that knowledge at that time lacked the two essential elements, i.e. the modifications suffered by the organism which was becoming immunised, and the fate of the microbes in the refractory organism.

The disappearance of the microbes in the cured or refractory animal had indeed been observed;[22] the inflammatory reaction of the organism in the course of immunisation had been noted;[23] microbes had long ago been observed inside the white globules of pus;[24] but, either an erroneous interpretation was given to the facts observed, or, rather, the links of causality between those factors failed to be established because they were observed solely in the complicated organism of superior beings. Humoral theories, less easy to test, preserved an appearance of generality and were easily admitted.

Such was the state of the question when Metchnikoff approached it from a naturalist's point of view. He knew the life of unicellular beings and that of the lower multicellular organisms in their complete simplicity;[170] he knew their mode of defence

74

by ingestion and intracellular digestion. Having become familiar with these phenomena, visible in the single cell, he was better able to see his way in the complicated milieu of higher beings. He was therefore able to discover the connection between the divers factors which other scientists had observed singly. He was able to prove that it is the combination of these factors, i.e. inflammation, the ingestion of living and virulent microbes, and their disappearance by means of intracellular digestion which makes immunity possible. He demonstrated that "there is but one permanent element in natural or acquired immunity, and that is phagocytosis."

The extension and importance of this factor, applicable to the whole animal kingdom, proved the truth and general scope of the phagocyte doctrine of immunity.

In 1900, Metchnikoff presented to the International Congress in Paris a complete tabulation of his researches and fought his contradictors for the last time, after which, convinced that his deductions were solid, he began to write a work on Immunity in Infectious Diseases. In it he epitomised, as in a great harmonious chord, the results of his researches, reaching over a period of nearly twenty years; he affirmed and gave final expression to his doctrine of immunity, based on the comparative study of the mechanism of that phenomenon and of its evolution along the whole scale of living beings; he related his controversies, analysed the objections to his doctrine, expounded the theories of other scientists concerning immunity, and gave a general view of the present state of the question. This book is a living picture of a[171] long and important part of Metchnikoff's scientific achievements.

The question of immunity is of such great importance, the mechanism of this phenomenon and the physiology of intracellular digestion are so complicated, that I have thought it useful to epitomise here the exposition given of it by Metchnikoff in his book. Readers who do not care to go further into the subject can pass over the next few pages without hindering their comprehension of the following chapters.

Diseases affect all living beings, and the greater number of plants and animals would cease to exist without innate or acquired immunity.

Unicellular beings are generally immune against infectious diseases, which are rarely observed in them. Their body being almost entirely made up of digestive protoplasm, the microbes which they absorb are directly introduced into a noxious medium and are destroyed therein like any other food. If the microbes are indigestible, they are immediately rejected; hence, in the majority of cases, they cannot become harmful.

This resistance of unicellular beings to many microbes and microbian toxins is due not only to the intense digestive power of the cell but also to the extreme sensitiveness which rules over the choice of food. Owing to this protoplasmic sensitiveness (chimiotaxis) protozoa are attracted towards certain microbes or substances (positive chimiotaxis) and repelled by others (negative chimiotaxis). Thus, many ciliate infusoria choose bacteria only for their food; they are sharply repelled by dead infusoria, etc.

[172]

Therefore, in the natural immunity of unicellular beings, two fundamental elements may already be observed: sensitiveness and intracellular digestion. No researches have yet been made on the possibility of conferring on protozoa an artificial immunity against certain pathogenic microbes and their poisons. But unicellular beings, insensible to microbian poisons, are the reverse to many chemical substances which, in their normal life, they have no opportunity of ingesting.

It has been proved by experiment that, against many of those chemical substances, an artificial immunity may be given to the protozoa by accustoming them gradually. Very diluted solutions are added at first to the medium in which they live and, by gradually concentrating those solutions, an artificial immunity is conferred; the negative chimiotaxis becomes positive, allowing the protozoa to absorb and digest the poison, now become a food.

Habit is therefore the fundamental condition of artificial immunity; it must be that also of immunity naturally acquired. Having accidentally digested enfeebled microbes or having suffered an attack of disease, the unicellular being becomes accustomed to a stronger virus and becomes immune against it. The fact that so many unicellular beings have become thus accustomed is therefore connected with their sensitiveness and their digestion. Accordingly, sensitiveness, habit, and digestion are the fundamental factors of the mechanism of immunity in protozoa; this immunity thus indisputably belongs to the category of purely cellular phenomena.

Having arrived at this conclusion, Metchnikoff thought that the same mechanism of immunity must be found in other primitive and analogous cells, such[173] as the phagocytes of multicellular beings. This was proved by a whole series of observations and by the fact that the immunity of higher animals is connected with an intense phagocytosis. In fact, as he ascended the scale of beings and studied their natural and artificial immunity, he ascertained that, in all of them, the essence of immunity, masked by the complexity of the organism, reduced itself to the phagocytes becoming accustomed to noxious agents. The mechanism of immunity in protozoa could therefore really be compared with that of immunity in multicellular beings.

Becoming accustomed and becoming immune are phenomena of a general order, for they can be manifested not only by animals, but also by plants. They, too, have to defend themselves against numerous diseases. Lower vegetables, such as myxomycetes (beings which stand on the limit between the animal and vegetable kingdoms), have an amœboid phase, in which they are but a simple heap of formless protoplasm. During that stage of their life, myxomycete behave towards noxious agents exactly in the same way as unicellular beings and, like them, acquire immunity by becoming gradually accustomed.

In higher vegetables, the mechanism is different because of their structure. The cells of nearly all plants are immobilised by rigid membranes; therefore they cannot surround their prey, but protect themselves by the production of tough membranes (cicatrisation) and by the secretion of various juices. Certain of these juices (gums and resins) become solid when exposed to the air and constitute a sort of natural (dressing); others (essences) are antiseptic. The secretion of these cellular juices in plants is[174] therefore a powerful means of defence. This defence is due to the extreme sensitiveness of the protoplasma of vegetable cells: they react against irritation by a defensive secretion. Vegetables, as well as unicellular beings, can accustom themselves or become artificially accustomed to noxious influences and acquire immunity.

As to animals, Metchnikoff had already proved long ago that they defend themselves against morbid agents by phagocytosis, i.e. by intracellular digestion. It is always to be found in cases of immunity and is indispensable to it, on the same grounds as in unicellular beings. The organism of multicellular animals possesses various cells which play the part of phagocytes. There are some in the blood and humors, as also in the divers organs and in the tissues. These phagocytes are either mobile—leucocytes, or fixed—tissue-cells. However, all those cells may be classed into two principal groups: the microphages and the macrophages. Both categories of cells are capable of digesting microbes, but it is chiefly done by the microphages, whilst macrophages more especially digest figured elements (cells) of animal origin and poisons. It may be said that the microphages are vegetarians whilst the macrophages are chiefly carnivorous.

What, then, is the mechanism of phagocytic digestion?

Intracellular digestion by phagocytes is accomplished by means of digestive ferments, similar to those of our own digestive organs. "In both cases," says Metchnikoff, [175]"a diastasic action is due to soluble ferments produced by living elements. In intracellular digestion, the diastases digest within the cells, whereas in extracellular digestion the phenomenon takes place outside the cells, in the cavity of the gastro-intestinal tube."

Only gradually has intracellular digestion given place to the digestion by secreted juices. The link between these two modes is to be found in certain transparent Invertebrates, such as the floating mollusc Phyllirhoë. The nourishment is first digested in the cavity of the digestive tube by secreted juices, and its treatment is completed within the amœboid cells of the cæcum.

In higher animals, the digestion of food is due to several digestive ferments (rennet, pepsin, trypsin, enterokinase, etc.) produced by divers organs (stomach, pancreas, intestines). The phagocytes also manufacture several digestive ferments; their principal digestive juice is a soluble ferment of the trypsin category, to which Metchnikoff gave the name of cytase.[25]

To the morphological difference of the phagocytes corresponds also a difference in the properties of their cytases, which are suited to the digestion of this or that food. The cytases are kept within the interior of the cells and only escape into the humors when the phagocytes are damaged (Pfeiffer's phenomenon). This kind of ferment does not withstand a temperature above 55° to 58° C. In natural immunity, it plays the principal part by digesting morbid agents inside the phagocytes like any other food. But, in artificial immunity, other soluble ferments come into play, developed in consequence of vaccination.

The principal of those is the fixator.[26] It is less [176]sensitive than cytasis to high temperatures and can bear a temperature of 65° to 68° C. It is incapable, by itself, of killing and digesting, but by fixing on them, it bites them, so to speak, and makes them sensitive to the action of the phagocytic cytases, which can thus digest them more easily.

The fixator may be compared to enterokinase, a special ferment in the small intestine of higher animals which also does not by itself digest food but which activates in a high degree the digestive power of pancreatic ferments. However, it has the property of fixing itself on fibrin; it is obvious that enterokinase and the fixator have the same essential properties. This similarity again proves that the destruction of morbid agents by the phagocytes really corresponds with actual digestion.

It is in consequence of the digestion of vaccinal products that the phagocytes manufacture the fixator. Created at the expense of a given vaccinal substance, the fixator has a specific character which corresponds with that substance, whereas the cytase already existing within the phagocytes never has a specific character.

Artificial immunisation generally produces the formation of so great a quantity of fixators that the phagocytes are unable to retain them and excrete them in part in the ambient humors, i.e. the blood plasma, or serum. When, afterwards, virulent morbid agents (microbes or figured elements) are introduced into an organism which has been immunised against them, they are at once faced, in the humors, with fixators, which immediately exert a biting action on them and render them sensitive to the action of the intracellular cytasis of the phagocytes. The same[177] mechanism explains the specificity of the serums of vaccinated animals.

The quantity of specific fixators in the humors depends on the surplus production of that ferment by the phagocytes and is not always the same. That is why different serums are preventive in different degrees. They are inactive if the phagocytes have not produced enough fixators to pass any out into the humors. For a serum is only preventive when it brings into the new organism into which it is injected a sufficient quantity of fixators ready to sensibilise the morbid agents afterwards introduced into the organism.

The over-production of antibodies—fixators or antitoxins—corresponds up to a certain point with the frequency and quantity of vaccinal injections; that is why serums are usually preventive in artificial immunity and very rarely so in natural immunity. Through successive inoculations, the cells become accustomed to digesting the microbes, or figured elements, and manufacture, in consequence of that digestion, growing quantities of fixators.

In natural conditions, on the other hand, morbid agents do not usually penetrate into the organism in massive or repeated doses; therefore digestion under natural conditions results in a less abundant production of fixators which can be contained in the interior of the phagocytes without leaking into the humors in sufficient quantities to render the latter preventive.

It might be thought that immunity against pathogenic microbes is accompanied by immunity against their toxins. In reality that is not always the case, and very often the organism, now made refractory to certain microbes, remains sensitive to their toxic[178] products. Thus antimicrobian immunity and antitoxic immunity constitute in most cases two distinct properties. In order to confer antitoxic immunity recourse must be had to vaccination by soluble poisons and toxins.

Immunity, acquired naturally, is so especially against microbes and not against toxins, for, in nature, it is almost always by microbes that the organism is threatened. As to antitoxic immunity, it is very probably due to the intracellular digestion of toxins by the different macrophages. This hypothesis is supported by the experiments quoted in the preceding chapter. During antitoxic vaccination, the macrophages manufacture, probably at the expense of vaccinal toxins, a certain quantity of antitoxins, substances which offer a great similarity with the fixators. Like them, they are specific; they are also produced in great quantities and excreted into the humors, which they render antitoxic when sufficiently abundant; finally, they are not very sensitive to high temperatures. That is why, in spite of the impossibility of proving their origin directly, it is quite probable that it is analogous to that of the fixators and that antitoxins are manufactured by cellular elements, the macrophages in particular. For it is they which absorb and digest toxins as well as soluble poisons.

This deduction is also supported by the antitoxic immunity which may be conferred on unicellular beings in which the cell alone enters into play.

Phagocytes no doubt manufacture many other soluble ferments corresponding with the elements which they absorb, for, in a vaccinated organism, divers new specific properties of the serum are to be[179] found, such as that of agglutination, precipitation, etc. Humoral properties may be more or less durable, in proportion as the products manufactured by the phagocytes are more or less rapidly evacuated by the organism.

All these humoral properties, traced back to their first source, depend upon the digestive activity of the phagocytes, since they are the products of that digestion. In cases where it has not yet been possible to make a direct demonstration of this, it becomes evident through analogy and experiments pointing in that direction.

To sum up, according to Metchnikoff, "Immunity in infectious diseases is linked with cellular physiology, namely, with the phenomenon of the resorption of morbid agents through intracellular digestion. In a final analysis, the latter (as also the digestion of food in the gastro-intestinal tube) reduces itself to phenomena of a physico-chemical

78

order; however, it is a real digestion accomplished by the living cell.... The study of Immunity, from a general point of view, belongs to the subject of Digestion."

Immunity against diseases is but one of the manifestations of an immunity on a much larger scale, always based, in final analysis, on the sensitiveness of the living cellular protoplasm. The sensitiveness of the nervous cells extends this phenomenon to the psychical domain. They also are capable of becoming accustomed to external irritations of all kinds, hence constituting a psychical immunity for the organism. We all know that one can become accustomed to many painful or violent sensations; and, as Metchnikoff says: [180]"... It is very probable that the whole gamut of Habit, starting from the unicellular beings, who accustom themselves to live in an unsuitable medium, to cultured men who acquire the habit of not believing in human justice, rests on one and the same fundamental property of living matter."

[181]
CHAPTER XXVII

Private sorrows — Death of Pasteur, 1895 — Ill-health — Senile atrophies — Premature death — Orthobiosis — Syphilis — Acquisition of anthropoid apes.

Metchnikoff's health had suffered from the numerous emotions provoked by the struggle in defence of the phagocyte doctrine and also from a series of sad events. In 1893, sickness and death fell upon our family; I lost a sister and a brother at a short interval and had myself to undergo a serious operation. My husband nursed me night and day, as a mother might have done, and went through the deepest anxiety on account of post-operative complications. All this told on him all the more that he had just endured cruel moral suffering during the experiments on cholera mentioned above. In 1894, an agricultural crisis in Russia influenced our material situation and gave him many worries. In the autumn of 1895, M. Pasteur's health became worse and, soon afterwards, he died.

This series of calamities depressed Metchnikoff, his old cardiac trouble returned, and he again became a prey to insomnia. We spent part of the holidays in the mountains, thinking it might do him good, but he did not care for a prolonged rest; he was preoccupied by the thought of his interrupted experiments and only thought of returning to the laboratory.

In 1898, he had some disquieting symptoms of[182] kidney trouble, a little albumen. He consulted the celebrated German physician, von Noorden, who found nothing serious, but this did not reassure him and he continued to worry about himself.

Already some time previously, theoretical considerations on senile atrophies had directed his thoughts towards old age. His reflections now turned towards the psychological aspect of the problem; he analysed his personal sensations and realised that he, at the age of 53, felt an ardent desire to live. This imperious instinct for life, in spite of the inevitable evolution towards personal death and old age, brought his thoughts back to the disharmonies of human nature. But now, through all his gloomy reflections, he was borne up by the unshakable conviction that Science would succeed in correcting those disharmonies and he continued to work with untiring energy.

He had prescribed for himself a hygienic diet, based on the idea that the cause of his own condition and senility in general was due to a chronic poisoning by intestinal microbes. This diet consisted in avoiding raw food in order not to introduce noxious microbes into the intestines, and in absorbing their useful enemies, the acid-forming microbes of sour milk. This diet was very favourable to his health.

After he had finished his book on immunity he at last allowed himself to pass on to the new questions which preoccupied him, i.e. senility and death.

He set forth a sketch of his ideas in 1901 in a paper which he read at Manchester (Wilde Lecture) on the "Flora of the Human Body." He reviewed this flora and pointed out the harmful effect of the microbes, especially those of the large intestine the toxins of which effect a chronic poisoning of the[183] cells of our organism and thus provoke their gradual weakening. He then indicated the means of combating this evil, on the one hand by stimulating the vital activity of the cells exposed to enfeeblement, by means, for instance, of small doses of specific cytotoxins, and, on the other hand, by direct action on intestinal microbes. He concluded by saying that "the intestinal flora is the principal cause of the too short duration of our life, which flickers out before having reached its goal. Human conscience has succeeded in making this injustice obvious; Science must now set to work to correct it. It will succeed in doing so, and it is to be hoped that the opening century will witness the solution of this great problem."

Metchnikoff considered that our chronic poisoning by intestinal microbes weakens our cellular elements; he supposed that the same cause might provoke senile phenomena, manifestly due to weakness of the tissues.

One of the first manifestations of senility being the whitening of hair, he began to study the mechanism of that. He had previously observed the dominant part played by phagocytosis in all phenomena of atrophy, and it occurred to him that it may be phagocytes which destroy the colouring matter of hair, a substance which, in the form of tiny granules, is enclosed within the hair cells. In fact, he found that the whitening process is accompanied by a stimulation of the amœboid cells which introduce their protoplasmic prolongations into the periphery of the hair. They absorb the coloured granules, or pigment, and digest it, partly on the spot, partly after carrying it into the root of the hair, often even[184] in the connective tissue which supports the hairy scalp. As the pigment becomes destroyed, the hair loses its colour and whitens. The cells which devour the pigment—pigmentophages—belong to the category of macrophages which, in general, absorb all the enfeebled cells in the organism.

Metchnikoff was able to note similar phenomena in divers other senile atrophies either by his own ulterior researches or by collaboration with his pupils (MM. Salimbeni and Weinberg).

In the same way that the whitening of the hair depends on the destruction of pigment by pigmentophages, the wrinkles of the skin, weakness of the muscles, friability of the bones, and senile degenerescence of divers organs are caused by the destruction of weakened cells which do not defend themselves and thus become the prey of the stronger and more resisting macrophages. Senility is thus no other than a generalised atrophy. What is it that provokes it? The answer is: The swarming microbes in our large intestine. They form the permanent source of a slow poisoning of our organism. This fact alone suffices to explain one of the principal causes of the enfeebling of our tissues. It is not simultaneous in all the cells because of their different powers of resistance. The struggle and destruction of the weak by the strong is the cruel law of nature; therefore the macrophages, more resisting to poisons, take advantage of the weakening of other cells in order to devour them, and this is one of the causes of senility.

These reflections and the biological researches which confirmed them allowed Metchnikoff gradually to build up a philosophical doctrine, which he expounded[185] in 1903 in his work, Études sur la nature humaine.

He considered "old age" as a pathological phenomenon. He saw in it one of the most important disharmonies of human nature, because of the fact that neither senility nor death is accompanied by a natural instinct. The accomplishment of every physiological function leads to satiety or to a desire for rest; after a busy day, man feels an instinctive need for rest and sleep. But, in his maturity, he has no desire to grow old, and in his old age none to die. It is rare that one should aspire to die, and nobody wishes to grow old. These facts are in contradiction with other natural phenomena; they are all the more discordant that they play an immense part in our psychical life.

After a general review of opinions on human nature, Metchnikoff analysed it from the biological point of view; he revealed its discords and concluded that it is far from being perfect. In his eyes, the lack of harmony in the human being is an inheritance from our animal ancestors; they have handed down to us a whole series of remains of organs which are not only useless but even harmful in the new conditions of human existence.

The large intestine, inherited from mammalian ancestors, holds the first place among those noxious organs. This reservoir of food refuse was very useful to our animal forebears in their struggle for existence; it allowed them not to interrupt their flight whilst pursued by their enemies. In man, whose life conditions are different, a large intestine of that size, without offering the same advantages, is a source of slow and continuous poisoning and a cause of premature senility and death.

[186]

Man, after acquiring a still higher development, realised these evils and made concentrated efforts to fight them and to soothe his own terrors. It is for that object that the divers religious and philosophical systems were created, in which humanity sought for consolation. Finding none there, man turned to Science, which, at first, neither solved his doubts nor eliminated his sufferings. But Science provided him with rational methods of research, owing to which he gradually progressed and conquered a series of truths, allowing him gradually to struggle against some of his troubles and to solve some of his problems. Science has already done much to diminish the diseases which are among the chief scourges of humanity. It has thrown light upon the causes of many of them and has found preventive and curative remedies for several.

Surgery, antiseptics, serotherapy, vaccinations already yield secure results. Hygiene and prophylaxis are in course of development, and a vast prospect is open to them in the future. But our heaviest burdens, senility and death, common to all, have yet scarcely been studied. Having expounded his views on senility and proved that it is a pathological phenomenon, Metchnikoff concluded that to struggle against it was quite as possible as to struggle against disease.

The principal causes which bring about premature senility are: alcoholism, chronic poisoning by intestinal microbes, and infectious diseases, headed by syphilis. Surely Science will discover efficacious means against all these.

The strengthening of the beneficent cells in our organism; the transformation of the wild intestinal flora into a cultivated flora, by the introduction of[187] useful microbes; the struggle against infectious diseases and alcoholism—all these are workable means of fighting pathological and premature senility.

When old age becomes physiological and no longer painful it will become proportionate with the other epochs of our lives and cease to alarm us. But how is the fear of death to be explained, since it is a general and inevitable phenomenon? How is it that we have no natural instinct for death? Metchnikoff supposes that this lack of harmony in our nature comes from the fact that death is as premature as senility and arrives before the natural instinct for it has had time to develop. This supposition is confirmed by the fact that old people who have reached an exceptionally advanced age are often satiated with life and feel the need of death as we feel a need of sleep after a long day's work. That is why we have a right to suppose that, when the limit of life has been extended, owing to scientific progress, the instinct of death will have time to develop normally and will take the place of the fear which death provokes at the present day. Both death and old age will become physiological and the greatest discord in our nature will be conquered.

Our manner of life will have to be modified and directed according to rational and scientific data if we are to run through the normal cycle of life—orthobiosis. The pursuit of that goal will even influence the basis of morals. Orthobiosis cannot be accessible to all until knowledge, rectitude, and solidarity increase among men, and until social conditions are kinder.

Man will then no longer be content with his natural inheritance; he will have to intervene actively in[188] order to correct his disharmonies. "Even as he has modified the nature of plants and animals Man will have to modify his own nature in order to make it more harmonious."

In order to obtain a new race, one forms an ideal in relation to the organism to be modified. "In order to modify human nature, it is necessary to realise what is the ideal in view, after which every resource of which Science disposes must be taxed in order to obtain that result. If an ideal is possible, capable of uniting men in a sort of religion of the future, it can only be based on scientific principles. And if it is true, as is so often affirmed, that it is impossible to live without faith, that faith must be faith in the power of Science."

In those words, Metchnikoff ends his book on Human Nature.

The public at large and many critics did not understand the deep and general meaning of Metchnikoff's thoughts. They reproached him with having an insufficiently exalted ideal, for they only saw in his doctrine the desire of postponing senility and living longer. They did not understand that to revolt against the lack of harmony in nature, through which all humanity has to suffer, not only physically but morally, was to aspire to perfection. They did not consider that, in order to attain that end, all human culture and the whole social state would have to be modified; that this could only be done through many virtues, intense energy, and great self-control. They had not understood the elevation and power of an ideal which aspired to perfect not only the direction of life but human nature itself. They had not understood[189] the audacious beauty of such a struggle, the benefit conferred by the belief that the human will and the human mind are capable of transforming Evil into Good according to a conceived ideal!...

In the meanwhile Metchnikoff, convinced that Knowledge is Power and that "Science alone can lead suffering Humanity into the right path," quietly continued his task.

One of the most characteristic symptoms of old age is the hardening of the arteries—arterio-sclerosis. He therefore especially wished to elucidate the mechanism of that phenomenon.

Whilst many, yet unknown, factors come into play in senility, one disease, syphilis, often provokes arterio-sclerosis, indisputably due to a morbid agent. Metchnikoff therefore began to study this disease, of which the origin is infectious—especially as he thought he could do so experimentally.

Long before this, he had conceived the idea that the study of those human diseases which cannot be transmitted to ordinary laboratory animals might be carried out on anthropoid apes, of all animals the nearest to man. He had spoken of it to M. Pasteur, but, at that time, the Institute could not afford to acquire these costly animals. In 1903, at the Madrid Congress, Metchnikoff received a 5000 fr. prize and utilised this money in the acquisition of two anthropoid apes. The same year M. Roux won the Osiris prize of 100,000 fr. which he devoted to the same object, and it was decided that the two together would undertake researches on syphilis. Other donations, 30,000 fr. from the Morosoffs of Moscow and 250 roubles from the Society of Dermatology and[190] Syphilography of the same city, completed the capital required to execute the projected plan.

The following is a short sketch of the researches that were undertaken and the results that were obtained.

The inoculation of anthropoid apes with syphilis was successful. The chimpanzee was found to be most sensitive to the disease; it manifests primary and secondary symptoms identical with those of man. Lower monkeys, though less sensitive, also contract syphilis but generally only show primary characteristic manifestations. The possibility of rapidly provoking in apes, even of the inferior kinds, syphilitic lesions similar to those of man has a very great importance, for it provides a sure means of diagnosis in doubtful human cases. Owing to the liability of apes to contract syphilis, experimental vaccination and serotherapy could be attempted on them; but, though these experiments were sometimes encouraging, the results obtained were not constant enough to justify their application to man. Thus, it was found possible to attenuate the virus by successive passages in certain lower apes, and yet, though attenuated for the chimpanzee, it did not confer upon him immunity against the active virus.

In 1905, Schaudinn discovered the syphilitic treponema in man. By using this discoverer's method, the same microbe was found in apes inoculated with human virus, which confirmed the specific character of the treponema.

An observation was then made which was of great importance on account of its consequences: it was ascertained that the syphilitic microbe was absorbed by the less mobile mononuclear phagocytes and remained localised near the entrance point long enough[191] to allow of a local treatment which might succeed in being curative as it had time to act before the microbes had passed into the general circulation of the organism. This supposition was proved to be correct by a series of experiments on monkeys, and, in 1906, a young doctor, M. Maisonneuve, inoculated himself with syphilis and applied the treatment with a perfectly satisfactory result.

It might have been thought that this simple, safe, and innocuous method would at once come into practice, but it was not so. Between opposition on the one hand, and carelessness of the subjects themselves on the other, this useful discovery remained for a long time without being utilised. All the above results were obtained through experiments on anthropoid apes, and the study of syphilis, until then purely clinical, entered at last into the field of experimental science.

Researches upon syphilis were but an interlude; Metchnikoff, returning to his principal work, resumed the study of senility and of the intestinal flora. During many years he applied himself to researches concerning the part played by the latter within the organism.

He was able to confirm the deductions expounded in his Études sur la nature humaine, and in 1907 he published a new work, Essais optimistes, in which he developed the same ideas, amplified by the results of his new researches, and answering the criticisms excited by his first book.

In the Essais optimistes he studied first of all the phenomena of old age in the different grades of the scale of living beings, of which he compared the life duration. He concluded that there was an indubitable[192] connection between this and the intestinal flora.

The shorter the intestine, the fewer microbes it contains and the longer the relative duration of life. As an example, he quoted the relatively great longevity of birds and bats. Those animals, adapted to aerial life, have to weigh as little as possible. To that end, they empty their intestine very frequently and this in consequence is not used as a reservoir for alimentary refuse; as it is but little developed, it contains a much smaller number of microbes. The longevity of flying animals is relatively much greater than that of mammals with a large intestine full of microbes, a constant source of slow poisoning.

After treating the question of longevity, Metchnikoff dealt with that of death.

Living beings die, in the great majority of cases, in consequence of diseases or accidents with an external cause; one involuntarily wonders whether there is such a thing as "natural death," i.e. arising exclusively from causes due to the organism itself. A review of known facts allowed Metchnikoff to draw the following conclusions: unicellular inferior beings have no natural death; they merely die by accident. Their individual life is very short and comes to an end by multiplication or division of a unit into two; there is no trace of a corpse in this loss of previous individuality.

Among superior plants, certain trees attain considerable dimensions (dragon-tree, baobab, oak, cypress), live for centuries, and die from external causes. Their organism presents no internal necessity for a natural death. On the other hand, a multitude of other plants have but a short life and their natural[193] death coincides usually with the ripening of the seed. It has even been observed that it is possible to retard the death of a plant by preventing it from fructifying. For instance, lawns made up of grass mown before it runs to seed remain green and living whilst grass allowed to flower and bear seed becomes yellow and dries up. It is a well-known fact that fruits and seeds are frequently poisonous. Therefore Metchnikoff supposed that the death of the plant may be due to an auto-intoxication by poisons manufactured by it in order to defend its seeds and ensure the next generation; in Nature, the individual does not count, but the species. Once the survival of this is ensured the individual may disappear.

A similar phenomenon of auto-intoxication is manifested by lower vegetables, yeasts, and microbes. Pasteur, who discovered the microbe of lactic fermentation, found that this micro-organism, which itself produces lactic acid, perishes because of the over-production of this substance. Yeasts, again, cannot bear an excess of alcohol, their own product. Thus the vegetable kingdom offers us examples of the absence of natural death as well as examples of a natural death due to an auto-intoxication of the organism.

In the animal kingdom examples of natural death are also to be found, but only very exceptionally. Those examples are provided by Rotifera (inferior worms) and by Ephemeridæ. Their adult life is reduced to the sexual act, almost immediately followed by death without an external cause. Their life is so short that they do not even feed and lack developed buccal organs. That in itself constitutes an organic cause of inevitable, i.e. natural, death.

[194]

Among human beings natural death is extremely rare. It sometimes occurs in very old people, under the shape of a peaceful last sleep. The likeness it bears to sleep is so striking that Metchnikoff thought himself authorised to form the following hypothesis concerning the analogy in their mechanism.

According to a theory of Preyer's, fatigue and sleep are due to a periodical auto-intoxication set up by the products of the vital activity of our organism. These products are destroyed by oxidation during sleep, after which fatigue disappears and awakening comes. According to Metchnikoff it may be that the mechanism of natural death also consists in an auto-intoxication by the progressive accumulation of toxic products during the whole of life. The analogy between sleep and natural death allows the supposition that, as before going to sleep an instinctive desire for rest is felt, in the same way natural death must be preceded by an instinctive desire to die. Moreover, this is confirmed by concrete examples. Thus that of an old woman of ninety-three who expressed that desire in the following terms to her great-nephew: "If ever you reach my age, you will see that death becomes desired just like sleep." The same thought had been expressed by the biblical patriarchs who fell asleep satiated with life.

When, owing to the progress of Science, men reach the development of the instinct of death, they will look upon Death with the same calm as do very old people, and it will cease to be one of the principal causes of pessimism. It is for that reason that we must learn to prolong life and to allow all men to realise their complete and natural vital cycle, thus ensuring their moral balance.

[195]

Psychological observations allowed Metchnikoff to conclude that pessimism is much more frequent in youth than in maturity or in old age. He attributes this to the gradual development of the vital instinct which is only completely manifested in middle age. Man then begins to appreciate life; made wiser by experience, he demands less and is therefore better balanced.

Metchnikoff proffers examples in support of his theory. He analyses the psychic evolution of Goethe as reflected in his Faust and describes that of "an intimate friend." These examples prove that natural psychological evolution already leads to a relative optimism. But, as long as senility is pathological and death premature, the apprehension that they inspire antagonises the normal evolution of optimism. A victory over those present evils will direct the normal course of life in the right way; one normal active period will succeed another; the accomplishment of individual and social functions corresponding with each period will become realisable; the death instinct will have time to develop, and Man, having been through his normal vital cycle, will sink, peacefully and without fear, into eternal sleep.

[196]

CHAPTER XXVIII

Researches on intestinal flora — Sour milk.

The problem of our intestinal flora is so vast and so difficult that it demands years of research. Numerous facts had already been accumulated by Science on this subject, but it was still far from being elucidated.

Certain scientists affirmed that microbes favour digestion by decomposing food residues in the intestine and are therefore not merely useful, but necessary to the organism. Others entertained a diametrically opposed opinion. The first thing, therefore, was to know which of the two opinions was founded on fact. Metchnikoff studied the case of the bat, in which the digestive tube is short and the large bowel not even differentiated. As he had supposed, a priori, in this animal, whose life duration is relatively long, the intestine contains few or no micro-organisms, which proves that digestion can be accomplished without their intermediary. Moreover, this was before long amply confirmed by the researches of MM. Cohendy, Wollman, and other scientists who succeeded in bringing up chickens and tadpoles in conditions of absolute sterility.

Having acquired the conviction that microbes are not indispensable to digestion, Metchnikoff studied the part they play in the organism. It is universally admitted that the products of putrefaction are toxic,[197] and he enquired whether the intestine sheltered putrefying microbes. This question had not yet been solved; certain bacteriologists thought that little or no putrefaction exists in a normal intestine. Metchnikoff ascertained through systematic researches that the intestinal flora includes several kinds of putrefying microbes which secrete highly toxic products.

With his pupils and collaborators, MM. Berthelot and Wollman, he carried out a series of experiments which established the fact that this intoxication is due to poisons of the aromatic group, such as phenols and indols. With these substances, they succeeded in artificially provoking arterio-sclerosis in the organs of animals, and also other modifications similar to those which are observed in senility. Having proved that putrefying microbes provoke the intoxication of the tissues, Metchnikoff set to work to find a means of struggling against those microbes.

It was known that they could only live in an alkaline medium which is precisely that of the intestinal juices. Metchnikoff thought that if means were found to render the intestinal contents acid, without harm being done to the organism, the putrefying microbes might thus be destroyed. It had been known for a long time that sour milk does not suffer putrefaction, that being prevented by the acid fermentation. The lactic microbes of this fermentation must therefore be antagonistic to the putrefying microbes. He drew a conclusion in favour of the utility of sour milk, containing acid-producing microbes; once introduced into the intestine, these should prevent the breeding of the noxious microbes which require an alkaline medium.

His hypothesis seemed confirmed by the fact that[198] populations who feed almost exclusively on curded milk live a very long time. In Bulgaria, for instance, whole villages, thus fed, are known for the longevity of their inhabitants. Starting from these considerations, he made experiments upon himself and systematically introduced into his diet sour milk carefully prepared with pure cultures of certain lactic bacilli. His health was benefited by it, and his friends followed his example. Certain doctors recommended sour milk, the use of which gradually spread as a hygienic food. Metchnikoff considered the result acquired as a first step towards the artificial transformation of the wild intestinal flora into a cultivated and useful flora.

Unfortunately, the study of the intestinal flora is extremely complicated because of the innumerable species of micro-organisms and the extreme difficulty of disentangling the many influences which cross each other. He therefore considered collective researches as indispensable, the life and science of one man being insufficient to solve so vast a problem. Up to a certain point he succeeded in realising this scientific collaboration within his own laboratory.

[199]

CHAPTER XXIX

The Nobel Prize — Journey to Sweden and to Russia — A day with Léon Tolstoï.

In 1908 Metchnikoff received the Nobel Prize, together with Ehrlich, for his researches on immunity. According to the statutes of that prize, the laureate is invited to give a lecture in Stockholm. Metchnikoff chose for his theme the "present state of the question of immunity in infectious diseases," and, in the spring of 1909, we went to Sweden and thence to Russia. The whole journey was a series of fêtes and receptions in his honour. He was touched and grateful at this welcome, but with his usual humour, declared that it was the Nobel Prize which, like a magic wand, had revealed to the public the value of his researches.

We only stopped for a short time at Stockholm, where the kindest hospitality was shown to Metchnikoff. Sweden made an unforgettable impression upon us. Her deep, dark waters, wild rocks, and sombre pines make of it a land of legends. Elie was impressed not only by Nature in Scandinavia but also by Scandinavian Art, which reproduces it admirably. He was specially pleased with Lilienfiorse's pictures, representing animals against a background at the same time real and legendary.

We went to Russia by way of the Baltic. The nights at that time were "white," and rocky islands[200] covered with pines emerged from the sea like ghosts, in the mysterious silvery midnight light; the impression was fairy-like.

A warm welcome awaited Metchnikoff in Russia. At Petersburg, as in Moscow, he was received with cordial and enthusiastic sympathy not only by scientific and medical societies, but by all the intellectual youth of those cities. This warm reception contributed to efface the bitterness sometimes aroused in him by distant recollections of the reasons which caused him to leave his native country.

During our stay in Russia we made the acquaintance of our great writer, Léon Tolstoï. We spent a day with him in his estate, Iasnaïa Paliana, and the day left a lifelong impression upon us.

It was at dawn that we reached the little railway station where a carriage had come to meet us. It had been raining in the night and now, in the first morning light, everything shone with dew. We were excited by the sight of the Russian country, cool meadows, forest, fields, all that simple landscape that we had not seen for so long, and we were also greatly moved at the idea of meeting Tolstoï.

The village appeared in the distance and, a little way apart, the wide open entrance gate of the old park of Iasnaïa Paliana. We entered a long shady avenue leading to the home of Tolstoï. The spring was at its best, flowers and perfumes everywhere. The house and the old park had the poetic charm of the ancient "nests of nobility" in Russia.

Tolstoï's daughter greeted us on the steps; her kindly simplicity at once put us at our ease. We had hardly entered the vestibule when we saw Léon Tolstoï himself coming down the stairs with a brisk[201] step. We knew him at once, though he seemed to us different from all his portraits. We were first of all struck by his eyes, deep, piercing, and yet as clear as those of a child. He had nothing of that hardness and severity that one is accustomed to see in his portraits; his features, too, seemed to us much finer and more idealised. He looked straight into our eyes as if he wished to read the depths of our souls. But we were at once reassured by the kind and benevolent expression of his whole face. He looked strong and healthy and did not seem old, but full of inner life. After the first words of welcome, he said to us, "You resemble each other; that happens after living happily together for a long time." He questioned us concerning our journey and on the impression made upon us by Russia after our long absence; then he said he had to finish his morning task.

His daughter and son took us for a walk through the park and the village, and the friendly words they exchanged with the peasants indicated excellent relations between the villagers and the people of the château. As soon as we came in, Léon Tolstoï reappeared, declaring that he gave himself holiday for the day. He questioned Metchnikoff on his researches, on the present state of hygiene, and on the application of scientific discoveries. He listened attentively and with visible interest. At the end of the conversation he declared that it was quite erroneously that he was thought to be hostile to Science, and that he only denounced pseudo-science, which has nothing to do with human welfare. "In reality," he said, "you and I are aiming towards the same goal by different lines."

All his words were impregnated with a deep love for, and an ardent desire to serve, humanity.[202] Literature and Art were mentioned; Tolstoï said that he was now so far from it all that he had even forgotten some of his own works and appreciated them much less than his writings on spiritual questions. He thought that sometimes beauty of form acted at the expense of the moral bearing of the subject. To the objection that Art embellishes Life, he answered that it has some value in that it serves as a link between men and makes them purer, but that its moral importance surpasses its æsthetic value by a great deal.

He related that he had conceived a new work on the social movement in Russia and, à propos of that, the conversation fell upon political reprisals. The subject of deportations, prisons, and executions was visibly painful to him; his eyes, now sad and suffering, revealed his vibrating soul.

On the agrarian question, he was in favour of the nationalisation of land, and showed great enthusiasm for Henry George. He thought the suppression of the commune in Russia a great mistake. Metchnikoff explained to him that his personal observations in Little Russia spoke, on the contrary, in favour of individual property, which gave better agricultural results. Tolstoï manifested perfect tolerance, and conversation flowed on peacefully concerning various subjects. In everything he said the beauty and elevation of his soul was perceptible.

After lunch he desired to have a serious conversation with Metchnikoff and took him out driving, he himself holding the reins. On the way he returned to the question of Science. He thought that humanity was so overwhelmed with misery and had so many urgent questions to solve that work ought to be[203] turned in that direction, and that we had no right to busy ourselves with abstract questions unrelated to life. "What good can it do man to have a notion of the weight and dimensions of the planet Mars?" he said.

Metchnikoff answered that theory is much nearer to life than it seems, and that many benefits have been acquired for humanity by scientific observations of an abstract order. Thus, the discovery of the great unchanging laws of Nature give to Man the consciousness of being submitted to logical laws instead of an arbitrary force, and that is a benefit. When microbes were discovered, their part in human life was not suspected, and yet this discovery was afterwards of the greatest service to human welfare since it enabled man to fight against disease.

On the way back, Tolstoï gave his place to his son and himself returned on horseback, an exercise in which he indulged almost daily, in spite of the approach of his eighty years. He still rode splendidly, sitting quite upright, and seemed even younger than before.

After that he went to take a little rest, whilst Countess Tolstoï gave us immense pleasure by reading to us two yet unpublished works by her husband, the charming story After the Ball and the tragic Sergius the Monk.

In the late afternoon a friend of our host, an accomplished musician, sat at the piano and played some Chopin. In the spring twilight the charm of that music filled us with emotion. Léon Tolstoï, seated in an armchair, listened; the lyrical beauty of the sound sank deeper and deeper into his soul, his eyes became veiled with tears, he leant his forehead[204] on his hand and remained motionless. Metchnikoff also was deeply moved, and the effect of music on two such men, the pleasure that it gave them, was the strongest plea in favour of pure Art.

"I do not know what takes place in my mind when I listen to Chopin," said Tolstoï a few moments later, after the closing sounds had vanished, "Chopin and Mozart move me to the depths. What lyrism! what purity!" Metchnikoff liked Mozart and Beethoven, but Tolstoï thought Beethoven too complicated. As to Wagner and modern music, they both agreed about it, thinking it unintelligible and lacking harmony and simplicity.

Around the tea-table conversation turned on senility, and Metchnikoff developed his theory of the discords of human nature. He illustrated his affirmations by the example of Goethe's Faust, who, according to him, formed the best picture of the evolution of human phases. To his mind the second part of Faust is but an allegory of the disharmonies of old age. It is a striking picture of the dramatic contest between the yet ardent and juvenile feelings of old Goethe and his physical senility. Tolstoï seemed interested by this interpretation and said he would read the second part of Faust over again, but that he himself would never offer an example of a similar lack of harmony. À propos of Metchnikoff's theory, according to which the fear of death exists because Death itself is premature, Tolstoï affirmed that he had no fear of death, but added, laughingly, that he would nevertheless try to reach the age of 100 in order to please Elie.

Our train only left late in the night, and, until we started, the conversation never ceased to be animated.[205] In every one of his words Tolstoï's exalted soul was perceptible, a soul in which there was room but for preoccupations of a spiritual order. He would have given the impression of floating above the earth if his ardent and compassionate heart had not constantly brought him back to the miseries and faults of human beings. The atmosphere around him was pure and vivifying as on high peaks, and the place seemed sanctified by his presence.

That interview had been a meeting of two superior minds, two exalted souls, but how different! The one, scientific and rational, always leaning on solid facts in order to soar and to spread his wings in the highest spheres of thought; the other an artist and a mystic, rising through intuition to the same spiritual heights; both pursuing the same goal of human perfection and happiness, but going along such different roads....

As we took leave of him, Léon Tolstoï said, "Not farewell, but au revoir!" And as we sat in the carriage and started to go, he appeared in a lighted window, as in an aureola, waving his hand, "Au revoir, au revoir!" he repeated for the last time.... The night was calm and beautiful under the immensity of the starry vault, and its greatness was confounded in our souls with the greatness of Léon Tolstoï.

[206]

CHAPTER XXX

Intestinal flora — Infantile cholera — Typhoid fever — Articles on popular Science.

When he returned home, Metchnikoff immediately resumed his work. He continued, with his collaborators, researches on the normal intestinal flora and on the microbian poisons which provoke arterio-sclerosis.

They were able to ascertain that certain microbes of the intestinal flora, such as the bacillus coli and Welch's bacillus, produce poisons (phenol and indol) which are reabsorbed by the normal intestinal walls and which provoke arterio-sclerosis and other lesions of the organs. A part of those poisons is eliminated by the urine, and the quantity found therein allows one to estimate the quantity contained in the organism. An exclusively vegetarian or carnivorous diet increases its production, while a mixed diet reduces it. During the rest of his life Metchnikoff made systematic and periodical analysis of his own urine in correlation with his diet.

From certain facts and certain experiments he concluded that the reciprocal influence of microbes might be utilised to attenuate or to eliminate the noxious action of some of them. Thus, by cultivating the lactic bacillus in the presence of those microbes which produce poisons belonging to the aromatic group, the[207] decrease in quantity and even the disappearance of phenol and indol is observed. All those facts confirmed anterior results which Metchnikoff had obtained, and indicated the route to be followed in his struggle against those toxins which gradually poison the organism and induce premature senility.

Having thus elucidated certain questions concerning the part played by microbes in a normal organism, he studied the pathogenic intestinal flora. He began by infantile cholera because this question is simplified by the fact that new-born children are fed exclusively on milk. It was then believed by practitioners that this intestinal disease of infants came from their mode of feeding, from summer heat, and other external influences. Metchnikoff, however, succeeded in demonstrating that the contents of the intestines of infants suffering from "cholera" always included a special kind of microbe, the B. proteus; he was also able to give the disease to young anthropoid apes by making them ingest food soiled by the intestinal contents of sick infants, thus establishing the infectious character of infantile cholera.

He then attacked another intestinal disease, typhoid fever, of which the microbe (Eberth's bacillus) had been known for some time, but had not been studied experimentally, ordinary laboratory animals being refractory. Metchnikoff had again recourse to anthropoids, and succeeded in infecting a chimpanzee by making him eat food soiled by the intestinal contents of a typhoid patient.

With the collaboration of Dr. Besredka, he undertook a series of experiments on anthropoid apes and on macaques. The former alone took typical typhoid fever, similar to that of man. It could be given them[208] by pure cultures of Eberth's bacillus, which definitely confirmed the specificity of that microbe.

Antityphoid vaccination by means of killed bacilli not being at that time either safe or durable, Metchnikoff advised measures of simple preventive hygiene: the use of cooked food, great personal cleanliness, cleanliness of streets and dwellings, and the destruction of insects, especially flies, which often infect food. In order to popularise these notions, he wrote a series of articles in newspapers. Later, several scientists found efficacious means of vaccination against typhoid fever.

In 1912 Metchnikoff, in collaboration with Dr. Besredka (the author of the antityphoid vaccination method by means of sensitised bacilli), demonstrated on anthropoid apes that antityphoid vaccination by living sensitised microbes is certain, and that it presents no danger of diffusing the disease, for these microbes, harmless to the vaccinated individual, cannot prove a source of danger for his entourage, since they are phagocyted at the very place where they are inoculated.

Metchnikoff always considered that it was very useful to keep the public at large informed of the results acquired by Science, because "it is only by becoming a part of daily life that measures of hygiene and prophylaxis will have efficacious results." He therefore lost no opportunity of spreading scientific principles and facts. In 1908 he had given in Berlin a lecture on "The Curative Forces of the Organism." In a Russian review, the Messenger of Europe, he developed the same subject and included an epitome of his lecture in Stockholm on immunity. In that article he expounded the phagocyte theory of immunity.[209] Among concrete examples of its application, he quoted the indications concerning the evolution of an infectious disease provided by the quantity of leucocytes in the blood, and the process employed by certain surgeons to diminish the danger of infection during an operation: just as, in case of an enemy menace, the Government mobilise an army, certain surgeons employ divers means to attract an army of phagocytes and to stimulate their activity in case any microbes should penetrate into the wound.

In 1909 he gave another lecture at Stuttgart, "A Conception of Nature and of Medical Science," in which he summed up his two works Études sur la nature humaine and Essais optimistes. The title of this lecture was intended to emphasise his view of human nature, according to which "Man, as he appeared on the earth, is an animal and pathological being belonging to the realm of medicine." But he ended his paper by the same optimistic thought which illumines the whole philosophy of his later years. "With the help of Science, Man can correct the imperfections of his nature."

He unveiled these imperfections and the ills which proceed from them, not only from a love of truth or scientific honesty, but always with the object of finding means to combat them. He never allowed sight to be lost of the fact that Science lights up the tortuous and painful path which leads to an issue that suffering humanity will find by gradually widening the limits of knowledge with the help of Work and of Will.

Thus all his writings offer us encouragement and support.

[210]

CHAPTER XXXI

A bacteriological expedition to the Kalmuk steppes, 1911.

During his preceding journeys in the Kalmuk steppes, Metchnikoff had often heard it said that tuberculosis was almost unknown there, but that the Kalmuks took it very easily when brought into contact with foreigners. As all means of combating this disease had hitherto given very unsatisfactory results, Metchnikoff thought that researches should be started along a new path. He had long thought that observations on the extreme liability of Kalmuks to tuberculosis might perhaps provide some new data. But the study of the question necessitated a very distant journey which he now at last had the opportunity of realising.

According to Metchnikoff's hypothesis, a natural vaccination takes place among us against tuberculosis which would explain the resistance of the majority of human beings in spite of the enormous diffusion of the disease. He concluded that some attenuated breeds of microbes become introduced into our organism during our childhood, thus vaccinating us against the virulent tuberculous bacillus. This supposition seemed to him plausible, for he had long ago found that some micro-organisms (Cienkovsky's bacillus, the cholera bacillus, etc.) become modified in different environment and conditions, both in form[211] and in virulence. He had described this phenomenon in 1888 in a memoir entitled Pleomorphism of Microbes. His hypothesis would explain the liability of the Kalmuks, since, if no tuberculous bacilli existed in the steppes, the inhabitants could not acquire a natural vaccination. When placed in an environment which was not free from tuberculosis, they became infected very easily, being in no wise prepared for the struggle against the virus.

The expedition to the Kalmuk country was therefore planned in order to ascertain whether tuberculosis was really absent from the steppes. This could easily be done by Pirquet's test,[27] which at the same time would show whether the number of Kalmuks infected increased from the centre to the outer limit of the steppes and corresponded with the greater degree of contact with the surrounding population. If the enquiry confirmed the hypothesis, there would remain to be seen which microbes might best be used as vaccines.

The expedition was also intended to elucidate a few questions on the etiology of endemic plague in the Kirghiz steppes. When this intention became known, the Russian authorities desired to add to it a local mission on the study of plague epidemics in the steppes. Metchnikoff, who was chiefly concerned with the question of tuberculosis, was only able to draw up a plan of work for the Russian mission and to start it going in one of the plague centres.

The Pasteur Institute expeditionary party comprised, besides Metchnikoff, MM. Burnet, Salimbeni, and Iamanouchi. They were joined at Moscow by[212] Drs. Tarassevitch and Choukevitch, and at Astrakhan by the physicians of the Russian plague mission. The Institut Pasteur party left Paris on May 14, 1911, full of spirits; Metchnikoff, eager to make the journey pleasant for his companions, was doing the honours of his country to the best of his ability; he fully succeeded, owing to the warm welcome and liberal hospitality which they received in Russia, where every one tried to contribute not only to the success of the expedition but to the comfort and pleasure of its members. The latter, indeed, preserved a most pleasant recollection of this journey, and, in later years, always spoke of it with pleasure.

Navigation on the Volga from Nijni Novgorod to Astrakhan was full of peculiar charm. That five days' journey was one of the rare periods of complete rest in Metchnikoff's life. He indulged in the dolce far niente as he watched the peaceful landscape on the passing banks. The Volga, then in flood, covered immense spaces. Here and there, whole forests emerged from the river which reflected them as in an enchanted dream. From time to time, little isolated villages appeared with the gilt cupola of a church or a monastery, then meadows, forests, steep cliffs, or gentle slopes down to the river. What poetry, what grandeur in simplicity! As in a kaleidoscope, types of varied populations and pictures of local customs followed upon each other.

Along the banks now and then were seen processions of pilgrims. Their humble, gray, stooping figures breathed deep faith and resignation. Sometimes popular songs arose from the Volga, sad, expressive, soul-penetrating chants.

This contemplative quietude was only interrupted[213] by stations in the ports of large towns where deputations of the educated inhabitants came to wish the mission welcome. These functions had a cordial and touching character, for it was obvious that such enthusiastic demonstrations had for their source a sincere cult for the knowledge whose representatives were being fêted; it was touching to see such a living ideal in this distant and oppressed land.

At Tsaritsine, several Kirghiz embarked on our boat in order to go to a large fair which the inhabitants of the steppes attended in numbers. Metchnikoff thought this was a unique opportunity to learn whether there were any carriers of the plague bacillus among those many natives coming from all parts of the steppes. He therefore decided that those members of the expedition who had come to study plague would go to the fair with the Kirghiz, whilst he, with the rest of the expedition, would make observations on the Kalmuks of the Astrakhan region.

A most hospitable welcome awaited us there; people vied with each other in their efforts to assist the expedition. The Governor-General of Astrakhan had ordered all preparations to be made, and the mission was provided not only with necessaries but with comforts which did much to alleviate the fatigue of the long journey.

Whilst waiting for our companions, we had time to verify several diagnostical reactions, the Kalmuks lending themselves willingly to the operation. We heard later that they thought they were being vaccinated against small-pox, a disease much feared in the steppes.

As soon as the plague mission arrived, we started towards the Kirghiz steppes, for there was a plague[214] centre north of the Caspian Sea. When we were out at sea, an intense north wind began to blow the waves away from the Kirghiz bank, and soon the depth lessened to such an extent that we could make no progress. The sailors were perpetually making soundings, and their repeated cries of "Two and a half feet!" became a regular nightmare. The situation seemed critical, and returning to Astrakhan was suggested; an idea which infuriated Metchnikoff; he would not hear of it. At last, after several incidents we reached the Kirghiz bank, the crossing having lasted three days instead of the usual twenty-three hours.

As we arrived, we could see from afar a sort of Valkyries' ride of natives clad in brilliant colours and riding up at full gallop with wild cries and exclamations. Before us spread a barren and sandy steppe, producing the sad impression of a land forsaken by God and man. How could life be possible there? But gradually, as we became captivated by the charm of the boundless space, the purity of the air, the harmonious colouring and the scent of wild heliotrope and wormwood which alone can grow in those sands, we began to understand that it was not only possible to live in those steppes, but also to love them.

The plague centre stood among sandy hills with low-growing grass; the summit of one of them was black with charred remains of burnt objects; the corpses were buried in the same place. Only a few wretched forsaken hovels remained. In order to throw light upon endemic plague in the steppes, it was first of all necessary to ascertain whether the plague microbes remained alive for some time in places where the scourge had raged; if they were preserved in dead bodies which had been singed[215] rather than burnt; if the worms, insects, rodents, and domestic animals on the spot were or were not carriers of the plague microbe, and could or could not transmit it to a distance from the initial focus.

After organising a small emergency laboratory, the corpses were exhumed, and Dr. Salimbeni made a post-mortem examination. These corpses, having been in the ground for three months, were in a state of advanced decomposition and contained no living microbes.

Having set the work of the plague mission going, Metchnikoff parted from it in order to accomplish the projected investigations on tuberculosis in the Kalmuk steppes. He made a very solemn entry into these steppes; a Kalmuk deputation welcomed the mission and presented Metchnikoff with a bronze Buddha.

The aspect of those natives is sad and humble, their movements are slow, their eyes dull. In this they contrast with their neighbours, the quick and intelligent Kirghiz, and one reason for it is that the latter, being Moslems, absorb no alcohol, while the Kalmuks consume fermented milk (alcoholic fermentation) which poisons them slightly but continuously; this observation had already been made by Metchnikoff at the time of his previous visit.

The Kalmuks live in tents covered with coarse felt; they transport these dwellings on camels from one place to another when their herds of sheep or horses have consumed the scanty pasture grass around the camp. There is no attempt at cultivation, and the steppes become more and more barren as the pastures become exhausted. In order to remedy this evil, the Russian administration has begun[216] various experimental plantations. In some places the steppes are covered with small tamarisk bushes or with silky grass, but, as a rule, the chief growth is of silver wormwood. The monotony is not so great as one might think, for the steppes, like a mirror, reflect all the divers light-changes, and wonderful natural phenomena take place there. During the great heat, mirages are to be seen in the distance—a river, lakes, reed-grown shores; sometimes a sand-storm supervenes, more infernal than fairy-like, called here "smertch." The wind raises the sand in tongues of flames or in funnels running up to the sky with giddy rapidity. Gradually, all the separate turmoils join in a gigantic wall of sand, advancing in an orgy of movement; the heavy clouds fall towards the ground, the sand rushes upwards, everything becomes confounded in darkness and chaos.

One feels so entirely in the power of natural forces that the fatalism of the poor inhabitants of the land is easily understood. The Kalmuks, primitive and nomadic, produce the impression of ghosts from distant centuries.

Metchnikoff noticed that since his last visit in 1874, fatal influences had worked havoc on the population. Four scourges, all of them coming from outside, are destroying the Kalmuks: syphilis, alcoholism, tuberculosis, and the Russians who are constantly pushing them back. Those poor people realise the fate which is awaiting them, and resign themselves like a sick man who knows his sickness to be incurable.

The spiritual life of the Kalmuks reduces itself to their religious cult. There are many Buddhist convents where children are being brought up for a[217] monastic life. Religious rites are performed by priests dressed in purple and brilliant yellow; for the uninitiated, their part consists in unrolling interminable bands on which prayers are inscribed, and in executing a religious music which seemed a mixture of a camel's grunt, a dog's howling, and an infinitely sad plaint. Of the pure cult of Buddha, nothing seems to remain but an empty form. However, there is a convent in the steppes—Tshori—a sort of religious academy, where an effort is being made to restore the cult to the original level of Buddhist doctrines.

Whilst gathering observations on tuberculosis, we traversed the steppes in a north-easterly direction as far as Sarepta. This town seemed like a civilised centre after the steppes, where the conditions of life were somewhat hard in spite of the cordial reception accorded us everywhere. The food, consisting solely in tinned goods and mutton, had caused intestinal trouble in nearly all the members of the expedition; on the other hand, we were greatly incommoded by the heat, lack of water, and abundance of insects of all kinds.

In spite of all, Metchnikoff had hitherto borne the journey fairly well. However, since we left Moscow he had had frequent cardiac intermittence, accompanied sometimes by sharp pains along the sternum. But the stay at Sarepta especially tried his health; the heat reached 35° C. (95° F.) in the shade and 52° C. (about 125° F.) in the sun; in the evening the windows could not be opened because of the mosquitoes. Metchnikoff, who had shown so much endurance, now became weak, drowsy, and nervous; he attributed his condition to the excessive heat. Yet he[218] could not leave Sarepta, for all the members of both branches of the mission had agreed to meet there in order to sum up the results of their observations.

The researches of the expedition for the study of plague were not finished, and the Russian mission had agreed to complete them. So far, it was established that neither the corpses—after a certain time—nor the ground, nor the surrounding animals contained any plague microbes, and no carriers had been found among the Kirghiz population.

The data gathered among the Kalmuk population justified Metchnikoff's hypothesis. In the centre of the steppes, where the Kalmuks were still isolated, tuberculosis was completely unknown; diagnosis reactions were negative. They became positive more and more frequently as we came nearer the periphery of the steppes and the Russian population. The extreme sensitiveness of the Kalmuks must therefore depend on the fact that they have suffered no natural vaccination in the steppes, which would support the idea that some natural vaccine exists amongst us. Metchnikoff therefore concluded that he might direct ulterior researches towards the quest of natural tuberculous vaccines. Such were the scientific results of the expedition.

Apart from that, the journey to Russia had a strong personal influence on Metchnikoff. He had formerly left his country under the impression of the fatal error committed by the revolutionaries in killing Alexander II., an error which had led to a protracted reaction. He had therefore remained very sceptical concerning the Russian revolutionary movement; he thought that the necessary reforms might come from a Government evolution. But, during his[219] sojourn in Russia, he was able to appreciate events which modified his ideas to a great extent. He was impressed by the contrast between the progressive aspirations of the "intellectuals" and the inertia or noxious activity of the rulers. The policy of Casso, the Minister of Public Instruction, who ordered regular raids in the universities, the persecution of Poles and Jews, the encouragement of the "black band" obscurantism, giving plenary powers to creatures of darkness like Rasputin and his peers, all these things excited indignation in a man who placed the free development of human culture above everything.

He thus ceased to count upon the progressive evolution of a Government which was incapable of solving the complicated problems of Russian life, and henceforward thought that those problems would be solved by the "intellectuals" apart from the Government and in opposition to it.

[220]
CHAPTER XXXII

Further researches on the intestinal flora—Forty Years' Search for a Rational Conception of Life.

Since Metchnikoff had conceived the idea that a considerable part was played in human life by the intestinal flora, his thoughts had centred around a study which he thought profitable: that of the influence of intestinal microbes on the normal and on the pathological organism.

So, on his return from Russia, he took advantage of the fact that an epidemic of infantile cholera had broken out in order to continue his former investigations of that disease. The numerous cases which he thus studied allowed him finally to establish the specific part of the B. proteus as well as the similarity between infantile cholera and Asiatic cholera. This time he succeeded in contaminating, not only young anthropoid apes, but also new-born rabbits, and that not only through sick children's excreta, but by pure cultures of the proteus, which eliminated every doubt of the specificity of this microbe.

Metchnikoff explained the contamination of children exclusively breast-fed, either by the presence of a carrier personally refractory, among the entourage, or by the transport of dirt, by means of flies, on the objects which infants so readily put into their mouths. He therefore advised preventive means of absolute[221] hygiene and cleanliness, especially where suckling infants are concerned.

During the year 1912, he studied the intestinal flora and the influence of divers food diets. He experimented upon the rat, an omnivorous animal whose mode of feeding resembles that of man. The rats were divided into three lots, of which one was kept to a meat diet, another to a vegetarian régime, and the third to a mixture of both. The meat diet was least favourable, and the best results obtained by the mixed food.

These observations led Metchnikoff to the study of other problems intimately connected with the same question.

He undertook a series of researches in collaboration with his pupils, MM. Berthelot and Wollman, on the conditions which cause the diminution within the organism of the toxic products of intestinal microbes. They found that the quantity of these products was very small in those animals which feed on vegetable or fruit containing much sugar, such as carrots, beetroot, dates, etc. This is explained by the fact that the products of the decomposition of sugar are acids which prevent the development of putrefying microbes. But the sugar, rapidly absorbed by the walls of the small intestine, only reaches the large intestine in a much reduced quantity, for it is only up to a certain point during its journey that the cellulose of vegetables, rich in sugar, protects that substance. The question, therefore, was to find the means of making it reach the large intestine in greater quantities. In the intestine of a normal dog, an innocuous microbe was found, the Glycobacter peptonicus, which decomposes starch into sugar.

[222]

Metchnikoff made some laboratory animals ingest this microbe together with food, and ascertained that it reached the large intestine and decomposed in it the starch of farinaceous food into sugar, of which the acid products prevented the swarming of putrefying microbes. By this process it is possible to reduce to a minimum and even sometimes to eliminate the production of phenol and indol in rats subjected to a mixed diet and made at the same time to ingest cultures of the lactic bacillus and of the glycobacter.

Metchnikoff applied these different diets to himself and to other individuals and obtained concordant results.

However, he ascertained that it is not only the food diet which regulates the quantity of microbian poisons contained in the organism; that quantity sometimes varies very much in spite of an identical diet. He thought that a very important part of influence is due to pre-existing microbes which prevent or favour the development of microbes of putrefaction. All these questions, complicated by the richness and variety of the intestinal flora, still demanded a long series of laborious researches.

At the end of the winter he felt tired, and we went to the seaside during the holidays. But the sharp sea air did not suit him; he had a beginning of cardiac asthma and nearly fainted during a walk. We therefore had to come away from the sea, and went inland, to Eu. At the beginning of our stay, Metchnikoff did not feel well, walking tired him, he suffered from cardiac intermittence; it was only gradually that his condition improved and he was able to write the preface to a Russian edition of his philosophical articles.

[223]

This book was entitled Forty Years' Search for a Rational Conception of Life, and the articles record the evolution of his ideas and his search "not only for a rational understanding of life, but also for the solution of the problem of death, which is so full of contradictions."

This collection of articles enables us at the same time to follow the gradual transition from the pessimism of his youth to the optimism of his maturity. His first writings[28] relate to the discords of human nature and the lack of a solid basis for morals.

But, already in 1883, he concluded an opening Causerie at the Naturalists' Congress in Odessa, by the following words: "The theoretical study of natural history problems, in the widest sense of the word, alone can give a sound method for the comprehension of truth and lead to a definite conception of life—or at least to an approach to it."

Another article, The Curative Forces of the Organism, sums up his phagocyte theory, and states the fact that the organism possesses special powers of struggle against enemy elements.

In 1891, he wrote The Law of Life, in which we find the dawning idea that the lack of harmony in human structure does not make a happy existence and a rational code of morals impossible. Morals must consist "not in rules of conduct adapted to our present defective human nature, but on conduct based upon human nature modified, according to the ideal of human happiness."

The Flora of the Human Body, published in 1901,[224] is a study in which Metchnikoff's optimism assumes a definite form, for he speaks of the efficacy of certain means of struggling with our lack of harmony.

The last chapter in the book, "A Conception of Life and of Medical Science," introducing the word Orthobiosis, strikes the optimistic chord, winged and conclusive, which must result from victory over the disharmonies of human nature. This is Metchnikoff's ultimate formula, summing up the problems of life and of morals:

The ethical problem reduces itself to this: to allow the majority of human beings to reach life's goal, that is, to accomplish the whole cycle of a rational existence to its natural end. We are still very far from that. We can but sketch the rules to follow in order to attain this ideal. Its final realisation will demand more scientific researches, which must be allowed the widest and freest scope. It is to be foreseen that existence will have to be modified in many ways. Orthobiosis demands an active, healthy, and sober life, devoid of luxury and excess.

We must therefore modify present customs and eliminate those extremes of wealth and poverty which now bring us so many evils. As time goes on, when Science has caused present evils to disappear, when men no longer tremble for the life and welfare of their dear ones, when individual life follows a normal course—then Man can attain a higher level and more easily devote himself to exalted goals.

Then Art and pure Science will occupy the place which is due to them and which they lack at the present moment in consequence of our many cares. Let us hope that men will understand their true interests and contribute to the progress of orthobiosis.

Many efforts are necessary, much self-sacrifice, but they will be attenuated by the consciousness of an activity directed towards the real goal of human existence.

[225]
CHAPTER XXXIII

First our pleasures die, and then
Our hopes, and then—our fears, and when
These are dead—the debt is due.
Dust claims dust—and we die too.
Shelley.

Unpleasant incidents — The fabrication of lacto-bacilli — St. Léger-en-Yvelines — Return to Paris — First cardiac attack — Evolution of the death-instinct — Notes on his symptoms.

The end of 1912 had some unexpected emotions in store for us.

Metchnikoff had always been able to congratulate himself on the cordial hospitality which he had found in France, and to the end of his life he remained deeply grateful for it.

But, in any country, incidents may occur about which it would be unjust to generalise when they are due to individuals or to particular limited circles, as was the fact in the present case. In spite of the broad and generous ideas so widespread in France, a sudden current of narrow nationalism became manifest, at this moment, in certain quarters. Foreigners were accused of invading the country, of occupying lucrative posts and increasing the difficulties of the bitter struggle for existence. At first, only vague allusions were made, but, little by little, the attacks of that nationalist circle went beyond all bounds of justice and decency and turned into brutal[226] provocations. The contemptuous word métèque was resuscitated.

One newspaper especially led a furious propaganda and hesitated at no means of overwhelming its victims, one of whom was Metchnikoff.

Those coarse attacks might have been ignored with the contempt which they deserved had they not been echoed by a writer in a serious publication. Dr. Roux then wrote a reply in the same paper, and the campaign ceased.

A proverb says with truth, "Slander away! something will always stick." And it was thus in this case. Metchnikoff was reproached with having made money by his scientific discoveries. The story of his whole life and the fact that he left no fortune should suffice to answer this calumny, yet I am obliged to dwell on it, though I should have preferred not to do so. The incident is too characteristic of Metchnikoff to be omitted in this biography, which must be a faithful testimony. The calumny was based on a real fact, but the interpretation of it was absolutely false. After Metchnikoff's experiments on the lactic bacillus, a notion of the hygienic power of pure sour milk began to spread among the public. A manufacturer had the idea of preparing it on a large scale, according to the new scientific principles, and wished to form a company to that effect; he asked Metchnikoff to recommend to him some one whom he could entrust with the technical work of preparing the pure curded milk. It happened that we were just then trying to find a post for a young couple in whom we were interested, and whose child was my husband's goddaughter. He trained his protégé in the technique required, and was therefore able to recommend him.[227] A short time later, the manufacturer declared that he could not be sure of the success of his enterprise without the guarantee of the name of Metchnikoff, whose researches had proved the advantages of the preparation in question. After consulting the legal adviser of the Pasteur Institute, Metchnikoff consented to this, without of course having any pecuniary interest in it; the formula chosen was, "sole provider of Professor Metchnikoff." The undertaking succeeded, and our protégé's future was assured. Metchnikoff himself, however, was attacked and accused most unjustly, though he had never made any personal profit whatever from the enterprise. And yet, when his friends told him that it had been very reckless on his part thus to expose himself, he answered that he thought it impossible to hesitate between the welfare of a whole family and the possibility of gossip. His reasoning was imprudent and perhaps erroneous, but he never hesitated between doing a kindness and the possible unpleasant consequences it might have for himself. If some people could not understand him, it was because he was far from the commonplace, "not like other people," a quality often misunderstood and unforgiven.

Such are the facts. "Honi soit qui mal y pense!"

The desire to lessen the ills around him was, in general, the cause of heavy anxieties in his later years. He had learnt that the discovery of an industrial process, of which the realisation required capital, would be an excellent investment. He immediately wished to make his friends profit by it, as well as himself, in order to alleviate material difficulties. But until the end of his life the undertaking had no[228] results, and he was obsessed by the fear of having given bad advice to those who followed him.

He knew not how to refuse, even when he should have done so; therefore he was odiously exploited. Often he worked, in his rare leisure moments, for people who were unworthy of his kindness. During the last years of his life, all these incidents grieved him so much that he used to say he felt the burden of existence. His soul was darkened, he felt very depressed, and his health suffered.

We spent the summer holidays of 1913 at St. Léger-en-Yvelines, a pretty place on the edge of the Rambouillet forest. In his choice of a holiday resort, my husband was always guided by the desire to find a place favourable to my sketching, and St. Léger answered the purpose wonderfully. The fields with their vast horizons, the forest with its graceful bracken and carpets of softly-tinted heather, the mysterious ponds, all went to compose an admirable symphony, full of artistic suggestion.

Elie himself was gay and full of spirits. He worked in the morning, and we spent the rest of the day in the forest. He often read aloud; he rested and enjoyed the peaceful calm, pure air, and verdure which he loved so much.

He had arranged to take advantage of these holidays to execute work of which he had been thinking for a long time. As it has been said above, he thought that the life instinct was only developed gradually and produced at the same time an optimistic conception of life; he wished to verify this personal impression by the psychological evolution of divers other thinkers. He turned to Maeterlinck, as a representative of modern ideas. This author,[229] mystical and pessimistic in his youth, had acquired in his maturity a far more optimistic conception of life. He himself explained this change by the influence of circumstances, but Metchnikoff saw in it a deeper cause, connected with the progressive evolution of the vital instinct which, by bringing equilibrium with it, suggests optimism. The study of Maeterlinck's works confirmed his opinion.

Time flowed peacefully between rest and these occupations; at the end of the holidays, we congratulated ourselves on their result on my husband's health; on our return, his friends thought him looking well. Yet on the 19th October, about seven in the morning, he had a terrible cardiac attack without any apparent cause. I found him seated at his desk, and was terrified by his appearance; his lips were blue, and he was breathing with difficulty. And yet he was writing, and this is what he was writing:

Sèvres, 19th October 1913, 7.45 A.M.

This morning, after a good night, my heart was working well; I had from 58 to 59 regular pulsations. But, as I rose, I suddenly felt acute pain along the sternum; at the same time began a strong crisis of tachycardia. I had never in my life felt anything like it....

Here he had to stop as the crisis was becoming intolerable, but a few hours later he took up his pen again:

19th October, 3 P.M.

The crisis lasted till one o'clock (six hours' duration).

There were times when the pain in the chest was unendurable.

I was thirsty and drank hot, weak tea; I vomited; I felt wind in the stomach and the intestine. About noon the pain decreased, but the heart-beats were frequent and extremely[230] irregular. I lunched in order not to alarm my wife, though I feared to aggravate the attack by filling my stomach.

But the opposite happened. From the first mouthfuls (I naturally eat very little) the pain became more tolerable and the pulse less frequent. After lunch, everything became normal again; the pain ceased, the pulsations slackened (78-80 per min.) and became much more regular. Intermittence was rare, and I several times counted 100 regular beats in succession. I remained absolutely conscious during the whole crisis, and what chiefly pleased me is that I felt no fear of death, which I was expecting at every moment. It was not only reasoning which made me understand that it was better to die now, whilst my intellectual powers had not yet gone from me and I had evidently accomplished all of what I was capable; I resigned myself also in feeling, and quite serenely to the catastrophe which was coming upon me and which would be far from unexpected.

My mother, who had suffered from heart attacks during a great part of her life, died at 65. My father died of apoplexy in his 68th year.

My eldest sister succumbed to an œdema of the brain; my brother Nicholas died at 57 of angina pectoris.

Undoubtedly my cardiac heredity is a bad one. Already in my youth, I suffered from my heart. At 33 I had such cardiac pains that sometimes I had to rest after walking a few paces. At 34, I had much giddiness and a feeling of heaviness in the head. I could not read a few lines, a poster even, without a painful sensation. In 1881, during relapsing fever, I had severe cardiac intermittence, very fatiguing and only relieved by small doses of digitalin.

I afterwards had periodical attacks of intermittence but never any tachycardia, at least none that lasted more than a few seconds. A little tincture of strophanthus used to relieve me during intermittence. I ended by consulting Dr. Vaquez, but the treatment he prescribed gave me no relief. As I attributed my condition to poisoning by the toxins of intestinal microbes, I resolved to give up raw food and to purge myself now and then with Carabaña water. The success of this[231] treatment was indisputable, and in 1897 the intermittence ceased. In the autumn of 1898 I was beginning to suffer from polyuria; I consulted Albaran, who counselled Contrexéville water, but this cure caused the appearance of albumen in my urine. In 1898 I consulted Norden at Frankfort and Leube in Paris during the Exhibition of 1900. Neither found anything alarming. Norden had told me that I had symptoms of arterio-sclerosis inherent to my age (53). I adopted a mixed diet; I took, regularly, sour milk prepared with cultures of the Bulgarian lactic bacillus, and, during some years, my health was quite satisfactory.

It was only after my journey to Russia in 1909 that a notable aggravation supervened. I felt acute pains in the chest, along the sternum, especially after eating or walking.

In 1911 the intermittence reappeared. In January 1911, I consulted Dr. Heitz in order to know whether I could undertake an expedition in the Kalmuk steppes, where hygienic conditions are very unfavourable. Dr. Heitz found my heart hypertrophied, some slight galloping noise, the blood-pressure (Pachon's apparatus) 17-16-15. He said, however, that I might undertake the journey, but added, "People die suddenly with less the matter than that with their hearts." The journey went well, though I suffered from frequent intermittence and pains along the sternum when I walked.

After my return, my heart was fairly satisfactory.

What consoles me especially is that I have preserved my activity, my passion for work, and my intellectual powers. But, naturally, I am ready to die at any moment.

100

At the beginning of the summer I was sounded by Dr. Manoukhine and Professor Tchistovitch; both thought the heart-sounds satisfactory, but Manoukhine was rather struck by the weakness of the first aortic sound whilst the second was very strong. I had frequent intermittence, but with intervals of normal pulsations. Latterly I have felt better in that respect, and the pain along the sternum only occurred in exceptional cases.

Whilst preparing for my end, I am glad that I can face it with courage and serenity.

[232]

As I look back upon my life, it seems to me to have been as "orthobiotic" as possible.

If it may seem premature to die at 68 years and 5 months, it must not be forgotten that I began to live very early (I published my first scientific work at 18); that I have had many emotions during my life; that I was, so to speak, in a state of continual ebullition.

The polemics concerning phagocytosis might have killed or finally enfeebled me much earlier. At times (for instance, I refer to Lubarsch's attacks in 1889 and those of Pfeiffer in 1894) I was ready to rid myself of life.

Moreover, I only began to follow a rational hygiene (according to my opinion) after I was 53 years old and already had symptoms of arterio-sclerosis. I have been fairly successful in combating intestinal putrefaction (phenols and indols),[29] but I could not succeed in getting rid of abundant clostridium butyricum which were implanted in my intestine.

To sum up, I rejoice that I have had an existence not devoid of sense, and I feel some satisfaction in considering my conception of the problem of life as being accurate.

As I prepare to die, I have not the shadow of a hope of a life beyond, and I calmly look forward to complete annihilation.

It is possible that having very early begun a very intense life, I have attained at 68 a precocious satiety of living, just as certain women cease to menstruate earlier than the great majority.

El. Metchnikoff.
P.S.—I believe everything is in order in view of my end (my will, my affairs, etc.).

P.S.—Let those who think that, according to my principles, I should have lived a hundred years, "forgive" me my premature end in view of the extenuating circumstances above-mentioned (intense and precocious activity, excitable temperament, nervous disposition, and late beginning of the rational diet).

E. M.
[233]
The very next day he felt well enough to return to his work.

101

When urged to settle down in Paris in order to avoid the fatigue of the journey, he replied that the peace and pure air of Sèvres were indispensable to his health, that the journey did not fatigue him in the least, but on the contrary provided him with wholesome exercise and a pleasant walk. Knowing how prudent he was, I did not dare to insist for fear of mistaking what was really best for him. And life gradually resumed its normal course....

For a long time Metchnikoff had been observing himself very attentively; he took regular notes on the influence of the food diet which he followed; by the analysis of his urine, he sought for indications respecting the toxic products of his intestinal flora; he studied upon himself the advance of senility, whitening of hair, etc.

Since his crisis he had adopted the habit of writing occasional notes on his psychical state. This is what he wrote on the 23rd December 1913 at Sèvres:

Two months and more have passed since I wrote the preceding lines. During that period my health has been satisfactory; nevertheless I have wondered every day whether it would be my last.

I am therefore hastening to write my memoir on infantile cholera.

The cardiac intermittence has been more or less frequent, yet every day I have had periods of regular pulsations (58-66-72 per minute) as usual.

The day before yesterday I contracted a bad cold, accompanied by a little fever. Wondering if it would degenerate into pneumonia, I faced anew the possibility of a near end, and I resumed the analysis of my thoughts, feelings, and sensations.

[234]

As my 70 years draw near to their close, it seems to me that a feeling of satiety with life, what I call the "natural death instinct," is gently beginning to evolve.

When, in autumn 1910, experimenting with typhoid cultures, I had soiled my face and mouth, I naturally said to myself that it might give me typhoid fever. I washed my face and beard with soap and a solution of sublimate without considering that I was safe against the infection. I reasoned that it would be preferable to contract the disease and to die of it. (At my age typhoid fever is almost always fatal. I had never had it, and might therefore consider myself in a state of receptivity.) It is fine to fall on the battlefield, especially at an age when life and activity are already on the wane. But all that was pure reasoning; instinctively I still felt a great desire to live, and it was with joy that I counted the days which separated me from the danger of having contracted typhoid fever. I felt much relieved a fortnight after the incident, considering that the limit of incubation was passed.

Thus reasoning and feeling or instinct were not in accord.

Since then, in the three following years, a modification has taken place in my psychical condition.

The prospect of death frightens me less than before. During my cardiac crisis of the 19th October 1913 I even felt no fear of death, and my satisfaction at my recovery was less than before.

I think it is that difference in quantity which constitutes the first symptoms of indifference towards death, an indifference which is hardly perceptible at first.

Satiety with life is sometimes observed in old people of 80; it is not surprising to feel the first approach of it about 70, especially in the case of a man like myself who began very early to lead a very intense life.

Other special circumstances influence even more this precocious satiety of life. As I become more indifferent to my own life I feel a more and more acute anxiety for the health, life, and happiness of those who are dear to me.

I am especially troubled by a consciousness of the imperfection of modern medicine. In spite of the progress[235] realised in these latter days, it is still powerless against a multitude of diseases, threatening us on all sides.

Pulmonary lesions (tuberculosis, pneumonia, etc.), the nephrites, and an infinite quantity of other diseases can yet neither be prevented nor cured. So we live in constant fear for those we love. When medicine shall (as I am persuaded) have conquered all these evils, one cause of the bitterness of life will cease—but that is not yet the case.

That is why, besides the weakening of the life-instinct, a resignation towards death grows in us, as a means of no longer feeling the ills which afflict our neighbours.

With time, when that source of unhappiness has been eliminated by medicine, old age will be more attractive, and an orthobiotic life will become normal and realisable.

At the ages of 50, 60, 65, I felt an intense joy in living, such as I described in my Studies on Human Nature and Optimistic Essays. In the last few years it has lessened markedly.

Scientific work still provokes in me an invincible enthusiasm, but I am becoming more indifferent to many of the pleasures of life.

And indeed he no longer had the joyous soul of former days; into his life a funereal note had crept, low but continuous and obstinate. He gave all the more energy to the study of those questions the solution of which was to bring about the reign of orthobiosis. He spent the whole winter in researches on the intestinal flora and on the completion of his studies on infantile cholera.

In the spring, on the occasion of his anniversary, he wrote the following:

Sèvres, 16th May 1914.

I have to-day entered my 70th year; it is a great event for me. As I analyse my feelings, I realise more and more the weakening of my "life-instinct."

In order to verify my impressions, I wished to hear again[236] the musical compositions which formerly used to make me shed tears of enthusiasm (for instance,

103

Beethoven's 7th Symphony or Bach's aria for the violin). Well, my impressionability towards music has very much lessened. In spite of the facility with which old people weep, I hardly shed a single tear, save with rare exceptions.

I observe the same change in other circumstances.

This spring, the blossoming of flowers, buds, bushes, and trees, all this renascence of nature, has not excited in me a shadow of the emotion of preceding years.

Rather I felt a melancholy, not on account of my coming end, but because of the consciousness of the burden of existence.

There is no question for me now of the old joy of living; my predominant feeling is infinite anxiety for the health and happiness of those I love. I now so well understand Pettenkoffer, who committed suicide at 84 after losing all his family. Their death had evidently been precocious because of the impotence of medicine. At every step, one comes across cases where neither hygiene nor therapeutics can do anything. How many are infected with tuberculosis, no one knows how or where. What is to be done to avoid it? And the consequences of measles, of scarlet fever, perhaps of a simple sore throat, followed sometimes by tuberculosis or nephritis!

What is the use of being able to foretell, by means of the proportion of urea in the blood, the precise moment of the death of an "azotemic" patient when you cannot prevent it or cure him?

This imperfection of medical science prevents many from reaching true orthobiosis, and it is understandable that, seeing the present state of medicine, the feeling of the "burden of existence" may be precocious, as in my case.

But it is indubitable that, in spite of the slowness with which medical science is developing, it will in the future reach a degree which will enable us to cease to tremble any longer before all sorts of incurable diseases. Orthobiosis will then appear, no longer under its present incomplete form, but as the solid and essential basis of life.

[237]
CHAPTER XXXIV

Return to St. Léger-en-Yvelines — Norka — Studies on the death of the silk-worm moth — War declared — Mobilisation.

The drawback of the holidays consisted, for Metchnikoff, in coming away from his laboratory and in the impossibility of following his diet in a hotel or a boarding-house. We therefore resolved to hire a cottage in some quiet place, to organise a small laboratory, and to continue our usual mode of life.

St. Legér-en-Yvelines, where we had spent part of the preceding summer, answered all our requirements. We took a small villa there and called it "Norka," which means in Russian "little hole," "little refuge," and came there for the holidays in July 1914.

Elie seemed pleased to be there; thanks to the laboratory, he could easily vary his occupations, for continuous reading fatigued him. His reflections having led him to the problem of natural death, he had for some time been seeking for a subject on which he could study the mechanism of the phenomenon. He had formerly studied the May-flies (Ephemeridæ), predestined to a natural death by their rudimentary buccal organs, incapable of use in feeding. But the life of those insects, a life of a few hours or a few days at the most, was too short to allow the necessary researches. The males of the Rotifera, which are also deprived of buccal organs and even of[238] digestive organs, were too small in size for physiological experiments. Thus, those two examples of natural death among multicellular beings were unsuitable to the projected study.

He found a more favourable subject in the moth of the silk-worm (Bombyx mori); the rudimentary buccal organs of that insect make all feeding impossible and predestine it to a natural death. The dimensions of the silk-worm moth are large enough and it has a life duration of twenty-five or thirty days, therefore sufficient to allow the study of the mechanism by which its death is brought about. Metchnikoff procured a quantity of silk-worms, and soon the moths hatched and covered all the mantelpieces and tables in Norka with white flakes. He ascertained that it was not hunger which brought about the death of the moths, for their organism was not in the least exhausted.

The nutrition of the latter takes place at the expense of the fatty substance which remains after the metamorphosis of the chrysalis into a moth. The dissolution of this fatty substance produces toxins which pass into the urine. Thus the obvious cause of the death of the moth is an acid intoxication by toxic urine secreted in the bladder. As the latter does not empty itself, uræmia becomes inevitable.

The majority of moths contain no micro-organisms which could suggest death by infection.

The only theoretic objection against a natural death might consist in the existence of "invisible microbes." Indeed, the question of invisible microbes revealed in certain infections perturbed Metchnikoff's mind to such an extent that, during his last illness, he used to say that it would have been a curse to his[239] ulterior activity, a sort of ghost preventing all definite conclusions in problems connected with the absence or presence of microbes. The last word on natural death, he said, will only be spoken when, owing to the improvement of the microscope, those microbes which are as yet invisible to us will become visible. Nevertheless, as far as can be judged at present, the death of the Bombyx mori is due, not to external causes, but to the structure of the insect itself, and is therefore a natural death.

During these holidays, Metchnikoff also wrote reminiscences of his friend the physiologist Setchénoff.[30]

We went quietly for fairly long walks; Metchnikoff rested on the shores of his favourite lake (Vilpert), and his health was very satisfactory.

After the intense heat, some rain came and the weather became ideal; there was a perceptible lull in nature; the underwood was becoming purple with heather; the corn was ripening; harvest had begun, and sheaves stood up in the fields. All was calm and peaceful; we never tired of the charm of the forest, of the fields, of the beautiful rustic surroundings, and our souls sang in unison with Nature....

Suddenly, like a flash of lightning in the pure sky, the news of the war burst out!

The possibility had so often been mentioned in late years that no one believed in it. Even now, on the eve of the catastrophe, it was hoped that all would settle down....

Until the last moment Metchnikoff refused to believe in it; he could not admit that a pacific[240] solution was impossible. "How is it possible that in Europe, in a civilised country, mutual interests should not be reconciled without killing?" he said. "A war would be madness, even from the point of view of Germany, who risks having to face three great powers. No, war is not possible."

And yet war was spreading all over Europe.

The situation of France seemed critical, for the country had just gone through a series of internal storms. The labour question, that of income tax, and that of the three years' military service had raised sharp controversies; the Caillaux affair had revealed hidden sores in political life; the insane assassination of Jaurès, of which the reason was still unknown, gave rise to the blackest prognostications.

Already on the 28th July, date of the declaration of war by Austria against Serbia, anxiety had become intense, but it was hoped that Russia would settle matters between the two countries, and that the trouble would remain local.

On the 1st August, Germany declared war on Russia, and it became obvious that the storm was coming on apace. The aspect of life suddenly changed; a feeling of dread and expectancy unnerved everybody; mobilisation was mentioned; automobiles at full speed hurried along the roads; the harvest was hastily gathered.... We could no longer work, go for walks, or admire nature without a feeling of heavy anxiety.

We went about like automatons, all our thoughts centred on one point—the threatening, inevitable war. Everything had put on a sinister aspect, and Nature herself joined in the general gloom; the[241] weather became stormy, thunder rolled alarmingly, heavy clouds hurried and met in a gigantic struggle, evoking the image of other coming struggles. During the night of the 1st August the storm never ceased, we could not sleep; all night long, frenzied automobiles raced along the high road, sounding their lugubrious horns. In the middle of the night, we heard some one knocking at the doors of the police station opposite. What was happening? In the darkness, illumined by flashes of lightning, we saw horsemen with lanterns; they were messengers bringing the orders for mobilisation. It was proclaimed the next day.

The population gathered at the mairie, a grave, silent crowd; the few words exchanged only concerned war and partings. Old men, who had lived through 1870, were low-spirited; young ones, on the contrary, were excited.

We had to think of our return home, which might be difficult later. We went into the forest for the last time; the evening was mild and calm after the storm. The peace and beauty around us were such that we longed not to believe in the terrible reality. But we had to bid farewell to all that had charmed us. We went once again into the meadows near Norka. The hayricks were standing in rows, their soft, golden silhouettes harmoniously outlined against the hilly background purple with heather. We sat down on the mown grass. Suddenly, in the calm of the evening, bells began to sound. It was not the distant and poetic call for vespers, nor the sad sound of the passing bell, but the hard, sinister, ill-omened tocsin, warning the whole countryside, down to the most distant, most peaceful hamlets and to the[242] wood-cutters in the forest, that mobilisation had commenced....

Another storm broke out in the night. Again the rolling of the thunder shook our nerves and seemed like the echo of distant battles; again mysterious automobiles and horsemen raced along the road, and everything, every sound, every shadow seemed sinister.

We did not feel any fear, but a kind of insupportable nervous tension. Later, when we were much nearer real danger, we did not experience this electric, almost morbid feeling.

The next day, Germany had declared war on France.

It was only with much difficulty that we found a carriage to take us to the station. On the road we were constantly being passed by various vehicles, crowded with soldiers and young men going off. The little station was full of people, the train also. Moved and excited, the people shouted, "Vive la France!" and sent friendly salutes to unknown soldiers in the train. Women, seeing their men off, were trying to be gay; they encouraged the departing ones, and only wept after they were gone. The general impression, both moral and material, was excellent; every one seemed equal to his task, conscious of his duty, and desirous of fulfilling it well. The mobilisation seemed well organised, everything was being accomplished without any flurry or bustle, even the trains were almost punctual.

All small personal interests and party quarrels which had latterly poisoned life now suddenly disappeared; everywhere the desire to be useful was noticeable; people became better, there was more[243] sympathy, more solidarity; the distance between classes seemed to decrease, the common trial made all equal.

There was beauty in that moment, for it showed that the greatest of evils might yet exalt and purify the human soul.

[244]

CHAPTER XXXV

Return to Paris — The deserted Institute — Memoir on the Founders of Modern Medicine — Metchnikoff's Jubilee — Last holidays at Norka.

This was but the beginning of the war; soon it spread with vertiginous rapidity, and made its cruel destructive force felt.

On our return from Norka, we found everything on a war footing. The very next morning, Metchnikoff hurried to the laboratory. He only reached Paris with some difficulty, all means of communication being encumbered by soldiers. He had left the house nervous and excited but full of courage and energy. I shall never forget his return home....

I was awaiting him as usual, just outside the station, and, as he got out of the train, I did not recognise him. I saw a stooping old man, bent as under a heavy burden; his usual vivacity was gone, and had given place to the deepest depression.

He told me in a broken voice that the Institute was already deserted; that it was under the orders of the military authorities, and completely disorganised for scientific work. The younger men were mobilised; the laboratories empty; the animals used for experiments had been killed on account of the departure of the servants, and for fear of a lack of food. Everything that had been devoted to the service of science[245] and of research into means of preserving life had been handed over to the service of war. Normal and cultured life was arrested. And that was the outcome of civilisation.

Metchnikoff felt as if he had suddenly been dropped into the abyss of centuries, into the times of human savagery. He could not accustom his mind to the idea of such a fall; it seemed to him a paradox, an impossibility, that civilised peoples could not do without sanguinary fights in order to solve questions of mutual relations.

The events which were taking place agitated and depressed him all the more that he had not the possibility of becoming absorbed in scientific investigations; he was completely thrown off his balance.

And as, one by one, the news came of the death in action of several of the young men who had left the Institute, Metchnikoff's grief knew no limits. He could not bear the idea, now a terrible reality, that these brilliant young lives should be sacrificed, victims of those who should have directed the peoples towards peace and a rational life, and who, instead of that, threw the most precious part of humanity into the abyss of death. War became a dark, sinister background to his daily life. The victims of war were not only those who fell on the battle-field, but included him whose whole life-effort had been directed towards the conservation of human existence and the search for rational

107

conceptions. The contrast between his aspirations and the cruel reality had been to him a blow which his sensitive and suffering heart was not fit to bear.

The Germans were advancing rapidly. Then came the sad days of panic, when the inhabitants[246] were leaving Paris in numbers and the Government started for Bordeaux. At night, the sky was swept by the gigantic, luminous sword of the searchlights; the rumble of cannon could be heard in the distance....

Metchnikoff, however, had no personal fear whatever. He very simply decided on his course of action, which was to remain at the Institute if his presence there could be of use; if not, to retire to some quiet place where he could work. As there was hardly any staff left at the Institute on account of the mobilisation, he did not go away, but, on the contrary, we came to live in Paris, the communication with Sèvres being very difficult.

The day we arrived was that on which the first German aeroplanes appeared, and they dropped bombs near the St. Lazare station just as we were alighting from the train. For some time after that, they carried out a raid above Paris every Sunday.

In spite of the disorganisation of his whole life, Metchnikoff had succeeded in resuming his work to a certain extent. He took advantage of an opportunity to observe an old dog who was suffering from diabetes, and hastened to examine his organs as soon as he died, whilst they were still fresh. He had for some time supposed that diabetes might be an infectious disease; yet he was unable to discover any specific microbe either in the humors or in the organs of the dog. But he succeeded in provoking symptoms of the disease (traces of sugar in the urine) in a healthy dog, by inoculating him with the pancreatic gland of the diabetic dog. He was much encouraged by this result, and would have liked to continue his researches, but was unable to do so because[247] of the general disorganisation and the impossibility of obtaining animals for experiments. He had to content himself with continuing his memoir on infantile cholera and his observations on the silk-worm moth.

As he was almost altogether precluded from laboratory work, he began to write a study on "The Founders of Modern Medicine," in order to demonstrate, by concrete examples, the importance of positive science in its application to life. This is what he said in his preface to the book:

These pages were written under special circumstances. If not in the actual hearing of guns, it was in expectation of it that I had to spend several weeks in my Paris laboratory, now under war conditions. These meant an almost complete cessation of any scientific activity in our Institute.

For fear of a lack of food, the animals used for our experiments had been killed, which deprived us of the possibility of proceeding with our researches.

The stables of the Institute were filled with cows who provided milk for the hospitals and children's homes.

The greater number of our young collaborators, assistants, or laboratory attendants were mobilised, and only the female employees and old men remained. One of the latter, I found myself in the impossibility of pursuing my investigations and in possession of much leisure. I made use of it to write this book in the hope that it might be helpful.

It is not intended for physicians, for they know all that is expounded in it, but for young men who are seeking a scope for their activities.

We may be sure that the insane war which broke out in consequence of the lack of knowledge or of power of those who should have watched over peace, will be followed by a long period of calm. It is to be hoped that this unexampled butchery will, for a long time, do away with the desire for fighting, and that soon the need will be felt of a more rational[248] activity. Let those who will have preserved the combative instinct direct it towards a struggle, not against human beings, but against the innumerable microbes, visible or invisible, which threaten us on all sides and prevent us from accomplishing the normal and complete cycle of our existence.

The results acquired by the progress of the new medical science allow us to hope that, in a more or less distant future, humanity will be freed from the principal diseases which oppress it.

After describing the state of medical science before Pasteur, Lister, and Koch, Metchnikoff compared with it modern medicine, created by these three Founders, and showed the great horizons opened by them to the medicine of the future.

On the 26th of September 1914, whilst we were still in Paris, he had, in the laboratory, an attack of tachycardia, which lasted three hours but was much less violent than that of the year before. The winter, however, passed fairly well in spite of the emotions and continuous excitement caused by the war, and he had no other attack until April 1915, when again he had a slight tachycardiac crisis of a short duration. Yet he was very much changed: his hair was much whiter, his movements were slow, and his figure bent. His infectious gaiety and vivacity had disappeared, but he remained energetic and enthusiastic in his work, and gained more and more in serenity.

Little children in the street called him "Father Christmas," and came confidingly to ask him for presents. They knew him well, and were aware that his pockets were always filled with sweets for them. He used to say that his growing love for children was the revelation of the grandfatherly instinct, for which he had reached the proper age. He especially[249] loved one of his god-daughters, little Lili; he had become attached to the child on account of her kind heart and exceptional sweetness, and also because, from the cradle, she had shown a marked preference for him. And yet his love for children was not to him a source of joy, for anxiety on their account predominated over other feelings.

In spite of the physical change which had supervened, his brain continued to work untiringly as in the past, and he tackled new problems with youthful courage and boldness. He had planned a work on the sexual question, which, according to him, was treated erroneously, with the result that grave disharmonies occurred in human existence.

Thus he reached some quite revolutionary conclusions respecting education and marriage. He thought that morality should be set upon a quite different basis, new and rational; and that was the question which he prepared to treat.

The 16th of May of that year was his seventieth anniversary.

His satisfaction was great at having reached the normal limit of age, for he saw in that a conclusive proof of the efficacy of his hygiene. Indeed, he showed on that day a sort of rejuvenation: his aspect was quite different, he was gay and animated as he had not been for a long time.

The Pasteur Institute celebrated his jubilee. In spite of the absence from "The House" of many members on account of the war, the library filled with people, and the fête had a cordial and intimate character. Dr. Roux's speech[31] will remain the best description of E. Metchnikoff and of his scientific[250] activity. He himself responded to all those manifestations of sympathy by a spirited speech, in which, à propos of his own particular case, he expounded his ideas on senility and the duration of life in general. This is what he wrote on that same day in his note-book:

16th May 1915. To-day I have at last accomplished my seventy years! I have attained the normal limit of life, a limit mentioned by King David and confirmed by the statistical researches of Lexis and Bodio.[32] I am still capable of work and of reflection. But the changes in my psychical state which I had observed a year ago have become sensibly accentuated. The difference in acuteness both of pleasant and painful sensations is becoming more and more marked. Agreeable sensations are becoming weaker; I am now indifferent to many things which I used to appreciate very much.

It is useless to say that I am indifferent to the quality of my food; my need of musical impressions has become so much less that I hardly feel the desire to satisfy it. The charm of spring no longer touches me and only provokes sadness in my mind.

On the other hand, my anxiety for the health and happiness of those I love is getting more and more acute. I find it difficult to understand how I ever could bear it.

The powerlessness of medicine grieves me more and more, and, as a last straw, the war has interrupted all the work that had been undertaken against disease. In these conditions, it is not astonishing that I should feel a growing satiety with existence. Last year [16th May 1914 to 16th May 1915] I had two attacks of tachycardia, during which I should have been glad to die, but in general my health is satisfactory and that sustains me. What would have become of me if, to crown my misfortunes, I had fallen ill! I certainly no longer fear death, but I desire to die suddenly during a heart attack and not to go through a long illness.

[251]

My comparative longevity is not due to family heredity (my father died in his 68th year, my mother in her 66th, my sister also, my eldest brother at 45, my second brother at 50, the third in his 57th year; my grandparents I have not known). It is to my hygiene that I give the credit for having attained my 70 years in a satisfactory condition. I have taken no raw food for eighteen years and I introduce as many lactic bacilli as possible into my intestines. But it is but a first step; in spite of all, I am being poisoned by the bacteria of butyric fermentation. However, I have practically reached the normal term of life and I must be satisfied. I have, so to speak, accomplished the programme of a "reduced orthobiosis."

When macrobiotics become more perfect, when people have learnt how to cultivate a suitable flora in the intestines of children as soon as they are weaned from their mother's breast, the normal limit of life will be put much further back and may extend to twice my 70 years. Then, also, satiety with existence will appear much later than it has done in my case.

To-day they celebrated my jubilee at the Pasteur Institute, which touched me very much, in spite of my distrust of sentimental manifestations, for I realised their sincerity. I should have liked to set out a programme of the researches which should be accomplished by the Pasteur Institute, but I feared to detain my audience too long.

I believe that Science will solve all the principal problems of Life and Death and that she will enable human beings to accomplish their vital cycle by real orthobiosis, not by a reduced caricature of it as in my case. Nevertheless, I consider the experiment practised upon myself as having already given some result and that is to me a real satisfaction.

We spent that summer a few weeks at Norka, where Metchnikoff completed his researches concerning the death of the silk-worm moth.

We went for delicious walks; we spent all the afternoon by the lake or under the pines in the heather, reading and working. Once only, during a[252] walk, he had a strong cardiac intermittence, but as a rule he felt well. I could see, however, that he was obsessed by a grave preoccupation which he did not express. Later, during his last illness, he confessed to me that during the whole of that stay at St. Léger he had feared to die suddenly during one of our walks. The thought of my isolation weighed on his mind and he hid his anxiety so as not to alarm me....

With a view to the work which he had planned on the sexual question, he interested himself in the influence that their sentimental life had had on the activity of great men, and we read together the biographies of Beethoven, Mozart, and Wagner. Elie was more than ever desirous of making our holidays as pleasant as possible, as if he already felt that they were our last. Here are more extracts from his note-book:

St. Léger-en-Yvelines, 24th June 1916.

When saying that I did not fear death, I had in view the dread of annihilation. That fear, manifested during a long period of life and disappearing towards the end, may be compared with the fear of darkness which children instinctively feel and which also disappears gradually and naturally. When, towards the end of life, the fear of nothingness ceases, no desire remains for a future life, for the immortality of the soul. It would even be painful to me to think that the soul, surviving the body, could watch, from beyond, the misfortunes of those who remain on the earth. On the contrary, towards life's decline, a desire for complete annihilation becomes developed.

He spent the autumn collecting and preparing the materials he required for his book on the sexual function. It was a relief from the sad impressions of the war and the deserted laboratory. But new troubles were in store for us; I became ill, and had[253] scarcely recovered when we heard the news of the death of a nephew who was very dear to us. The death of the young had always deeply moved Metchnikoff, and it was so in this case. It was another weight thrown into the already descending scale.

In spite of all, he continued to work with enthusiasm, planting young trees that future generations might enjoy their shade.

[254]
CHAPTER XXXVI

Bronchial cold — Aggravated cardiac symptoms — Farewell to Sèvres — Return to the Institute — Protracted sufferings — Intellectual preoccupations — Observations on his own condition — The end — Cremation.

If in this sad last chapter I occasionally dwell on details which may seem insignificant in themselves, it is because, at this supreme moment of Elie Metchnikoff's existence, everything was full of significance, for everything converged to emphasise the powerful unity and the ascending and continuous progress of his ideas.

His attitude in the face of illness and death was a teaching, a support, and an example. That is why, relating the story of his last days, I piously describe everything.

Towards the end of November, he caught a slight cold, which did not prevent him from leading his usual life, but which, nevertheless, was the starting-point of the illness which took him from us.

On the 2nd of December, during a walk, he suddenly felt a cardiac commotion such that he thought he was dying. For hours, his pulse remained intermittent and very rapid, and from that day he felt unwell but continued to go to the laboratory.

On the 9th of December his condition became worse and forced him to interrupt his normal life. All the doctors were away or very busy on account of the war,[255] and it was only on the 11th that Dr. Renon could give him a consultation at the Laënnec Hospital. He found Metchnikoff's heart very tired and nervous, prescribed a treatment, and told us to come back in twenty-five days.

But the disease was making giant strides. In the night of the 12th to 13th a first attack of cardiac asthma supervened, an extremely painful one; we had the impression that the end was near. Elie suffered agonies but remained morally calm and ready for death, as he had ever been since his first heart attack, two years previously. He repeated that he had accomplished his task and run through his vital cycle; that what he could yet do would be but a supplement, and that it was better to die than to outlive his own decadence.

He only wished not to suffer too long, but that humble desire was not to be realised. We spent two more nights at Sèvres, terrible nights not to be forgotten if one had centuries to live, and we then decided to go to a nursing home in Paris, as it was imprudent to remain any longer isolated as we were.

Having heard of Metchnikoff's illness, Dr. Roux offered to receive us at the Pasteur Institute in a small lodging which was now free, the house-physician who had occupied it having been killed.

Dr. Widal, in whom Metchnikoff had absolute confidence, came to Sèvres on the 14th and found myocarditis. Thanks to an absolutely incomprehensible phenomenon, Elie had suddenly ceased to realise the rapidity of his pulse; he had 160 beats in a minute and only perceived less than half; it was therefore easy to keep the truth from him.

After a last night of suffering we left our Sèvres nest, which we had so loved. Leaning on my arm,[256] he slowly walked through the little garden and gazed for the last time at the home that we were leaving for the unknown.... He looked worn and bent under the weight of suffering, but he was quite calm, and his eyes, though firm and gentle, already seemed to me to be looking very far away.

The automobile bore us slowly from Sèvres to the Pasteur Institute, and we found ourselves in the small flat which had been inhabited by the young doctor who had been killed in the war. He had only spent a short stage of his life there. How long should we remain? And what road should we take when we left it? We tried to smile, though our hearts were terribly heavy, in order to cheer each other.

But, in the course of the day, we were surrounded by friends full of solicitude, the tension relaxed, and we felt a growing sense of comfort and security. No more nights of mortal dread and loneliness, with no help at hand! That thought alone inspired courage and hope. In case of need, I had only to send down to the next floor to ask for a doctor.

For a few days, Elie felt much better, perhaps on account of the mental relief, but his heart was weak and his pulse extremely rapid. Drs. Widal, Martin, Veillon, Salimbeni, and Darré came to see him every day; during the whole of his long illness, they never ceased to show him the most attentive and devoted care. They attempted by every means to save him from pain, for, alas, they had no hope of curing him. Nothing was neglected, and many still greater sufferings were spared him.[33]

The war was an inexhaustible and passionately interesting subject of conversation; Elie read a number of newspapers and listened with avidity to every news from private sources. Often, too, scientific questions were discussed, which continued to interest him intensely. These talks were an invaluable relaxation.

Feeling infinitely grateful towards his medical advisers and friends, he showed himself a most docile patient, following their prescriptions with absolute punctuality. When his condition grew worse and he felt no hope whatever of his recovery, he often used to say, "What is to be done? the doctors can do nothing, for medicine is powerless. Unhappily, it will remain so for a long time. Much work will have to be done to rid humanity of the scourge of diseases. But, surely, one day science will succeed in doing so; that will be chiefly through prophylaxis and rational hygiene. There will also be a new science—the science of death; it will be known how to make it less hard."

After lunch and a short sleep, he received the daily visit of his friend Dr. Roux, with whom he talked in the full intimacy of friendship and affection. He confided to him his apprehensions and desires, and felt unlimited gratitude for his kindness to us, often saying to me, with tears in his eyes, "I knew Roux was a kind man and a true friend, but I see now that he is incomparable." Other friends also did their utmost to serve him and to show their sympathy. He had the great joy of feeling himself beloved and surrounded with an atmosphere of real kindness. Many times he said to me, [258]"Now, only, have I appreciated the warm-heartedness of the French at its full value. Do not fail, in my biography, to emphasise how deeply I feel it, and how grateful I am. I want them to know it."

Yet all the care and devotion of which he was the object could neither arrest the fatal progress of disease nor spare cruel suffering to him who had thought of nothing but relieving the pains of others. All our efforts were as flowers scattered over a tomb; he, poor tortured one, was slowly, consciously sinking into it through the implacable logic of Fate. From the beginning of his illness, he foresaw the issue; he lived in constant expectation of death, on the threshold of which his calm and serenity remained as unalterable as were his patience and resignation.

After a temporary and comparative lull, which lasted until the end of December, the disease began to progress again, and almost every week brought a fresh alarming symptom. It was especially during the night that the pain, treacherously, reappeared. After dropping asleep fairly early, he would begin to breathe with difficulty and then awake in an indescribable state of anguish; perspiration drenched his head, neck, and chest, several towels often being required to dry him. His breathing was hard; during bad attacks, the wheezing of his bronchial tubes was terrifying.

He would sit up, his hands clenched, his face blue and contracted by suffering, his darkened lips apart, his eyes dilated—the face of a man on the rack. He gasped like a suffocating man; at last a tearing cough supervened, followed by expectoration, and the attack gradually subsided.

For a time we were able to relieve him without the use of narcotics. As long as there was a ray of hope[259]—not of recovery, but of a bearable life and further work—he wished at all costs to avoid the influence of narcosis. He breathed fumes of pyridin or ether, he smoked Escouflaire cigarettes, and inhaled various other things. In order to sleep after an attack, he ate a few biscuits, and I sprinkled his head with a menthol solution, with which I damped his temples and forehead. That eased him, and sometimes he slept again for a few hours.

But how many were the nights of insomnia and suffering! How many times did he call for death as a deliverer, and say that he resigned himself to live for my sake only!

And in spite of the martyrdom he endured, he always had gentle words, a caress, a consolation even! He constantly returned to the thought that he had nothing to complain of, that he had had a large share of happiness and good fortune in having accomplished his task, and even arrived at the development of the natural death-instinct.

All those who saw him every day knew that he was courageous and patient, every one admired his serenity, but no one could realise the degree of his courage and patience, for no one had seen and lived through those miserable nights.

Often, even, when asked how he was, he said "not bad!" after a terrible night, saying to me afterwards in explanation, "Why grieve them, since it cannot be helped?"

At the beginning of our stay in the Institute, he was not yet quite bedridden. After his morning toilet, he would lie for some hours on a sofa, reading almost continuously, newspapers, scientific reviews, and many works in connection with the book he had[260] planned on the sexual function, of which he wrote only the introduction and a few lines of the first chapter.[34]

Another question occupied him at that time, that of first-born children. Certain data led him to think that men of genius were but rarely the first-born of their parents, and he sought for every possible information on the subject. In his constant desire to improve life-conditions, he even thought that a demonstration of this fact might have a desirable influence on the increase of population in France after the war; if it were proved that the most successful children are not the first-born, perhaps the system of having two children only would be given up in order to have a chance of giving the country a more capable population.

His reflections on the sexual questions led him to seek for experimental means of studying gonorrhœa. He thought of inoculating the gonococcus into the eye of new-born mice and entrusted M. Rubinstein, the only worker left in the laboratory, with these experiments. The latter began them and obtained encouraging results, but he left Paris in the spring and the work remained unfinished.

Metchnikoff's mind never ceased to work unless[261] interrupted by acute pain; until the very end, his brain never failed him. He often used to say how far he was from any mystic aspirations, and how sure he was of remaining a rationalist until the end. And such was the case. Faithful to himself, not even in the most painful moments did he feel a desire to look for support outside the ideas and principles of his whole life. Yet his soul was sad and full of care; the war grieved him utterly, every newspaper he read renewed his sorrow. When a severe engagement, Verdun for instance, was going on, he lost the little sleep he had, and his agitation became painful.

He was deeply disillusioned by the Germans. Having always felt great esteem for their scientific work, he had believed in their high culture, and now he was absolutely disconcerted by the mentality which they manifested during the war.

Neither could he understand how the war had been allowed to come about. He thought it ought to have been avoided, and considered the authorities guilty for not having done so. He said that nothing could compensate the harm done by this insane butchery.

The deserted laboratories, the interruption of scientific work, filled his soul with melancholy. For, he said, all the great, all the real questions should have been solved by Science and were kept waiting....

He also had material worries, the war having brought great perturbation in his affairs. The fate of his mobilised pupils preoccupied him constantly. The least indisposition, however trifling, of those he loved made him unhappy. His sensibility, which had always been very marked, increased still more, and[262] consumed him; it surely was one of the causes that had worn his heart out. When already very weak and ill, he constantly thought of giving pleasure to those who were with him; he read innumerable reviews and periodicals, and would tell each friend what he had found of particular interest to the latter, even when speech was difficult to him. His gentleness and cordiality were most touching during the whole of his illness, though he preserved his usual outspokenness.... It seemed to me that this offended no one; they all understood Elie now.

He sought a refuge from his sufferings in his own ivory tower; these sufferings themselves were to him a source of observations. He studied his body and his soul as he would have studied any subject under experiment. Every day he wrote down his auto-observations, and carefully read the diary which I kept for him.

During the whole of the winter he had ups and downs. Towards the end of December the cough and respiratory symptoms increased, and at the beginning of January he expectorated clots of blood, due to a passive congestion of the right lung.

On the 19th January, some liquid appeared in the pleura on the same side. Pleurisy persisted for a whole month and necessitated three punctures. Every time we feared to tell him that the puncture was necessary, but he received the news with complete coolness, saying that he had always been in favour of radical measures.

After the third puncture, which took place on the 19th February, a marked relief supervened, and the improvement lasted for some time; it was the only moment when we saw a ray of hope.

[263]

Though keeping to his bed, he worked a great deal, read, and received not only his friends but other visitors. At the beginning of March and at the end of April he again expectorated blood, and the terrible, tragical nights began again. Yet the days were fairly good.

During that period, he had the pleasure of seeing some of his pupils again, and of receiving several Russian deputies and journalists. They talked to him of political events, of the war, of the moral state of Russia. All that interested him immensely; he plied them with the most varied questions. It must be remembered that, before that interview, we had lost all touch with Russia.

During the whole of May he again had ups and downs, but the progress of the disease was indisputable.

Tachycardia was constant, urine more and more scanty, the swelling of the legs never decreased, cough and oppression occurred frequently even during the day. Elie awaited his seventy-first birthday with impatience. Often during the night, after a painful attack, he would count the days, hours, and minutes which separated him from that date. At last it arrived. Here are the lines which he added to his notes on that day:

16th May. Against all expectation, I have lived until this day. I have reached my 71 years. My dream of a rapid death without a long illness has not been realised. I have now been bedridden for five months. After several crises of tachycardia, following upon a slight grippe with asthma, I had congestion of one lung with pleuritic exudate. Though some improvement followed after that, nevertheless I am tormented by fits of sweating followed by cough and oppression.[264] I suffer chiefly in the night from those attacks; they provoke insomnia which can only be combated by pantopon.

My psychical state is twofold. In one way, I should like to get well, but, on the other hand, I see no sense in living any longer. Illness has not provoked in me any fear of death, and I am more deprived than formerly of the joy of living. The reawakening of spring leaves me quite indifferent. There can be no question for me of that pleasure which convalescents often feel, nor indeed of any pleasure. To the despair that I feel in the face of medicine's powerlessness to cure the ills of my friends is added the feeling of its powerlessness towards my own illness. I think that my desire to recover and to continue to live is connected with practical causes.

The war has compromised our finances, our income from Russia has practically disappeared. If I die, my wife may find herself in a very difficult situation. Given her lack of practical notions, that may lead to very sad results. Yet it is quite impossible to straighten our affairs before the end of the war and the re-establishment of normal conditions.

These were the last words he wrote in his book of notes; his hand had become weak and trembling; he tired very soon, and henceforth I wrote under his dictation. On the 18th June, one month before his cremation, he dictated to me for the last time, and this is what he said:

This is the seventh month that I have been ill and it brings my thoughts back to the gravity of my condition. I therefore continually realise how much satisfaction I have derived from life during my long years. The gradual disappearance of my "life-instinct," which already began a few years ago, is now more marked, more precise. I no longer feel that degree of pleasure which I felt only a few years ago. My affection for my nearest and dearest shows itself much more by the anxiety and suffering provoked by their diseases and[265] sorrows than by the pleasure I derive from their joys or normal health.

Those to whom I describe my feelings tell me that satiety with living is not normal at my age. To that I oppose the following: Longevity, at least to a certain point, is hereditary. Now I have already mentioned, on the occasion of my 70th anniversary, that my parents, sister, and brothers died before reaching my present age. I knew neither of my grandparents, which shows that they could not have been very old when they died.

Let us now turn to the profession, since it is an established fact that it has an influence on the duration of life. Pasteur died at 72, but for a long time he had been unable to do scientific work. Koch did not reach the age of 67. Other bacteriologists died at a much earlier age than I (Duclaux, Nocard, Chamberland, Ehrlich, Büchner, Loeffler, Pfeiffer, Carl Fraenkel, Emmerich, Escherich).

Among those bacteriologists of my generation who are still living the majority have already ceased from working. All that should indicate that my scientific life is over and confirm at the same time the fact that my "orthobiosis" has actually reached the desirable limit.

He was anxious to prove that his end, which seemed premature at first sight, did not contradict his theories, but had deep causes such as heredity and the belated introduction of a rational diet. He had only begun to follow it at fifty-three. Facts corroborated him after his death, for the post-mortem examination showed that the heart lesions were of long standing. He himself thought they went back at least to 1881, when he had had a

116

very grave relapsing fever. The doctors even wondered how he had lived with his heart in such a state, and only accounted for it by the strict régime which he had followed during the latter part of his life.

And indeed when it is remembered how pugnacious,[266] how vehement he was—always, so to speak, in a state of ebullition, feverishly active, intensely sensitive—it must be admitted that his life really held more than an ordinary life of longer duration.

He was very desirous that the example of his serenity in the face of death should be encouraging and comforting. It should prove that, at the end of his vital cycle, man fears death no longer; it has lost its sting for him.

Early in June his condition became still worse. The nights were so painful that, every evening, recourse had to be had to pantopon.[35] It was with the greatest impatience that he awaited his "dear Darré and dear Salimbeni," as he called them.

After Dr. Darré had finished his complete and thorough medical examination, we three remained talking around Elie's bed for a short hour. He often recalled his personal or scientific memories when he was not too weary; we talked of the war, of medical questions; often, too, we would evoke, with Salimbeni, recollections of our journey to the Kalmuk Steppes.

We loved that peaceful hour, which ended by an injection of pantopon, the only relief, alas, that could be procured for him. He would thank Dr. Darré with gratitude, and drop his poor weary head on the pillow, awaiting in absolute security the blessed sensation of warm heaviness which pervaded him, for he knew that sleep and rest from his sufferings would not be long in coming. The spectre of tragical nights never ceased to haunt us.

Until the hot weather came, he was quite comfortable in the small flat in the Pasteur hospital; the temperature there had been perfectly regular all[267] through the winter; but now he began to be incommoded by the heat.

M. Roux then proposed that we should be transferred to Pasteur's old flat; the rooms were spacious and much cooler. This idea rejoiced and touched Elie very much. As he thanked M. Roux, he said to him: "See how my life is bound with the Pasteur Institute. I have worked here for years; I am nursed here during my illness; in order to complete the connection I ought to be incinerated in the great oven where our dead animals are burnt, and my ashes could be kept in an urn in one of the cupboards in the library." "What a gruesome joke!" answered M. Roux, really taking those words for a joke. But directly after he was gone Elie turned to me with an anxious look and said, "Well, what do you think of my idea?" I saw by his earnest expression that he meant what he said, and I answered that I thought it a very good idea. The Pasteur Institute had become his refuge, the centre of all his scientific interests; he loved it; he had spent his best years there. Let his ashes be laid there some day; it would be in perfect harmony with his past. Let us only hope that would not be too soon! But why had he given his words that jesting form which must have misled M. Roux? He explained it to me: knowing how deeply conscientious his friend was, he did not wish to express his desire as a dying wish in order that he should feel no obligation. A simple jest, on the contrary, left him absolutely free.

On the 26th June, Elie was carried into Pasteur's flat; it was a very great satisfaction to him, it brought him nearer his laboratory. Now and then, very seldom now, he thought he might return there one[268] day; he said I should wheel him there in his bath-chair. "I know I could scarcely work there myself. But perhaps I might still play the part of a ferment, be useful to my pupils by giving them advice. I am leaving so much unfinished work which it would be interesting to go on with: the question of intestinal flora, that of diabetes, which surely is an infectious disease—but that will have to be proved,—and my experiments on the subject were scarcely begun. I think the study of gonorrhœa will give very interesting results when they succeed in inoculating it in new-born animals. And the question of tuberculosis is well started! I could still help my pupils and encourage them if I were a little better!... But I have no illusions! I must live now only from day to day...."

Those words were uttered with heart-rending resignation.

He continued to get worse....

It was fortunate that pantopon should have given him good nights, for attacks of oppression now supervened several times during the day; tachycardia was continuous, the heart was weakening. The quantity of urine diminished; it often did not surpass 250 cubic centimetres, and no diuretic succeeded in increasing it; the legs remained swollen, ascitis was beginning to become visible; in the night he occasionally grew slightly delirious.

At the beginning of July he wished to sit up; he spent part of the afternoon in an armchair, his legs lying on cushions. We thought it was a good sign, but in reality he found it difficult to breathe lying down. Several times he asked me to play to him, very soft music, as noisy sounds wearied him. I[269] played him some Beethoven, some Mozart; the last time it was a Chopin prelude.

On the 9th his temperature went down in an alarming way to 35.2° C. (95 F.). For the first time he would not write down his ordinary observations. "What is the good?" said he, "it has no longer any interest." Yet the next day he did so, for the last time. On the 11th and 12th he put down his temperature, and glanced superficially at the notes I had written. On the 12th, about five o'clock in the morning, he had a bad fit of breathlessness followed by coughing, and brought up large clots of very red blood. He smiled faintly. "You understand what that means," he said, adding some tender words.

I wheeled him to his bed, which he never left again.

On the 13th, in the early morning, he felt very ill. Calmly and gently he warned me to be ready. "It will surely be to-day or to-morrow."

My heart breaking, I asked him why he said that; was he feeling very weak? or suffering very much?

"No," he said, "it is difficult to say what I feel; I have never felt anything like it; it is, so to speak, a death-sensation.... But I feel very calm, with no fear. You will hold my hand, will you not?"

How can I describe those last three days? He preserved all his lucidity and serenity, often smiling at me and drawing me towards him. He inhaled oxygen very often, as breathlessness became almost continuous.

On the 14th there was to be a matinée performance of Manon Lescaut, and remembering that his god-children had long wished to see that opera, he had had a box taken for them. He was now quite uneasy about it. "What ill-luck," he said, [270]"if it happened just before and prevented them from going. In any case they must not come here on their way to the theatre, so that if it happens they will not know, and can still enjoy the performance."

Thanks to pantopon, he spent a very good night. He awoke about five o'clock, but remained so quiet that I thought him asleep. When I rose about six he held out his hand to me and told me he had been awake for a long time. He talked to me tenderly, in the full intimacy of our affection; he spoke sweet, unforgettable words. He made me promise once again not to give way to grief. "At first, our friends will help you, and then work, that infallible remedy, and duty.... You will have that of writing my biography. Remember how much I wish the last chapter to be complete. You alone can write it, for you have seen me all the time; I have told you all my thoughts, and yet...." I understood that he had occasionally, out of pity for me, hidden his sufferings and his sad thoughts. But he did not

118

know how often I guessed what he did not say; love and pain have a dumb language, more eloquent than any human words.

"You will hold my hand when the moment comes," he repeated. "But do not think I am afraid, now that it is near. No, I assure you, I have an absolute serenity of soul! I spent a divine night. It seemed to me that I was already half outside life. This night has taught me many things.... Everything which troubled me, everything that seemed so disturbing, so terrible, like this war for instance, seems so transitory now, such a small thing by the side of the great problems of existence!... Science will solve them some day." He ceased speaking. He seemed[271] illumined by a very exalted feeling; it was like the last chord of his harmonious soul. What a consolation if he could have died then!

But life is cruel. He lived through two more days of suffering. On the 14th he inhaled oxygen almost continually. He asked for pantopon, but we feared to give him too much. I told him it would induce such continuous sleep that he would not even be able to enjoy it. "But an eternal sleep is precisely what I want! Do understand that now nothing is left to me but pantopon. What is the good of making me last? Is this a life? A few days or a month have no importance when one is not going to recover. And you cannot wish to prolong my sufferings." His breathlessness increased; he said, "Give me your hand; stay near me!" I knew what he meant; he had the "death-sensation."

His poor hands were hot and warmed my cold ones.... The next day I could not warm his hands, ice-cold for ever.

The whole day he awaited with impatience the hour for pantopon. About nine o'clock, when Dr. Darré came in, he said, "Dear Darré, at last!"

There was no talk that evening, he was so weary. With what anguish I awaited the stroke of midnight, which ended those two dread days! He had been mistaken by barely one day. The night was not bad, in spite of breathlessness and some fits of coughing. The next morning he felt better. He had not read the papers the day before, to-day I read him the communiqués in the Petit Parisien, he said it was enough. He also turned the pages of a book he had recently begun to read, La Science et les Allemands.

[272]

I told him how pleased I was to see him better. "It is true," he said, "to-day I have no death-sensation, but I beg you, have no illusions!"

Always that preoccupation of breaking the shock for me. He made me bring a pocket-book with some money in it and a few envelopes; in each of them he made me place notes of similar value, then with his already shaking hand, he himself wrote on each envelope the value of the notes multiplied by their number, and explained that it was to help me to find quickly what I should require after the catastrophe.

He ate better at lunch than he had done lately; but already at two o'clock the breathlessness increased. Yet he did not look pale; he had preserved his rosy complexion. As he inhaled the oxygen, he was shaken by a hiccough. He pressed my hand. "It is the end," he said, "the death rattle; that is how people die." He looked at his watch on the small table, it marked four o'clock.

"No," he said, "it must have stopped. Four o'clock struck some time ago." And he smiled. "Is it not strange that it should have stopped before I? Go and see what time it is."

I ran out to see the clock from the window of another room; it was twenty minutes to five. I met some one in the passage and asked him to go quickly to fetch one of the Institute doctors. Then I begged Elie not to have such ideas, and tried to cheer him.

"But, my child, why do you want to calm me? I am quite calm; I am only stating facts," he said, adding tender words.

119

At that moment Salimbeni came in. Elie said to him: "Salimbeni, you are a friend; tell me, is it the end?" And as he protested, he added, [273]"You remember your promise? You will do my post-mortem? and look at the intestines carefully, for I think there is something there now." MM. Roux and Martin then arrived. The feeling of weight in the intestines of which he complained was mentioned. He did not know that he had ascitis in the peritoneum.

As I was attending to him I felt him move suddenly, and said, "I beg you, do not make such sudden movements; you know it is not good for you." He did not answer. I raised my head; his was thrown back on the pillows, his face had assumed a blue tinge, the white of the eyes alone could be seen under the half-closed lids.

Not a word, not a sound.

All was over.[36]

Then an abyss of oblivion....

I saw him again, stretched on his deathbed. He was white, cold, and dumb. His face bore a calm and very serious expression. He looked like a martyr who had at last entered into rest. Death had marked his face with no dread seal. The lids had closed of their own accord, and he seemed to be sleeping after great lassitude; one might have thought that, with his usual kindness, he wished to spare us all too painful an impression....

All through the night and the next morning his face preserved the same expression.

In the afternoon Salimbeni performed the autopsy. Then he was laid in his coffin; twenty-four hours had elapsed since the end. Wrapped in a white sheet, which framed his fine face, he had the appearance of a biblical prophet.

Now his expression had assumed absolute serenity,[274] illumined by gentleness and kindness. He had a look of elevation, grandeur, and beauty which was really divine. It was an apotheosis. His beautiful soul beamed in its full purity; neither suffering nor any earthly preoccupation had any hold on it. He gave an impression of eternal rest.

It was his final image, a splendid one, the last ... for ever.

The bier was closed and covered with a heavy black pall. On life also a blacker and heavier pall had fallen. The light had gone out.

Two days later, on the 18th July, he was carried to the cemetery of the Père Lachaise, to be cremated in all simplicity, as he had wished. Faithful to his ideas, he had wished for a lay funeral, with no speeches, flowers, or invitations.

His bier disappeared into a large sarcophagus; on each side black curtains fell to hide what was going on.... Then one hour of heavy silence whilst the poor body was being consumed by the flames....

A death silence....

And that was all....

The mercurial, vivacious child, good-hearted, intelligent, and precocious; the young man, ardent, impetuous, passionate, a lover of science and of all that was exalted; the mature man, a bold thinker, an indefatigable investigator, eager, generous, tender, and devoted; the old man, in everything faithful to himself, but progressing in serenity, shining with an ever softer light, like a mountain peak in the setting sun; the martyr at last, enduring suffering with patience and resignation, seeing the approach of death without fear, observing it as he had observed life....

[275]

The hour of silence was over; the incineration accomplished. Of his body, little was left—a handful of ashes. They were enclosed within an urn and placed in the library of the Pasteur Institute.

But his beautiful, ardent soul, his audacious and fertile ideas, all that rich inner life which had developed into a harmonious and puissant symphony, all that cannot be dead, cannot disappear! The ideas, the influence we give to life must persist, must live; they are the sacred flame which we hand on to others and are eternal.

[276]
EPILOGUE

The life and work of Elie Metchnikoff are so intimately bound together that, in a biography, it is impossible to separate them. That is why the description of his work necessarily has been dispersed along the story of his life; but, just as, in order to judge of a work of art, one has to draw back and contemplate the whole, we must also, after following the evolution and successive stages of E. Metchnikoff's scientific works, take a full view of his work as a whole.

He was a born biologist; everything connected with life interested him. In his childhood, he observed plants and animals. At the age of fifteen, he became acquainted with microscopic beings; they aroused in him such powerful interest towards the primitive forms of life that, from that moment, not only his future path was marked out for him but also his method of starting from the simple to elucidate the complex. He was imbued with Darwin's theory of evolution; having begun by the study of inferior animals, he began to look for their connections with other groups.

He endeavoured to establish the continuity and the unity of phenomena in all living beings. According to his method of studying first what was simplest, he turned to embryology, for in the egg and the embryo it is possible to follow step by step the transformation[277] of the simple to the complex and to see the origin and development of all the constituent parts of the organism. Moreover, the embryo is exempt from secondary complications, due to the multiple external conditions of post-embryonic life.

Metchnikoff was able to establish, from embryological data, that the development of lower animals takes place according to the same plan and under the same laws as that of higher animals. In all of them, the segmentation of the egg is followed by the formation of embryonic layers, of which each gives birth to cells and to definite organs. Superior forms repeat, in their embryonic life, the evolution cycle of inferior forms.[37]

This common plan in the embryology of all animals established their genealogical continuity and strengthened the Darwinian theory.

Metchnikoff's studies, carried out on the various groups of animals, contributed towards the foundation of comparative embryology. Owing to the comparative method, he had made himself familiar not only with the morphological and functional continuity of divers organisms, but also with that of their constituting cells; a comparison between the latter and unicellular beings was inevitable. That is why, having ascertained that the mobile cells of the lower Metazoa absorbed foreign bodies by inclusion, he naturally concluded that that phenomenon was similar to digestion in unicellular beings.

Having established the fact of intracellular digestion in lower animals, he extended it to certain cells [278]of the higher animals; thus his phagocyte theory was born.

Seeing that unicellular beings, like the mobile cells of Metazoa, englobe, not only food, but foreign bodies, he asked himself whether this was not at the same time a defensive action. Such a possibility brought no surprise to a zoologist, accustomed to see that, in the struggle for existence, animals often devoured their enemies.

All the materials for the building up of the phagocyte theory were therefore ready in Metchnikoff's mind when he asked himself, as by an intuition, whether the white globules of our blood, globules so similar to amœbæ, do not play the part of a defensive army in our organism when they envelope in accumulated masses intrusive bodies injurious to the organism.

The thought was but the result of a preparatory work already accomplished; it was the butterfly escaping out of the chrysalis.

Metchnikoff had recourse to his method of simplification in order to solve the question.

The organism of the higher animals being extremely complicated, he went down as far as the transparent larva of the starfish (bipinnaria) in order to watch with his own eyes the phenomena which take place within it. He introduced a rose-thorn into the transparent body of the larva, and noted the next day that the mobile cells in the latter had crowded towards the splinter, like an army rushing to meet a foe.

The analogy of this phenomenon with inflammation and the formation of an abscess was striking. Metchnikoff said to himself that since most diseases[279] in the higher animals are accompanied by inflammation and provoked by microbes, it was chiefly against these microbes that our defensive cells had to struggle. He named the defensive cells phagocytes.

He confirmed his hypothesis by another observation, equally simple. In a little transparent crustacean (Daphnia) infected by a small parasitic fungus, (Monospora bicuspidata), he was easily able to observe the struggle between the animal's mobile cells and its parasites.

These two simple observations served as foundation and supports to the bridge by which Metchnikoff connected normal biology with pathological biology. Having entered the domain of the latter, he studied various microbian diseases, and asked himself why the organism was sometimes liable and sometimes refractory. In order to elucidate this question, he turned again to lower animals, in which he could easily observe the most intimate phenomena, simplified.

He ascertained that liability in an animal corresponded with the fact that microbes introduced into the organism remained free and invaded it, whilst immunity coincided with the inclusion and digestion of the microbes by phagocytes.

He also found that, in artificial immunity, the phagocytes are accustomed gradually, by preventive inoculations, to digest microbes and their toxins.

Thus he established the fact that phagocytosis and inflammation are curative means employed by the organism.

All his ulterior researches, his studies on the various categories of phagocytes and their properties, on their digestive liquids, on the formation of antitoxins, on the different properties acquired by the[280] blood, etc., were but the natural development of those premises.

He had proved that the part played by the phagocytes consists, not only in the struggle against microbes and their poisons, but also in the destruction of all the mortified or enfeebled cells of the organism, and that atrophies are nothing more than the absorption of cellular elements by the phagocytes.

He found that senile atrophies have the same cause, and asked why the cells of old people's organisms should become enfeebled.

He demonstrated that the principal cause is the chronic poisoning of the cells by toxins manufactured by microbes in the intestine. Premature senility was the result—a phenomenon as pathological as any disease.

The source of the evil, therefore, resides in the intestinal flora. Accordingly he started to study the latter, as also senility, in order to find means of struggling against both.

His researches enabled him to indicate a series of means, based, on the one hand, on the struggle against microbes, and, on the other, on the defence of the noble cells against destructive ones.[38]

The study of old age led him to that of syphilis, a disease which provokes an arteriosclerosis which is similar to that of old people; the study of the normal intestinal flora was followed by that of intestinal diseases, such as typhoid fever and infantile cholera.

Finally, he progressed towards the last phenomenon, the most mysterious in nature, Death.

[281]

Researches on the silk-worm moth—a rare example of an animal the life of which ends in natural death—allowed him to conclude that the latter is due to an auto-intoxication of the organism.

But he only just raised the veil of the great mystery; it was his last work....

Metchnikoff's philosophical evolution ran on parallel lines with his scientific researches.

When studying the laws and the unity of vital phenomena he found that their harmony was occasionally broken by the collision of internal conditions with the environment and that regrettable consequences ensued. He saw an example of that in human nature, full of disharmonies due to its animal origin.

These considerations caused the pessimism of his youth. But his energetic, pugnacious temperament could not remain content with a passive acceptance of facts.

He started to study the lack of harmony in human nature and its causes, and sought for means to combat these causes. Gradually he reached the conclusion that the greatest human disharmonies are provoked by the rupture of the normal cycle of our life, by the precocity of senility and of death, chiefly arising from a chronic poisoning by the toxins of intestinal microbes.

But having acquired the conviction that it is possible to struggle against that intoxication, he concluded that science, which has already done so much to fight diseases, would also find means of struggling against premature old age and precocious death, thus leading us to the normal vital cycle, orthobiosis.

Then disharmony, transformed into harmony, will cause the greatest of ills to disappear.

[282]

Faith in the power of Science and in the possibility of modifying human nature itself through Science was the foundation of the optimistic philosophy of his maturity. Thoughts full of strength and hope shine like leading stars all along his philosophical works.

"Alone, Rational Science is capable of showing humanity the true path."

"The real goal of human existence consists in an active life in conformity with individual capacity; in a life prolonged until the appearance of the death-instinct, and until Man, satisfied with the duration of his existence, feels the desire for annihilation."

"Man is capable of great works; that is why it is desirable that he should modify human nature and transform its disharmonies into harmonies."

"If an ideal capable of uniting men in a sort of religion is possible, it can only be founded on scientific principles. And, if it is true, as is often affirmed, that man cannot live without faith, it must be faith in the power of Science."

Thus Elie Metchnikoff had begun by the study of nascent life in inferior beings; by a logical and continuous chain, he had followed the whole cycle of development of living beings in their continuity and their whole.

From the initial question of intracellular digestion he had reached the most exalted problems which can occupy our minds, the harmonising of human discords through knowledge and will.

Such is the harmonious edifice which he has built.

No vital question was indifferent to him. He tackled the most difficult and most mysterious among them with courage, moved by an invincible impulse[283] towards Truth and sustained by enthusiasm and faith in the power of Science.

The beauty of a work of art consists in the harmony and unity of a realised conception.

Thus a Gothic cathedral, by its graceful and harmonious lines, expresses an impulse towards higher spheres; it leans solidly on the earth only in order to soar better towards the heavens.

Such is also the character of Elie Metchnikoff's life-work.

[285]
BIBLIOGRAPHICAL APPENDIX

WORKS OF ELIE METCHNIKOFF
1865.   "Beiträge zur Kenntniss der Chaetopoden," Zeitschrift für wissenschaftliche Zoologie, xv. 3, p. 328.

"Über einige wenig bekannte Thierformen," Zeit. f. wissen. Zool. xv. 4, p. 450.

"Über Geodesmus bilineatus Nob. (Fasciola terrestris), eine europäische Landplanarie, Mélanges biologiques" (Bull. de l'Académie des Sciences de Saint-Pétersbourg, vol. v.).

1866.   "Untersuchungen über die Embryologie der Hemipteren (vorläufige Mitteilung)," Zeit. f. wissen. Zool. xvi. 1, p. 128.

"Zur Entwicklungsgeschichte von Myzostomum," Zeit. f. wissen. Zool. xvi. 1, p. 326.

"Apsilus lentiformis, ein Räderthier," Zeit. f. wissen. Zool. xvi. 3, p. 1.

"Embryologischen Studien an Insecten," Zeit. f. wissen. Zool. xvi. Entgegnung auf die Erwiederung des Her. Prof. Leuckart in Giessen, in Betreff der Frage über die Nematodenentwicklung (Göttingen, Verlag von Adalbert Rente).

1867.   "Beiträge zur Naturgeschichte der Würmer," Zeit. f. wissen. Zool. xvii. 4, p. 539.

"Embryology of the Sepiola" (in Russian), Archives des Sciences physiques et naturelles, Genève, vol. 21.

1868.   "Beiträge zur Kenntniss der Entwicklungsgeschichte der Chaetopoden" (in collaboration with Ed. Claparède), Zeit. f. wissen. Zool. xviii.

1869.   "Embryology of Nebalia" (in Russian), Mélanges biologiques de l'Académie de Saint-Pétersbourg, vi. p. 730.

"Untersuchungen über die Metamorphose einiger Seethiere, Tornaria," Zeit. f. wissen. Zool. xx. p. 131.

"Über ein Larvenstadium von Euphausia," Zeit. f. wissen. Zool. xix. 4, p. 179.

"Über die Entwicklung der Echinodermen und Nemertinen," Mémoires de l'Acad. de Saint-Pétersbourg, xiv. 8, p. 33.

1870.   "Bemerkungen über Echinodermen," Bulletins de l'Acad. de Saint-Pétersbourg, xiv. p. 51.

"Embryologie des Scorpions," Zeitschr. f. wissen. Zool. xxi.

1871.   "Über die Metamorphose einiger Seethiere," Zeit. f. wissen. Zool. xxi. 2, p. 235.

124

[286]   "Entwicklungsgeschichte des Chelifers," Zeit. f. wissen. Zool. xxi. p. 513.

"Über den Naupliuszustand von Euphausia," ibid. Bd. xix.

1872.   "Zur Entwicklungsgeschichte der einfachen Ascidien," Zeit. f. wissen. Zool. xxii. 3, p. 339.

"Vorläufige Mitteilung über die Embryologie der Polydesmiden," Mélanges biologiques des Bullet. de l'Académie des Sciences de Saint-Pétersbourg, vol. viii.

"Zur Entwicklungsgeschichte der Kalkschwämme," Zeit. f. wissen. Zool. xxiv. p. 1.

"Studien über die Entwicklung der Medusen und Siphonophoren," Zeit. f. wissen. Zool. xxiv. p. 15.

"Embryologie der doppelfüssigen Myriapoden," Zeit. f. wissen. Zool. xxiv. p. 253.

1874.   "Embryologisches über Geophilus," Zeit. f. wissen. Zool. xxv. p. 313.

1876.   "Beiträge zur Morphologie der Spongien," Zeit. f. wissen. Zool. xxvii. p. 275.

1878.   "Spongiologische Studien," Zeit. f. wissen. Zool. xxxii. p. 349.

1879.   "Spongiologische Studien," Zeit. f. wissen. Zool. xxxii. p. 374.

1880.   "Über die intracelluläre Verdauung bei Coelenteraten," Zoologischer Anzeiger, No. 56, p. 261.

"Untersuchungen über Orthonectiden," Zeit. f. wissen. Zool. xxxv. p. 282.

"Über die systematische Stellung von Balanoglossus," Zoologischer Anzeiger, pp. 139, 153.

1881.   "Zur Lehre über die intracelluläre Verdauung niederer Tiere," Zoologischer Anzeiger, p. 310.

Vergleichend-embryologische Studien:

1. Entodermbildung bei Geryoniden.

2. "Über einige Studien der Cunina," Zeit. f. wissen. Zool. xxxvi. p. 433.

1882.   3. "Über die Gastrula einiger Metazoen," Zeit. f. wissen. Zool. xxxvii. p. 286.

"Die Embryologie von Planaria polychroa," Zeit. f. wissen. Zool. xxxviii. 3, p. 331.

1883.   "Untersuchungen über die intracelluläre Verdauung bei wirbellosen Tieren," Arbeiten d. zool. Instituts zu Wien, v. 2, p. 14 (Quarterly Journal of Micr. Science, vol. 93).

"Untersuchung über die mesodermalen Phagocyten einiger Wirbeltiere," Biologisch. Centralblatt, No. 18, p. 560, Bd. iii.

1884.   "Embryologische Mitteilungen über Echinodermen," Zoologischer Anzeiger, vii. Nos. 158, 159.

"Über eine Sprosspilzkrankheit der Daphnien; Beitrag zur Lehre über den Kampf der Phagocyten gegen Krankheitserreger," Virchow's Archiv, vol. 96, p. 177.

"Über die Beziehung der Phagocyten zu Milzbrandbacillen," Virchow's Archiv, vol. 97, p. 502.

"Über die pathologische Bedeutung der intracellulären Verdauung," Fortschritte der Medizin, 1884, p. 558, No. 17.

1885.   Vergleichend-embryologische Studien:

4. "Über die Gastrulation und Mesodermbildung der Ctenophoren," 648.

[287]

5. "Über die Bildung der Wanderzellen bei Asterien und Echiniden," Zeit. f. wissen. Zool. xlii. p. 656.

1886.   "Medusologische Mittheilungen," Arbeiten d. zool. Instituts zu Wien, vi. 2, p. 1.

125

Embryologische Studien an Medusen, ein Beitrag zur Genealogie der Primitivorgane, Wien, 1886.

1887.   "Sur l'atténuation des bactéridies charbonneuses dans le sang des moutons réfractaires," Annales de l'Institut Pasteur, i. p. 42, No. 1.

"Über den Kampf der Zellen gegen Erysipelkokken, ein Beitrag zur Phagocytenlehre," Virchow's Archiv, vol. 107, p. 209.

"Über den Phagocytenkampf bei Rückfalltyphus," Virchow's Archiv, vol. 109, p. 176.

"Sur la lutte des cellules de l'organisme contre l'invasion des microbes," Annales de l'Institut Pasteur, i. p. 321, No. 7.

"Kritische Bemerkungen über den Aufsatz des Herrn Christmas-Dirckinck-Holmfeld, I. V.," Fortschritte der Medizin, 17, p. 541.

1888.   "Über die phagocytäre Rolle der Tuberkelriesenzellen," Virchow's Archiv, vol. 113, p. 63.

"Pasteuria Ramosa, un représentant des bactéries à division longitudinale," Annales de l'Institut Pasteur, p. 165, t. ii. No. 4.

"Über das Verhalten der Milzbrandbakterien im Organismus," Virchow's Archiv, vol. 114, p. 465.

"Réponse à la critique de M. Weigert au sujet des cellules géantes de la tuberculose," Annales de l'Institut Pasteur, ii. p. 604.

1889.   "Recherches sur la digestion intracellulaire," Annales de l'Institut Pasteur, iii. p. 25, No. 1.

"Contribution à l'étude du pléomorphisme des bactéries," Annales de l'Institut Pasteur, iii. p. 61, No. 2.

"Note sur le pléomorphisme, etc.," Annales de l'Institut Pasteur, iii. p. 265, No. 5.

Studies on Immunity:

1. "Immunité des lapins contre le bacille du rouget des porcs," Annales de l'Institut Pasteur, iii. p. 289, No. 6.

1890.   2. "Le Charbon des pigeons," Annales de l'Institut Pasteur, iv. p. 65, No. 2.

3. "Le Charbon des rats blancs," Annales de l'Institut Pasteur, iv. p. 193, No. 4.

1891.   4. "L'Immunité des cobayes vaccinés contre le Vibrio Metchnikowii," Annales de l'Institut Pasteur, v. p. 465, No. 8.

"Sur la propriété bactéricide du sang de rat" (in collaboration with Dr. Roux), No. 8.

"Recherches sur l'accoutumance aux produits microbiens" (in collaboration with Dr. Roudenko), Annales de l'Institut Pasteur, v. p. 567, No. 9.

"Beiträge zur vergleichenden Pathologie der Entzündung," Virchow Festschrift, vol. 11.

1892.   "La Phagocytose musculaire" (in collaboration with Dr. Soudakevitch), Annales de l'Institut Pasteur, vi. p. 1.

Leçons sur la pathologie comparée de l'inflammation. Paris, 1892.

"On Aqueous Humour, Micro-organisms and Immunity," Journal of Pathology, i.

[288]   Studies on Immunity:

5. "Immunité des lapins vaccinés contre le microbe du Hogcholéra," Annales de l'Institut Pasteur, vi. p. 189, No. 5.

"Atrophie des muscles pendant la transformation des batraciens," Annales de l'Institut Pasteur, vi. No. 1.

"Note au sujet du mémoire de M. Soudakevitch (Parasitisme intracellulaire des néoplasmes cancéreux)," No. 3.

"Über Muskelphagocytose," Centralblatt für Bakteriologie, 1892.

"La Lutte pour l'existence entre les diverses parties de l'organisme," Revue scientifique, 10 sept. 1892, No. 11.

1893.   "Recherches sur le choléra et les vibrions, 1er mémoire" (Sur la propriété préventive du sang humain vis-à-vis du vibrion de Koch), Annales de l'Institut Pasteur, vii. p. 403, No. 5.

2. "Mémoire," idem (Sur la propriété pathogène des vibrions), tome vii. p. 562, No. 7.

Comparative Pathology of Inflammation. Lectures at the Pasteur Institute. Paul: London, 1893. 8vo. (The name of the translator is not stated.)

1894.   3. "Mémoire," idem (Sur la vaccination artificielle du vibrion cholérique), Annales de l'Institut Pasteur, viii. p. 257, No. 5.

4. "Mémoire," idem (Sur l'immunité et la réceptivité vis-à-vis du choléra intestinal), tome viii. p. 529, No. 8.

"L'état actuel de la question de l'immunité" (Rapport du Congrès international de Budapest), Annales de l'Institut Pasteur, viii. p. 706, No. 10.

1895.   Studies on Immunity:

6. "Sur la destruction extracellulaire des bactéries dans l'organisme," Annales de l'Institut Pasteur, ix. p. 433, No. 6.

1896.   "Toxine et antitoxine cholériques" (in collaboration with Drs. Roux and Salimbeni), Annales de l'Institut Pasteur, x. p. 25, No. 5.

"Quelques remarques à propos de l'article de Gabritchevsky sur la fièvre récurrente," Annales de l'Institut Pasteur, x. No. 11.

Recherches sur l'influence de l'organisme sur les toxines:

1897.   1st Memoir. "Recherches sur l'influence de l'organisme sur les toxines," Annales de l'Institut Pasteur, xi. p. 801.

"Réponse à M. Gabritchevsky," Annales de l'Institut Pasteur, xi. No. 3.

"Immunität," Weyl's Handbuch der Hygiene. Jena, 1897.

"Recherches sur l'influence de l'organisme sur les toxines" (Communication faite au congrès de Moscou en août 1897), Annales de l'Institut Pasteur, xi. No. 10.

1898.   2nd Memoir. "Influence du système nerveux sur la toxine tétanique," Annales de l'Institut Pasteur, xii. No. 2, p. 81.

3rd Memoir. "Toxine tétanique et leucocytes," Annales de l'Institut Pasteur, xii. No. 4, p. 263.

1899.   "Résorption des cellules," Annales de l'Institut Pasteur, xiii. No. 10, p. 737.

1900.   Researches on the Influence of the Organism on Toxins:

4ème mémoire. "Sur la spermotoxine et l'antispermotoxine," Annales de l'Institut Pasteur, xiv. p. 5.

"Sur les cytotoxines," Annales de l'Institut Pasteur, xiv. No. 6. p. 369.

"Recherches sur l'action de l'hémotoxine sur l'homme," Annales de l'Institut Pasteur, xiv. No. 6, p. 402.

[289]1901.   Biological Studies on Old Age:

1st Memoir. "Sur le blanchiment des cheveux et des poils," Annales de l'Institut Pasteur, xv. No. 12, p. 865.

L'Immunité dans les maladies infectieuses. Paris, 1901.

1902.   Biological Studies on Old Age. "Recherches sur la vieillesse des perroquets" (in collaboration with Drs. Mesnil and Weinberg), Annales de l'Institut Pasteur, xvi. No. 12.

The Nature of Man. Studies in optimistic philosophy. The English translation by P. Chalmers Mitchell. Heinemann: London; Putnams: New York, 1903. 8vo.

1903.　　　Studies on Human Nature: Paris, 1903.

Études expérimentales sur la syphilis (in collaboration with Dr. Roux):

1st Memoir. Annales de l'Institut Pasteur, xvii. No. 12, p. 809.

1904.　　　2nd Memoir. "Études expérimentales sur la syphilis" (in collaboration with Dr. Roux), Annales de l'Institut Pasteur, xviii. No. 1, p. 1.

3rd Memoir. Id. No. 11.

1905.　　　4th Memoir. Id. Annales de l'Institut Pasteur, xix. No. 11.

Immunity in Infective Diseases. Translated from the French by F. G. Binnie. University Press: Cambridge; The Macmillan Co.: New York, 1905. 8vo.

1906.　　　5th Memoir. Id., Annales de l'Institut Pasteur, xx. No. 10.

The New Hygiene: three lectures on the prevention of infectious diseases. Translated and a preface written by E. Ray Lankester. Heinemann: London, 1906. 8vo.

[Another edition.] Chicago Medical Book Co.: Chicago, 1906. 8vo.

1907.　　　[Another edition.] W. T. Keener & Co.: Chicago, 1907. 8vo.

"Sur la prophylaxie de la syphilis" (Paper read at the XIIth International Congress in Berlin), Annales de l'Institut Pasteur, xxi. No. 10.

The Prolongation of Life: optimistic studies. The English translation edited by P. Chalmers Mitchell. Heinemann: London, 1907. 8vo.

Essais optimistes.

1908.　　　"Études sur la flore intestinale," "Putréfaction intestinale," Annales de l'Institut Pasteur, xxii. No. 12.

1909.　　　Idem. "Roussettes et microbes" (in collaboration with MM. Weinberg, Pozersky, Distaso, Berthelot), Annales de l'Institut Pasteur, xxiii. No. 12.

Notes on Sour Milk and other Methods of administering Selected Lactic Germs in Intestinal Bacterio-therapy. J. Bale, Sons & Co.: London, 1909. 8vo.

1910.　　　Idem. "Poisons intestinaux et scléroses," Annales de l'Institut Pasteur, xxiv. No. 10.

The Prolongation of Life. New and revised edition, Heinemann: London; Putnams: New York, 1910. 8vo.

1911.　　　"Sur la fièvre typhoïde expérimentale" (Metchnikoff et Besredka), Annales de l'Institut Pasteur, xxv. No. 3.

Annales de l'Institut Pasteur:

Tome xxv. No. 6. Quelques remarques sur la vaccination à propos du mémoire de M. Choukevitch sur le choléra.

Tome xxv. No. 6. Réponse de MM. Metchnikoff et Besredka à M. le Dr. Vincent (remarques sur la vaccination antityphique).

[290]　　　Tome xxv. No. 11. El. Metchnikoff, E. Burnet et L. Tarassevitch, "Recherches sur l'épidémiologie de la tuberculose dans les steppes Kalmouks."

Tome xxv. No. 12. El. Metchnikoff et A. Besredka, "Des vaccinations antityphiques (2nd Memoir)."

1912.　　　Tome xxvi. No. 11. El. Metchnikoff et Eug. Wollman, "Sur quelques essais de désintoxication intestinale," "Bactériothérapie intestinale."

The Warfare against Tuberculosis—being the Priestley Lecture of the National Health Society for the year 1912. Published in Bedrock, January 1913. Constable: London.

1913.　　　Études sur la flore intestinale.

Tome xxvii. No. 8. "Des vaccinations antityphiques" (El. Metchnikoff et A. Besredka).

Tome xxvii. No. 11. "Toxicité des sulfoconjugués de la série aromatique."

1914.   Tome xxviii. No. 2. "Études sur la flore intestinale" (4ème mémoire). "Les diarrhées des nourrissons."

1915.   Tome xxix. No. 8. "Causerie de El. Metchnikoff à l'occasion de son jubilé."

Tome xxix. No. 10. "La Mort du papillon du mûrier."

"Founders of Modern Medicine: Pasteur, Lister, Koch" in Russian (a French translation to appear shortly).

1915-16.   "Introduction à 'Études sur la fonction sexuelle'" (posthume, dans Le Mercure de France, 1917).

1916.   The Nature of Man. Popular edition. Heinemann: London, 1916. 8vo.

Note.—Sources consulted: British Museum Catalogue; English Catalogue; American Catalogue.

[291]

FOOTNOTES

[1] He received an honorary degree at Cambridge in 1891, and also attended the International Medical Congress in London in that year. In 1901 he gave a lecture at Manchester on the intestinal flora. In 1906 he gave a course of three lectures in London on "The New Hygiene." I translated them for him, and they were published as a little volume by Heinemann.

[2] By Prof. Hertwig of Munich.

[3] Ungainly open carriage on high wheels and without springs.

[4] Metchnikoff himself insisted upon the recital of this episode, for which he had felt some remorse. He considered that, in a biography, disagreeable traits were not to be omitted.

[5] Chronicle of John Neculua.

[6] This Boyar was no doubt a nephew of the Great Spatar.

[7] He made researches on a very singular annulate worm, the Fabricia.

[8] All this episode was described by Metchnikoff in 1866 in a separate publication with great restraint and in a very moderate tone.

[9] In later years Metchnikoff often dwelt on the fact that Fritz Müller was not fully appreciated and that it was he who had most efficaciously contributed to the confirmation of Darwinian theories.

[10] A degree preceding that of Doc.Sc.

[11] The latter affirmed that the nervous system of Ascidia originated from the upper layer, whilst Elie believed that it was the lower layer which gave birth to it. It was Kovalevsky who was right, as Elie himself declared later.

[12] He ultimately developed these considerations in a paper entitled Education from an Anthropological Point of View, of which mention will be made hereafter.

[13] Rural administration.

[14] "Elie" is the French form of Elijah, in Russian Ilia, and was ultimately adopted by Metchnikoff.

[15] Migration of the white blood corpuscles (leucocytes) through the walls of blood-vessels.

[16] Arbeiten des zool. Inst. zu Wien, Bd. v. Heft ii. p. 141. "Untersuchung über die intracelluläre Verdauung bei wirbellosen Tieren," E. Metchnikoff.

[17] It was only in 1892 that he completed and developed his observations. He found that the cells of the sarcoplasma of the muscular tissue devoured its contractile part, the myoplasma.

[18] This paper was entitled "Forces curatives de l'organisme."

[19] Virchow's Archiv, vol. 96, p. 177.

[20] Aqueous humor, the exudate of aseptic œdemata.

[21] Naegeli, Büchner, Gravitz.

[22] Chauveau.

[23] Büchner.

[24] Hayem, Birsch, Hirschfeld, Kleps, Recklinghausen, Waldeyer, and Virchow.

[25] It is also called alexine or complement by other writers.

[26] Designated by other writers by various synonyms: preventive, or sensibilising substance, immunising body, amboceptor.

[27] A cutaneous scarification by tuberculin which provokes local inflammatory redness on the scarified point in tuberculous subjects only.

[28] Education from an Anthropological Point of View, The Matrimonial Age, The Conception of Human Nature, The Struggle for Existence in a General Sense. See Bibliography.

[29] 28th June 1914.—I have again analysed my urine and I again find indican in fairly large quantities in spite of a diet which is as rational as possible. I am trying to elucidate this strange contradiction.

[30] In the Russian Review, Messenger of Europe.

[31] Annales de l'Institut Pasteur, Jubilé d' E. Metchnikoff, 1915.

[32] Annales de l'Institut Pasteur, 1915.

[33] For instance, Dr. Widal, very early in his illness, had advised a saltless diet, which caused the infiltration in the tissues to remain comparatively slight.

[34] He expounded the theory that ideas on the sexual function had been falsified through fear of venereal diseases at a time when people did not know either how to avoid or cure those diseases. He showed that the condemnation of a natural function by divers religions was based on that fear. He analysed the deplorable consequences of that, and set forth the necessity of returning to more wholesome ideas, more in conformity with nature and allowing the study and avoidance of many evils. He thought that, in this connection, a new direction should be given to the education of children and to marriage. He then examined the part played by the sexual function in the lives of men of genius and, with that object, read many biographies and literary works. During his illness he read books concerning Victor Hugo and Napoleon, J. J. Rousseau's Confessions and even parts of the Nouvelle Héloïse.

[35] Pantopon is a narcotic drug prepared from opium.

[36] It was 5.20 by the conventional war time, 4.20 in reality.

[37] Thus the parenchymella, phagocytella, and gastrula stages correspond in the embryo with the adult form of certain very primitive Metazoa and even to a colony of unicellular animals.

[38] Replacement of the wild and noxious flora of the intestines by antagonistic cultivated microbes; strengthening and vaccinating of noble cells.

Made in the USA
Middletown, DE
06 December 2016